THE MAKING OF CHINA'S WORKING CLASS

Marc Blecher presents a seminal analysis of the development of the urban working class in China. Chinese workers have been the subjects of a great deal of analysis by scholars, documentation by journalists and activists, and portrayal by writers, filmmakers, and artists. *The Making of China's Working Class: A World to Lose* seeks the foundation for all this in three questions: What kind of class is China's working class? What are the historical forces and processes that have formed it? And how does the pattern of class formation help explain the working class's reactions historically, presently, and prospectively?

Blecher offers a contribution not just to scholarship on Chinese labor politics, but on the country's politics and the state's hegemony more widely as well as to comparative labor politics. Combining usefulness, thoroughness, and clarity, *The Making of China's Working Class* is an outstanding resource for educators and students, a bookshelf staple for understanding Chinese politics and comparative working class politics.

Marc Blecher is James Monroe Professor of Politics and East Asian Studies at Oberlin College. He has served as a Senior Research Fellow at the University of California, Berkeley Center for Chinese Studies, a Visiting Professor of Political Science at the University of Chicago, and a Visiting Fellow at The Institute of Development Studies (IDS), University of Sussex. His specialty is Chinese politics, on which he has published five books and dozens of articles on political science, rural and urban politics, popular participation, political economy and political sociology.

Conceptualising Comparative Politics: Polities, Peoples, and Markets
Edited by Anthony Spanakos (Montclair State University) and Francisco Panizza (London School of Economics)

Conceptualising Comparative Politics seeks to bring a distinctive approach to comparative politics by rediscovering the discipline's rich conceptual tradition and inter-disciplinary foundations. It aims to fill out the conceptual framework on which the rest of the subfield draws but to which books only sporadically contribute, and to complement theoretical and conceptual analysis by applying it to deeply explored case studies. The series publishes books that make serious inquiry into fundamental concepts in comparative politics (crisis, legitimacy, credibility, representation, institutions, civil society, reconciliation) through theoretically engaging and empirically deep analysis.

11. Authoritarian Gravity Centers
A Cross-Regional Study of Authoritarian Promotion and Diffusion
Thomas Demmelhuber and Marianne Kneuer

12. Politics as a Science
A Prolegomenon
Philippe C. Schmitter and Marc Blecher

13. Populism in Global Perspective
A Performative and Discursive Approach
Edited by Pierre Ostiguy, Francisco Panizza, Benjamin Moffitt

14. Populism in Power
Discourse and Performativity in SYRIZA and Donald Trump
Giorgos Venizelos

15. Right-Wing Populism in Latin America and Beyond
Edited by Anthony Pereira

16. Is There Such a Thing as Populism?
3 Provocations and 5 1/2 Proposals
Benjamin Arditi

17. The Making of China's Working Class
A World to Lose
Marc Blecher

THE MAKING OF CHINA'S WORKING CLASS

A World to Lose

Marc Blecher

Routledge
Taylor & Francis Group
NEW YORK AND LONDON

Designed cover image: Getty Images

First published 2026
by Routledge
605 Third Avenue, New York, NY 10158

and by Routledge
4 Park Square, Milton Park, Abingdon, Oxon, OX14 4RN

Routledge is an imprint of the Taylor & Francis Group, an informa business

Library of Congress Cataloging-in-Publication Data
Names: Blecher, Marc J., author.
Title: The making of China's working class: a world to lose / Marc Blecher.
Description: New York, NY: Routledge, 2026. | Series: Conceptualising comparative politics | Includes bibliographical references and index. |
Identifiers: LCCN 2024016664 (print) | LCCN 2024016665 (ebook) |
ISBN 9781032854496 (hardback) | ISBN 9781032769110 (paperback) |
ISBN 9781003518228 (ebook)
Subjects: LCSH: Working class–China–History. | Labor–China–History |
Social classes–China–History. | China–Politics and government–1949-Classification:
LCC HD8736.5.B54 2026 (print) | LCC HD8736.5 (ebook) |
DDC 331.0951–dc23/eng/20240426
LC record available at https://lccn.loc.gov/2024016664
LC ebook record available at https://lccn.loc.gov/2024016665

ISBN: 978-1-032-85449-6 (hbk)
ISBN: 978-1-032-76911-0 (pbk)
ISBN: 978-1-003-51822-8 (ebk)

DOI: 10.4324/9781003518228

Typeset in Times New Roman
by Deanta Global Publishing Services, Chennai, India

For Sharon

— educator *extraordinaire*
— resolute shop steward
— copilot on our wild ride
— the world I somehow won

CONTENTS

FIGURES

TABLES

ON THE COVER

Cotton mill workers on strike, Beijing, revolutionary era (photographer unknown, via Bettmann Archive and Getty Images).

Workers train at the Anshan Iron and Steel Works seamless tube plant, Anshan, 1956 (photograph by Tom Hutchins, via Getty Images).

Machinists sewing toys in a factory, Shenzhen, 2002 (photograph by Peter Parks, via Getty Images).

PREFACE AND ACKNOWLEDGMENTS

This book's main title can justifiably be experienced as presumptuous, comparing itself as it does to E. P. Thompson's masterpiece *The Making of the English Working Class.*[1] On the contrary, I mean it as an *homage* to one of its models. Thompson was engaged in social history; I am a political scientist with a decidedly multi-disciplinary bent. Thompson sought "to rescue the poor stockinger, the Luddite cropper, the 'obsolete' hand-loom weaver, the 'utopian' artisan and even the deluded follower of Joanna Southcott, from the enormous condescension of posterity."[2] Precisely because of the avalanche of scholarship stimulated by scholars such as Thompson, that can no longer be counted among the myriad problems facing workers and working classes around the world. Thompson's inspiration for me lay in his conception of working class formation as a lengthy and "active process, which owes as much to agency as to conditioning."[3]

The Making of the English Working Class has been one among many touchstones for scholarship on American political development (APD), with its emphases on the historical origins of political institutions as decisive explanatory factors (rather than just useful, obligatory background) and on the study of

1 E. P. Thompson, *The Making of the English Working Class* (New York: Open Road Media, 2013), Kindle edition. I have made one minor but, to me, significant change in adopting his renowned title. *The Making of the Chinese Working Class* might imply that there is something distinctively Chinese about the country's working class. In some respects, this could well be the case. But I mean to examine China's proletariat using theoretical and analytical apparatuses that treat it as a case of working classes more generally (and, only briefly in the commentaries at the end, comparatively). Hence, *The Making of China's Working Class.*

2 Ibid., 153.

3 Ibid., 76.

the trajectories and path dependencies they created. That, in turn, has been an inspiration for this book as well, which seeks to provide what I believe to be the first work on what could be called "Chinese political development" focusing on the working class. *The Making of China's Working Class* aims to bring into the rich literature on the country's working class politics a perspective informed by APD. A key example is the argument that the White Terror of 1927—during which the Guomindang slaughtered thousands of workers and Communists in Shanghai (and up to a million people elsewhere)—proved to be a non-ergodic moment that severed what up until then had been the close linkage between the Communist Party and the working class.[4] Never again would workers provide more than a tiny minority of the Party itself or its social base. This had profound consequences for labor politics during the rest of the revolution as well as the radical state socialist and structural reform periods that followed.

Hence the subtitle of this book—*A World to Lose*. The gesture is, of course, to the stirring coda of *The Communist Manifesto:* "The proletarians have nothing to lose but their chains. They have a world to win."[5] Here, the influence of comparative historical sociology, APD and the dialectic of structure and agency come into play, and the wording matters. It would be too deterministic (and, obviously, unverifiable) to argue that all was necessarily lost for China's working class in 1927—"a world they were bound to lose." Moreover, the working class itself did not act as if anything like this were the case. It continued to struggle for its class interests in every decade up to the present, albeit in very different ways that are charted in this book. But its battle would, ever after, be severely constrained by its shortage of power and influence in the Communist Party, which built and wielded hegemony over the proletariat. The consequences for the Party, the working class, the politics between them, the country and the world have been profound.

...

This is not the book I planned to write. In the wake of the 1989 popular risings in China and the Party's steely determination and unique success, compared with its kindred parties in Russia and Eastern Europe, in remaining in power, I began, along with many colleagues, to focus hard on where Chinese politics was heading. I had spent the formative two decades of my career working on the politics of Chinese farmers. But I now began to reflect on what I took to be one of the core arguments of Barrington Moore's *Social Origins of Dictatorship and Democracy*—still a classic, and the breakthrough to an entirely new field

4 See p. 9.
5 See p. 1.

of comparative historical sociology[6]—that while rural revolts could destabilize *anciens régimes,* it was rising urban classes such as the bourgeoisie or the proletariat who would primarily determine whether a revolution would be made on that basis. *Ergo*, the key to China's post-1989 fate lay in the cities. So I closed out my work on politics within communes and villages and set off in 1995 to make my fortune studying working class politics.

I had already begun some forays into teaching Marxian theory and labor politics. Of course, Marx and Engels's clarion call set up a deep problematic, since the workers of the world were not uniting and the world they could win seemed to be moving farther away by the hour. It was the scholarship of Michael Burawoy—a contemporary in graduate school at the University of Chicago—that got my juices going. In a series of books and articles based on participant observation in industrial workplaces in the U.S., the state socialist countries of Eastern Europe and Africa, he took a Gramscian position which, while itself fundamentally Marxian of course, reached a quite different conclusion: that given the nature of the capitalist shop floor, workers themselves were producing and reproducing capitalist hegemony there. That, in turn, sent me scurrying to immerse myself in Gramsci. I packed him along on my first research trips to China on workers' politics starting in 1995. My dream was to take up Burawoy's questions and methods there.

In my initial meetings with factory, labor bureau and union officials, I asked about landing a volunteer job in a factory, a request which tested to the limits their capacities for demurring politely and hiding their puzzlement at the strange things foreigners say. I finally gave up and contented myself with doing my ethnography at one remove via systematic, in-depth interviews, a method at which I had become very practiced from my previous work on rural politics and on the Cultural Revolution. I also conducted a survey. This yielded material rich enough for several articles.

But as I pondered the significance of my own findings and those of a small but growing number of colleagues, I began to be transported from the very micro to the very macro. In 2002, I published an article in *The China Quarterly* on "Hegemony and Workers Politics in China."[7] When it surprised me by becoming the most oft-cited publication I ever produced (but who's counting?), I thought I might be on to something after all. It described a refrain my interviewees with a wide range of characteristics and origins articulated regularly but implicitly—I never asked about such matters directly—and enacted in their lives and their descriptions of their families' and fellow workers': they basically

6 It is still top of my "desert island" list of the handful of books that I would take along in existential exile.

7 Marc Blecher, "Hegemony and Workers' Politics in China," *The China Quarterly* 170 (June 2002): 283–303.

accepted and often supported the structural reforms even when they were disadvantaged by the radical shift in China's political economy. This stood at odds with the drumbeat of strikes and factory protests that were developing at the time, and also with the theories and political positions of the small left in China and the larger one outside it. Moreover, it posed the question of how this surprising new hegemony had come about and how durable it would prove to be. I wondered if the deeply historical and macro-level theories and approaches of Gramsci and his scholarly progeny, and of comparative historical sociology, political development and class formation might help unlock an answer. Hence this book. As it goes to print, I am still wondering.

...

"What soon grows old? Gratitude." When I first encountered it, my untutored interpretation of this Aristotelian aphorism took "old" to mean "tiresome," consistent with the sentiment Shakespeare expressed in scripting Bolingbroke in *Richard II*: "Evermore thanks, the exchequer of the poor." But as I myself have grown older, the time finally came to research the matter. The original Greek *τί γηράσκει ταχύ; χάρις* points to something much nobler, linking gratitude to human dignity and "the idea of giving oneself" with lasting consequence.[8] So many people have done just that in connection with this project.

First come the dozens of workers who gave me their time and straightforward accounts of factory life, and my many colleagues and friends in China who helped connect me with them. Because of the current political environment in China, they have to remain anonymous. At least they know who they are and how grateful I am to each and every one of them.

The American Philosophical Society, the National Endowment for the Humanities and Oberlin College provided funding at key stages of the project so I could journey to China year after year to undertake the research.

My wife Sharon and my children Ian, Jacob and Joel put up with—or possibly were relieved by—my frequent absences to do the work in China, and then when I retreated to my desk for countless hours drafting. Many colleagues—most notably Joel Andreas, Steve Crowley, Sarah El-Kazaz, David Goodman, Chris Howell and Dorothy Solinger—took an interest in the project and offered me their sage advice. My son Joel Blecher, title-smith *extraordinaire,* consulted on mine. Vimbai Shire and Robert Harries, my brilliant copy-editors, smoothed out the entire unwieldy manuscript. For the second time, Tony Spanakos played an indispensable role in getting a project off my computer and onto the pages you are reading. And following his concept, Steve Crowley, Elaine Sio-ieng

8 Lillian Quinones, "Living in Gratitude: Insights from Aristotle, G. K. Chesterton, and C. S. Lewis," *World Youth Alliance*. https://wya.net/living-in-gratitude-insights-from-aristotle-g-k-chesterton-and-c-s-lewis/ (accessed March 31, 2025).

Hui and Paul Pierson took the time and effort to make their written contributions, which so enrich this book. (And it's a special thrill to have Paul here, since he was my first honors student!) Vijay Bose, Charlotte Christie and Natalja Mortensen at Routledge organized the publication with aplomb and high professionalism. Givers of themselves indeed, one and all.

Marc Blecher
New York City, June 26, 2025

SERIES EDITORS' FOREWORD

What can Western political science offer in explaining politics in China? Is the Chinese communist party truly a political party or, at least, can scholars assume that it is enough like what one expects of a political party so that it can be treated as a member of the same set as other communist (or other) parties?[1] Was the Chinese empire an empire, and when it shed its imperial name did it become a nation-state?[2,3] Do international relations theories apply without serious modifications?[4,5,6] What sort of state did China, the site of early administrative states, have prior to 1949?[7,8] And what of Chinese

1 Yongnian Zheng, *The Chinese Communist Party as Organizational Emperor: Culture, Reproduction, and Transformation* (New York: Routledge, 2009).
2 Gungwu Wang, *Renewal: The Chinese State and the New Global History* (Hong Kong: Chinese University Press, 2013).
3 Yongnian Zheng, *Discovering Chinese Nationalism in China: Modernization, Identity, and International Relations* (New York: Cambridge University Press, 1999).
4 David Kang, *East Asia Before the West: Five Centuries of Trade and Tribute* (New York: Columbia University Press, 2012).
5 Tingeing Zhao, *All Under Heaven: The Tianxia System for a Possible World Order*, trans. Joseph E. Harroff (Oakland: University of California Press, 2016).
6 Feng Zhang, *Chinese Hegemony: Grand Strategy and International Institutions in East Asian History* (Stanford: Stanford University Press, 2015).
7 Victoria Tin-bor Hui, *War and State Formation in Ancient China and Early Modern Europe* (New York: Cambridge University Press, 2005).
8 Patricia M. Thornton, *Discipling the State: Virtue, Violence, and State-Making in Modern China* (Cambridge: Harvard University Asia Center, 2007).

capitalism?[9,10] Should China be understood on its own terms[11] because the differences (philosophical, religious, historical, and so on) between China and the West are so great?[12]

Yet understanding China is fundamental if one is to understand the world today (if not at any historical moment). It is striking that one of the most commented upon recent global histories of the nineteenth century is by a Sinologist.[13] It is also telling how scholars in the West, often drawing on research of Chinese and other non-Western colleagues, have re-envisioned their understanding of China.[14,15] makes the compelling case to understand the First and Second World Wars and the Chinese Civil War within a single framework, and[16] correctly points attention to what she calls "the other great game" in East Asia.

There is much yet to be explained, then, in that the Chinese communist party has survived various terminal moments in history, has pursed capitalist and administrative reforms that might have been unthinkable, and retains some sort of communist rhetoric even when its representatives are championed as defending (possibly saving) globalization and free market capitalism at Davos.[17] Given the rise of China, geopolitics, the incredible story of the transfer of wealth and reduction of poverty, and so much else, it is easy to lose sight of the working class. Indeed, where is the working class in China? What is it? Were they involved in the increase in mass incidents during the early twenty-first century? What happened to them during the period of reform, which itself may be a series of periods? How much power did the working classes in China have and why and how did they relinquish power?

The poor in China had long been aware of their suffering. Blecher's title, recalling Marx, notes that they had quite a bit to lose in not organizing and

9 Yasheng Huang, *Capitalism with Chinese Characteristics: Entrepreneurship and the State* (New York: Cambridge University Press, 2008).

10 Yongnian Zheng and Yanjie Huang, *Market in State: The Political Economy of Domination in China* (New York: Cambridge University Press, 2018).

11 Yaqing Qin, "Why Is There no Chinese International Relations Theory?" *International Relations of the Asia-Pacific* 7, no. 3 (2007): 313–40.

12 Francois Jullien, *On the Universal: The Uniform, the Common and Dialogue between Cultures* (Malden: Polity, 2014).

13 Jürgen Osterhammel, *The Transformation of the World: A Global History of the Nineteenth Century* (Princeton: Princeton University Press, 2015).

14 S. C. M. Paine, *Imperial Rivals: CHina, Russia and Their Disputed Frontier* (New York: Routledge, 1996).

15 S. C. M. Paine, *The Wars for Asia, 1911–1949* (New York: Cambridge University Press, 2014).

16 Sheila Miyoshi Jäger, *The Other Great Game: The Opening of Korea and the Birth of Modern East Asia* (Cambridge: Belknap Press, 2023).

17 Anthony Petros, Spanakos, Francisco E. Panizza, Larry Elliot, and Graeme Wearden, "Xi Jinping Signals China Will Champion Free Trade If Trump Builds Barriers," *The Guardian*, January 17, 2017, accessed February 21, 2024, https://www.theguardian.com/business/2017/jan/17/china-xi-jinping-china-free-trade-trump-globalisation-wef-davos.

politicizing. What did they gain and, how much of that, did they subsequently lose. This book includes Blecher's careful study of working class formation in China as well as perceptive comments from Stephen Crowley, Elaine Sio-leng Hui, and Paul Pierson, to which he, ultimately, responds. With each building on his or her respective expertise (Crowley on Russia, Hui on hegemony and China's working class politics, and Pierson on political institutionalization and path dependence), they contextualize the contributions of this excellent. The careful reader of this work has so much "to win."

Anthony Spanakos and Francisco Panizza

INTRODUCTION

> The proletarians have nothing to lose but their chains. They have a world to win.
>
> —*Karl Marx and Friedrich Engels,* The Communist Manifesto

In one sense, Marx and Engels were right: China's working class *has* brought about a fundamentally new world—just not at all in the way they projected. It has provided the engine of China's astonishing rise, but also, amid the country's sweeping socialist revolution, its own demise. Following Adam Smith, David Ricardo, Karl Marx and plain old common sense, labor is the source of all material value. *Ergo,* China's working class is the source of all the wealth churned out there. But only with their economic, social, cultural and political accession to the forces financing, mobilizing and exploiting their labor could they have produced those vast quantities of value. The core argument of this book is that a key precondition for that acquiescence is the nature of the working class itself—more specifically, the pattern of working class formation in China from its origins around the turn of the twentieth century to the present day.

China's workers have been the subjects of a great deal of analysis by scholars, documentation by journalists and activists, and portrayal by writers, filmmakers and artists. Light has been shone on the rich tapestry of economic, social, cultural and political forces driving them into low-paid, dangerous, degrading, alienating, mind-numbing, transient employment, on the obstacles to improvement, on workers' understandings of their world and their lives in it, on their passivity and resistance, and on the effects of their responses. *The Making of China's Working Class* seeks the foundation for all this in three questions: What kind of class is China's

DOI: 10.4324/9781003518228-1

working class? What are the historical forces and processes that have formed it? And how does the pattern of class formation help explain the working class's reactions historically, presently and even prospectively?

An analogy may help. Aficionados of crime literature, drama and film will recognize a familiar trope: a mountain of evidence points toward a culprit with the motive, the opportunity, the resources, no alibi, and even the suspicious look. But along comes the clever detective who has developed a sense of who the suspect is, and believes they are just not the sort of person who would or could commit the crime. Soldiering on doggedly in the face of disbelief and derision, the investigator, focusing *not just on the details of the crime but also the nature of the criminal*, finally serves up justice by apprehending the real culprit.

Likewise, scholarship on labor politics in China tends to focus directly on its manifest activities: Of what do those politics consist? What stimulates them? What forms do they take? Who leads? Who participates in them (and who does not)? What obstacles do they face? What are their goals, tactics and strategies? Do they target employers, the government, or both? What ideological formations do they entail? What results do they achieve? These and related questions can be best approached in the context of a prior set: Who are China's workers? What is China's working class? How has it developed since its birth over a century ago? As such, the focus here is on *working class formation*, understood as a noun and a verb: What is the working class qua class, and how did it become, over a long period of time, what it is?

Our inquiry draws inspiration from scholarship on *political development*, which has contributed so much to understanding American and Western European politics by seeking the roots of present-day outcomes in their historical origins.[1] It pays attention to questions of *path dependency*—the ways in which economic, social, cultural and political *institutions* (including formal and even legal ones but also widely shared norms and practices) arose and became settled in ways that came to be taken for granted, proved difficult to change, and as such had enormous if often overlooked implications for outcomes ever since. It also focuses on historical *sequences* and *conjunctures* as causal or influencing mechanisms in themselves.[2] As such, *The Making of China's Working Class* also aims to begin to fill a curious lacuna in scholarship on Chinese politics: that in the study of so ancient and historically continuous a civilization, country and polity, the past

1 Here, "political development" eschews the meanings the term took on in the heyday of modernization theory in the 1960s and 1970s when it referred to processes of capitalist economic growth, social and cultural "modernization" and political democratization and stabilization.

2 "For instance, it arguably mattered a good deal for the trajectory of domestic politics whether left-wing or right-wing parties happened to be in power at the time when a cataclysmic event, the Great Depression, hit a particular country." Paul Pierson, *Politics in Time* (Princeton, NJ: Princeton University Press, 2004), 11.

is still deployed mainly as background or context (and an often reified one), but not as itself a dynamic space in which the durability or discontinuity of institutions, and the concatenation of specific forces at specific moments, has actually shaped outcomes in specific ways.

...

Already, three major conceptual and theoretical problems have arisen. First, for the past 175 years, Chinese politics have demonstrated significant *path independence* and *radical discontinuity*. The political development approach as applied to China, therefore, must de-emphasize positive feedback loops and institutional self-reinforcement that are central to its analyses of real-existing democracies[3] and capitalist political economies in favor of the politics of radical change. Yet this can be completely consistent with the political development approach by emphasizing the moments when new pathways began to be forged and then themselves went off the rails after mere decades and had to be replaced with new ones. The very fact of rapid-fire disjunction itself produced important political effects on each new pathway, as *The Making of China's Working Class* will demonstrate.[4] Finally, political development's foci on the analytical importance of conjuncture and sequence is particularly useful in explaining disjuncture, since they are central to the formation of path dependencies in the first place.

Second is the question of "working class," which conjures up a thicket of conceptual, theoretical, analytical and political problems. Starting with the first of its elements, should conceptualization focus on the nature of work itself, in which case it would include anyone who engages in manual labor, even if they are self-employed and perform their work outside a factory—as, for example, a woman spinning cotton or working a loom at home on a putting-out basis, or a self-employed gardener bulking up muscles and pouring out sweat beautifying suburban tract homes? Does it include mental or professional work, such as that done by doctors or even professors who write sentences such as this one? Or should it be grounded in the economic, social and political relations of work, so that it features those toiling, together with fellow workers, for a wage in factories? Turning to the second element, do large numbers of "workers," however defined, always form a "working class"? Or is that better conceived as something greater than merely the sum of its parts—*i.e.*, a large body of

3 "A 'real-existing' democracy (or RED, in my terminology) has three characteristics: (1) it calls itself democratic; (2) it is recognized by other self-proclaimed democracies as being 'one of them;' and (3) most political scientists applying standard procedural criteria would code it as democratic. Its relationship to democracy as advocated in theory or as described in many civics texts is coincidental." Philippe Schmitter, "The Future of 'Real-Existing' Democracy," *Society and Economy* 33, no. 2 (2011): 399–428.

4 For example, labor activism in the structural reform period is shaped and restricted by workers' antipathy toward any return of Cultural Revolution-style political conflict.

workers unified by the kind of work they do, the terms on which they do it, or their relations to each other?

Now add "formation" into the mix. If there is a "working class," how is it formed historically? Should the process be thought of in rather strictly—or, as critics would have it, "vulgar"—Marxian terms as a teleology that begins with shared exploitation[5] and punishing manual labor, which produce oppressive social relations with employers and shared bonds among workers, that in turn engender collective "class consciousness," all of which lead workers to band together politically to do something about it? Or is the process more indeterminate, recursive and complex than that?

Ira Katznelson has developed a conceptual framework to help sort through these issues. At its core is the idea that class has four distinct aspects,[6] which can be denoted in shorthand as economic, social, cultural and political. The *economic* is the strictly materialist one rooted in the mode of production. For capitalism, class is a function of the commodification of labor and capital, the wage relationship and the exploitation of labor through the creation and extraction of surplus value. In state socialism, it is structured by the decommodification of labor in favor of treating it as a "use value,"[7] compensation delinked from actual labor contribution, and appropriation of the product for social distribution and of the surplus mainly for direct reinvestment. Even Marx and Marxists, not to mention analysts and actors of other theoretical and political persuasions, have long realized, of course, that the economic aspect of class is necessary to conceptualize a working class theoretically and for it to form historically, but also that it can never suffice to explain or even chart the social, cultural or political life of the proletariat.[8] In capitalism, the stark facts of private ownership of the

5 This rhetorically loaded word is deployed throughout in its coolly analytical meaning: the appropriation of surplus by one who did not produce it.

6 Katznelson uses the term "levels" and even prefers merely to enumerate rather than name them (level 1, etc.). Since, however, his ultimate point is that there is no necessary or underlying logical, historical, theoretical, or analytical hierarchy among them, it seems best to adopt the more analytically neutral "aspect." (A more dialectically inflected theoretical conceptualization might prefer "moment." But since that word can also refer to a specific point in time, its deployment could add ambiguity to the present, temporally grounded, empirical approach.) See Ira Katznelson, "Working-Class Formation: Constructing Cases and Comparisons," in *Working-Class Formation: Nineteenth-Century Patterns in Western Europe and the United States*, ed. Ira Katznelson and Aristide Zolberg (Princeton, NJ: Princeton University Press, 1986), 1–41. The shorthand terms are mine, not Katznelson's.

7 In classical political economy, the senses in which a commodity satisfies a want or need, in contradistinction from "exchange value"—its price in relation to other use values.

8 Hence Marx's famous distinction between a class in and for itself. "Economic conditions had first transformed the mass of the people of the country into workers. The combination of capital has created for this mass a common situation, common interests. This mass is already a class as against capital, but not yet for itself." See Karl Marx, *The Poverty of Philosophy* (New York: International Publishers, 1963), 173.

means of production (and the working class's exclusion therefrom), wage labor, and appropriation of the products of labor by capitalists do not by themselves imply anything very specific even about workers' incomes, wealth and economic conditions.[9] Much less do the relations of production and exploitation lead directly to specific patterns of working class social life, "consciousness" or politics. Nonetheless, the latter are bound to be shaped by the basic economic structures and processes of the mode of production in a particular place and time, including income, payment systems, labor recruitment mechanisms, employment security and the labor process.

The *social* aspect of class is "the social organization of society lived by actual people in real social formations"[10] that affects the ways workers experience the mode of production and their place in it. By contrast with the cold, bare material aspects of class and labor, here the focus is on the existential, quotidian and phenomenological. It includes elements that are not strictly economic or determined by the basic facts of the mode of production, such as the size and composition of the working class, the relationship between workplaces and residential spaces,[11] social status, and social and power relations and hierarchies within the factory.

The *cultural* aspects of class refer to workers' shared dispositions—"the ways people construct meaning to make their way through the experienced world," the "plausible and meaningful [thought] responses to the circumstances workers find themselves in."[12] Katznelson rejects the term "consciousness" as too deterministic and teleological, preferring more open-ended questions about the kinds of social and political affinities that workers conceive as most important or salient. How and how much do workers think of themselves as having something in common with other workers who are similarly situated within the structures and processes both of the mode of production and of daily life (*i.e.*, the *economic* and *social* aspects)? Beyond class, how and how much do they identify with the nation? Their place of origin? Their gender? Their secret society? Their institutions such as parties or unions? It also takes in the content and tenor of working class political predispositions. Are they forward-looking or atavistic? Optimistic or pessimistic? Accommodative, syndicalist, socialist or something else? How do they interact with other identities?

9 After all, highly paid baseball players who sell their labor to team owners are, strictly speaking, exploited—an idea that is not so fanciful when it is recalled that they have organized unions and gone on strike.

10 Katznelson, "Working-Class Formation," 16.

11 Ira Katznelson, *City Trenches: Urban Politics and the Patterning of Class in the United States* (New York: Pantheon, 1981). Indeed, he gives particular emphasis to the spatial array of workplace and home, building it into a theory in which it provides an *explanans* for various other facets of working class formation—the construction of hegemonic "trenches" that orient working class politics toward either labor-based issues or community-based ones.

12 Katznelson, "Working-Class Formation," 18–19.

Finally, for Katznelson the *political* aspects of class refer to organization and collective action. What are the institutions of working class politics: parties, unions, other kinds of associations and social movements? What are the stimuli, repertoires and demands? Is it contentious?[13] In what ways does collective action depend on the emergence of political opportunities to create openings?[14] Is it patterned as isolated incidents or waves, or in rhythm with economic upturns or downturns? How politicized is it: Do workers target the state, employers, foreigners or "others"? Do they form unions, parties, movements, or other collectivities? Do they strike, hold political demonstrations, or engage in other political actions? Then, there is the question of the state's response: How does it mix coercion, cooptation, manipulation and accommodation?

Katznelson's major conceptual and methodological point is that there is no simple or straightforward theoretical or historical relationship among these four aspects of class. He seeks, for example, to undermine simplistic "base-superstructure" theories, according to which, implicitly or explicitly, economic factors lead to certain forms of working class life (*e.g.*, the way capitalism brings workers together in factories and subjects them to increasing homogenization, impoverishment and exploitation) that in turn foster burgeoning class consciousness leading to organization and action. He argues that the process of class formation is "the conditional (but not random) process of connection" among the four aspects of class.[15] The explanatory arrows can run in a number of directions and even be recursive. For example, following E. P. Thompson, working class consciousness can grow out of contentious collective action as well as bring it about in the first place, and there is evidence of this in China.[16] The political can also shape the cultural in other profound ways, though. For example, the existence of the franchise and the organization of parties in American urban neighborhoods induced workers to focus on issues of community rather than class.[17] Likewise, of course, collective action reshapes the economic and social structures of capitalism that affect workers.

13 Sidney Tarrow distinguishes between "collective action" and a subset he calls "contentious collective action." The former "can take many forms—brief or sustained, institutionalized or disruptive, humdrum or dramatic. Most of it occurs within institutions, on the part of constituted groups acting in the name of goals that would hardly raise an eyebrow. Collective action becomes contentious when it is used by people who lack regular access to institutions, who act in the name of new or unaccepted claims, and who behave in ways that fundamentally challenge others or authorities." Sidney Tarrow, *Power in Movement: Social Movements and Contentious Politics*, 2nd ed. (Cambridge: Cambridge University Press, 1998), 3.

14 See the discussion of Tarrow's theory of political opportunity structure in Chapter 1.

15 Katznelson, "Working-Class Formation," 21.

16 Elizabeth J. Perry, *Shanghai on Strike: The Politics of Chinese Labor* (Stanford, CA: Stanford University Press, 1993), 8.

17 Katznelson, *City Trenches.*

The four aspects of class do not form a theory of class formation. Katznelson's argument is that there cannot be a robust theory that explains working class formation always and everywhere. Rather, he offers a conceptual and analytical scheme for explaining and comparing particular cases. First, it helps pose important questions by deploying working class formation as a noun. How fully and coherently developed was working class formation in a particular time and place, and what were the political implications? For example, was the working class politically organized and active even as it did not fully share economic conditions, experiences or discourses (as happened to some extent in Maoist China)? Or did it have the opposite problem of being unable to build a political movement on its shared exploitation, experiences or thinking (as happened to some extent in China under structural reform)? And if so, which obstacles were most important, and how did they interact? Second, conceptualizing working class formation as a verb, how did the working class form over time? For example, can changes in its political activity be explained by shifting levels of immiseration or exploitation? By reorganizations of social life (brought about, for example, by developments in urban, housing, transport and communication infrastructures)? By systematic changes in workers' thinking? And were any such "cultural" changes produced by shared economic and social experiences or by political efforts such as literacy campaigns and cultural activities?[18] Turning matters around, did the material lives of workers change due to concerted political action? Many more meaningful lines of inquiry can spin out in potentially revealing, fascinating and, ultimately, recursive ways that explain working class formation in a particular time and place as both a thing and a process, neither of which is random or overdetermined but, rather, is contingent on the specificities of particular times and places.

...

The Making of China's Working Class is organized according to this analytical scheme. It is divided into three parts. First, before 1949, working class formation in China took place amid the crisis of the *ancien régime* and, after 1920,[19] the protracted struggle between two hegemonic projects:[20] one to build a Republic on the foundations of the nascent capitalist economy, and the other for socialist

18 Elizabeth Perry has emphasized their importance in China. See Elizabeth J. Perry, *Anyuan: Mining China's Revolutionary Tradition* (Berkeley: University of California Press, 2012).

19 1921 is the year commonly given for the birth of the Chinese Communist Party. In fact, Party organizations began to form the previous year in at least six Chinese cities as well as Paris. See James Pinckney Harrison, *The Long March to Power: A History of the Chinese Communist Party, 1921–72* (New York: Praeger, 1972), 30–31.

20 The systematic effort to construct hegemony, which itself involves the exercise of power through the active or passive consent of the ruled. Its modern usage in political science derives from the work of Antonio Gramsci. For a brief summary, see Philippe Schmitter and Marc

revolution. Second, from 1949 to 1978, the victory of the revolution led to titanic, contradictory exertions in the Party/state to construct a new hegemony around radical yet also developmental state socialism. Third, beginning in 1978, the Party/state sought to rebuild its hegemony around a new foundation of deep structural reform[21] of the economy and a demobilized politics centered on the preservation of its power.

For each period, *The Making of China's Working Class* conceptualizes working class formation in terms of the myriad interactions among the four aspects of class. How, for example, did changes in the mode of production and degree of exploitation reshape social life? And how did working class social life contribute to coping with or even reinforcing economic relations? How did the economic and social aspects of working class life find cultural expression (and, in turn, how did working class cultural formation reinforce or undermine material or social life)? How did the economic, social and cultural aspects shape labor politics (and *vice versa*)?

...

Working class formation has proceeded both in terms of particular dynamics within each period as well as some that transcended them. On the one hand, the "long century" since the dawn of China's industrial working class has been a time of radical discontinuity. On the other, distinctive features, sequences and conjunctures of working class formation in one era created path dependencies both within it as well as for the succeeding one(s). Yet they also brought the first two periods to their ends in path independent climacterics.

Chapter 1 covers the Republican/revolutionary decades (c. 1920–1949):

Blecher, *Politics as a Science: A Prolegomenon* (New York and Abingdon, Oxon: Routledge, 2021), 48.

21 The commonplace term for the vast changes that have taken place in China since 1978 is "reform." It is appropriate insofar as it refers to aspects of the process by which these transformations have occurred. Change has been pursued gradually and mostly peacefully. But "reform" can hardly capture the depth and breadth of the substance of the changes. Since 1978, China has not merely been tinkering with, perfecting, or toning down Maoist state socialism. Something far more thoroughgoing is afoot. The country has been seeking, often successfully, to excise, root and branch, the basic elements of its Maoist polity, economy, society and political culture. It has questioned almost everything that went before. Its leaders and people have sought to create new forms of political authority, economic activity, social organization and cultural expression that have no precedent in China or indeed the world. If revolution is defined as a "basic transformation of a society's state and class structures" (Theda Skocpol, *States and Social Revolutions* [Cambridge: Cambridge University Press, 1979], 4) then what China has been undergoing is no mere "reform," but rather something that would more aptly be called a "peaceful revolution." Another, perhaps less oxymoronic term to capture China's gradual and peaceful process toward "basic transformation of the state and class structures" would be "structural reform."

- Labor exploitation was intense throughout.
- To cope, workers elaborated a complex set of social relations and organizations.
- And to express their misery and shock, they developed and articulated ways of thinking that combined themes of class, nation and ardent humanism.
- Across much of this period, the working class took the initiative to organize itself in powerful but locally and regionally bounded waves of strikes and protest. This experience continued to propel labor activism in the radical state socialist and structural reform periods that followed.
- The Communist Party was founded in 1920 by radical intellectuals, not workers. It endeavored to provide political leadership to the working class, which did enable the labor movement to begin to transcend those boundaries in the early and middle 1920s and again in the latter 1940s when the Party could operate in some cities.
- The "White Terror" of April 1927, when Nationalist forces betrayed the working class and the Communist Party with which it had been allied, leading to subsequent defeats through the autumn, proved a watershed—a nonergodic moment the effects of which could not subsequently be canceled out.[22] It drove the Party into the countryside, separating it and the working class over the next two crucial, formative decades for both.
- That period was conjunctural with the rise of autocracy in urban China under the proto-fascist Nationalists and the Japanese occupation. As Aristide Zolberg has suggested, "the single most important determinant of variation in the patterns of working class politics …is simply whether, at the time this class was being brought into being by the development of capitalism…, it faced an absolutist or liberal state."[23] In China this had two effects.
  - It reinforced class-based labor politics by preventing the development of a reformist or community-based working class politics.[24]
  - It inclined the working class toward hostility to political authority more generally, though this would not become apparent until after 1949.
- At the same time, the working class lost its left-wing activists and Party leadership which were necessary for developing any capacity for organization and mobilization on regional, much less national scales.

22 Pierson, *Politics in Time*, 18.

23 Aristide Zolberg, "How Many Exceptionalisms?" in *Working-Class Formation: Nineteenth-Century Patterns in Western Europe and the United States*, ed. Ira Katznelson and Aristide Zolberg (Princeton, NJ: Princeton University Press, 1986), 397–455.

24 In the United States, by contrast, the residential separation of workplace and residence, combined with the wider context of "real-existing democracy," gradually shifted working class politics from focusing on labor to community. See Katznelson, *City Trenches*.

- Yet the working class continued to mobilize itself in various if limited ways under even the unfavorable conditions of Nationalist autocracy, Japanese occupation and civil, anti-imperial and, indeed, world war.
- These three developments—separation from the Communist Party, the autocratic context and political deficits at the regional and national levels—produced a working class politics after 1949 that was active, spontaneous, radical and hostile to political leadership and authority.
- Meanwhile, the Party became consolidated and battle-hardened in relative isolation from the working class over the same two decades after its expulsion from the cities.
- Thus, the working class emerged into the state socialist period with considerable political experience. Yet it also had definite autonomy from and disillusionment with political authority, born not just of the failure of the Communist Party to lead forward but, even worse, the working class's decimation as a result of following Party leadership and the Party's inability to protect it from slaughter at the hands of the Guomindang (GMD). Moreover, thereafter it was left with little in the way of left-wing leadership or membership, and it suffered for two more decades under the Guomindang and Japanese.
- And as it came to power the Party faced the prospect of ruling with little if any base in the working class.
- The attenuation at best, and estrangement at worst, of ties between the Party and the working class during their formative decades had major, yet qualitatively different, consequences for labor politics in China in both the radical state socialist and structural reform periods that followed—encouraging but then deserting it in the former, and suppressing it in the latter. It is an example of what Arthur Stinchcombe called "'historical causation,' in which dynamics triggered by an event or process at one point in time reproduce themselves, even in the absence of the recurrence of the original event or process."[25]

Chapter 2 explores the radical state socialist period of the People's Republic from 1949–78:

- The new Party/state was founded before any institutional or political incorporation of the working class. It did not significantly increase working class representation, much less power, within its ranks—a path-dependent effect of its separation and alienation from them after 1927 as well as a product of newer élite-level conflicts over the role of workers in industrial management and politics itself.

25 Pierson, *Politics in Time*, 11.

  - Put in terms of political development, the Party was an "early arriver"[26] in creating and filling the new and radically expanded political space starting in 1949. To be sure, early arrival does not guarantee success in holding that space over the medium, much less long term.[27] And the Maoist wing's penchant for fomenting instability and, indeed, actual ("Cultural") revolution provided political opportunities that the working class took to assert itself.[28] Yet the Party's profound Leninist organizational, ideological and political DNA, combined with its long experience with managing revolutionary politics and internal fissiparousness, as well as with the working class's long estrangement from the Party and its lack of organization and leadership of its own, made it unable to overcome the Party's early strategic advantages in building and occupying political space.
  - Moreover, early on the sidelining of labor was not necessarily a conscious move by the Party so much as an unconscious effect of the path-dependent alienation of the Party and the working class in revolutionary times.[29] Yet by the start of the First Five-Year Plan, many in the Party did suppress working class self-assertion around the "East China" system of participatory management and shopfloor democracy. And that crackdown, along with the path-dependent effects of the cultural and political aspects of working class formation—*i.e.*, the legacy of spontaneous working class politics before 1949—can in turn help explain the eruption of radical working class contention during the Cultural Revolution in the next decade.
- Despite all this, the Party significantly improved wages, benefits and labor conditions, exalted workers' social status, and concentrated them in all-encompassing factory-run communities. But these were not just gifts *from* the new government; they were very much the products of working class activism over previous decades, which could now begin to be realized at last *through* that government. But those gains were short-lived. By the time of the Second Five-Year Plan and the Great Leap Forward in the late 1950s, compensation and living standards began to stagnate; Chinese workers did not receive a raise after 1957.
- In terms of the social aspects of class formation—workers' lived experience—the working class expanded significantly with the rapid industrialization. It was broadly homogeneous: workers mostly hailed from the cities in which they worked and in which they had been settled for some time, they

26 Ibid., 72 and *passim.*

27 Kathleen Thelen, "Timing and Temporality in the Analysis of Institutional Evolution and Change," *Studies in American Political Development*, 14, no. 1 (2000): 101–108.

28 Again, see the discussion of Tarrow's theory of political opportunity structure in Chapter 1.

29 As Pierson points out, "an understanding of path-dependent dynamics may suggest alternative explanations for arrangements that are too easily attributed to power relations." Pierson, *Politics in Time*, 47.

were paid according to fairly uniform scales (and they opposed wage differentials), they lived together in factory communities, and rural emigration was tightly restricted. Yet the limited incorporation of farmers during the Great Leap Forward (who were then forced back home), and of contract workers sent subsequently to urban factories by rural communes, and the extrusion of urban workers to remote cities or rural projects, did produce inequalities and frictions that became major flashpoints in the Cultural Revolution.

- Working class "social capacities"—"the stock of available [material, technological, organizational, and ideational] resources in social life"—also increased sharply.[30] But those of the state developed even more.
- Culturally, the working class evinced a "workerist" sensibility, political self-confidence and sheer gumption *vis-à-vis* the Party. These were grounded in its experience of self-directed activism in the Republican/revolutionary period, its hostility to Guomindang proto-fascism and Japanese colonial fascism, and its attenuated links with the Party during that time.
- The previous three points help explain the puzzle of rising levels but also increased politicization of labor politics in the early years even despite improving material conditions at that time. Workers mobilized early, spontaneously, repeatedly, and, in contrast with their previous focus on material issues, often for radical political changes, especially within their factories, many against the Party/state and many stimulated by the Maoist left.
- But this politics also explains the working class's ultimate defeat. Sequencing matters: radical working class political offensives in the early years of the People's Republic were defeated before the rise of Maoist radicalism in the run-up to the Great Leap and then in the Cultural Revolution, which gave renewed voice and official *imprimatur* to those early concerns. Context was also crucial: the Cultural Revolution proved too chaotic a cauldron for the working class to be able to press its concerns effectively. And finally, the fact that the social capacities of the state grew more than those of the working class proved significant when push came literally to shove in ringing down the curtain on the popular mobilization phase of the Cultural Revolution in 1967–68 and in preventing it from returning during the rest of the Cultural Revolution decade.

Chapter 3 turns to the structural reform beginning in 1978. In industry, it remained tentative and contested through 1993, when it began to take off and powered the rest of the economy to do the same. The working class formation approach can help explain the shifts both overall and also between the first fifteen years and the subsequent ones.

30 Pierson, *Politics in Time*, 74.

- In the 1980s, labor radicalism of the Cultural Revolution remained fresh in the minds of workers, managers and officials, cowing the latter two groups and delaying structural reform.
- By the early 1990s, though, labor "reform" broke through alongside "reforms" of prices, planning, ownership and management. The Party/state began to dismantle factory communities and the housing, services and benefits they provided. It also carried out massive layoffs in the service of closing "unprofitable" enterprises.
- Thus, wages and economic life waxed and waned, while the working class was knocked off the social and cultural pedestal on which the Party/state had placed it decades earlier.
- The most massive and rapid wave of proletarianization in world history occurred with the addition to the working class of hundreds of millions of farmers hired into burgeoning low-wage private firms.
- Thus, the working class became far more socially heterogeneous and widely distributed across the country. Yet within industrial areas, it grew both more dispersed in one sense (with the end of factory-provided housing) but also more concentrated in another with the rise of gargantuan factory towns and the return of the pre-1949 practice of dormitory housing for single young workers.
- The working class also became more heterogeneous culturally, evincing patterns of atavism (especially in rustbelts), acquiescence (generally among urban residents in functioning industrial areas) and attraction/repulsion (among rural migrants in the new export hubs).
- Labor protest became endemic—China is now home to more of it than any other country—but also, in contrast to the Maoist period, defensive and apolitical. The quantity continues the working class's long traditions of self-organized protest. Qualitatively, depoliticization and deradicalization were grounded in:
    - the political defeats of, and disillusionment with, the radicalism of Maoist-era labor politics;
    - the gradualism of labor reform, itself attributable to lingering effects of radicalism in the 1980s; and
    - the tidal wave of rural entrants into the working class.
- In the end, workers came to accept broadly the hegemony of capitalist and market relations, and of aspects of state rule (especially its use of law).[31]

31 Elaine Sio-ieng Hui, *Hegemonic Transformation: The State, Laws and Labour Relations in Post-Socialist China* (New York: Palgrave Macmillan, 2018); Ching Kwan Lee, *Against the Law: Labor Protests in China's Rustbelt and Sunbelt* (Berkeley: University of California Press, 2007).

...

Amid this complex admixture of continuity and discontinuity, of path dependence and path independence, working class politics demonstrated a key commonality that repeatedly drove it to heroic activism and tragic defeat. On the one hand, the working class took the initiative to mobilize itself politically in each era. It acted frequently and spontaneously (rather than in a manner produced within or by developed institutions) to resist the depredations being visited on it and, in the Maoist period, to advance its vision of a better world. It was not generally the tool of élites, and, with the exception of three moments in the mid-1920s, mid-1940s and the mid-1960s, it did not take advantage of them to provide the energy, organization, discourse, tactics or strategy for its political interventions. But on the other hand, *it engaged in politics very differently in each period because its resistance was fundamentally shaped by the economic, social, cultural and political hegemony of the time.* Thus, in the Republican/revolutionary period, it struggled hard to protect itself from the despotism of China's nascent capitalism, developing its own spontaneous tactics, wildcat unions and associations, and a discourse that wove together themes of class and nation. In the mid-1920s and latter 1940s, it relied on the Chinese Communist Party (CCP) mainly to help it coordinate its fragmented local efforts into wider movements. In the Maoist era, much of the working class, exalted at least early on materially, socially and culturally by the new radical state socialism, went on the political offensive to press the new state socialist political economy even further leftward, advancing a powerful syndicalist program grounded in a "workerist" sense of extremely bold self-confidence, even as it did so within but also against *ad hoc* organizations created by shifting groups emerging out of the Party/state and the intellectuals, students and politicians who drove the left forward. During the transition to structural reform, it reverted to a generally defensive but still highly active pattern of resistance, while still succumbing to the new hegemony by not criticizing the new capitalistic[32] economic and social forces or deploying lenses and language of class. In short, *over more than a century of dizzying, path-independent change, working class formation in China has proceeded in a dialectic in which it has resisted the hegemonic forces acting on it in ways fundamentally stamped by those very forces.*

The consequence is that *this helps explain why the working class ultimately lost out in each period, albeit in very different ways.* In the Republican/revolutionary period, the revolution won, but the working class was never incorporated significantly into the Party or able to drive or even underpin revolutionary

32 This term is meant to elide the debate about whether structural reform—with its adoption of private capital, wage labor and markets—amounts to capitalism or, because of the heavy role for the Party/state, something else.

politics. That ultimately left it in a weak position *vis-à-vis* the new Party/state, and therefore vulnerable when the deep contradictions of Maoist politics erupted into crisis during the Cultural Revolution. That defeat of the working class opened the door for the structural reforms which, in turn, knocked the working class off its Maoist-era pedestal and subjected it to new depredations redolent of pre-revolutionary factory despotism and labor markets. Ultimately, and more in line with Gramsci's theory of hegemony than the revolutionary optimism of Marx and Engels in their concluding battle cry of *The Communist Manifesto*, Chinese workers, despite their best efforts, lost the world they might have made.

1

REVOLUTION

The Making of China's Working Class

While there is evidence that a class of propertyless, legally free wage workers began to form in China as early as the sixteenth century,[1] industrial working class formation started in earnest in the late nineteenth century and flowered in the first half of the twentieth, when the country underwent its first transition to capitalism. In 1895, China's humiliating defeat in the Sino-Japanese War forced it to agree to the Treaty of Shimonoseki, which gave Japan—and, therefore, other Western imperialists—the right to establish factories in China. That in turn stimulated the rise of the Chinese bourgeoisie at one pole and the proletariat at the other.[2] Thus, China's working class began to form around 1900, at the midpoint of China's century of "total crisis."[3]

1 S. A. Smith, *Like Cattle and Horses: Nationalism and Labor in Shanghai, 1895–1927* (Durham, NC and London: Duke University Press, 2002), 16; William T. Rowe, "Modern Chinese Social History in Comparative Perspective," in *Heritage of China: Contemporary Perspectives on Chinese Civilization*, ed. Paul S. Ropp (Berkeley: University of California Press, 1990), 242–62.

2 By 1933, Chinese-owned factories outnumbered foreign-owned ones by a factor of ten, employed nearly three-fourths of the industrial working class, and produced two-thirds of China's industrial output. See Victor Lippitt, "The Development of Underdevelopment in China," *Modern China* no. 4 (1978): 264.

3 Tang Tsou, *The Cultural Revolution and the Post-Mao Reforms* (Chicago: University of Chicago Press, 1999), xxxi–xxxv.

DOI: 10.4324/9781003518228-2

The new proletariat[4] grew at breakneck speed: by 1919, there were 1,500,000 industrial workers in China.[5] It was subjected to extraordinary material depredation, profoundly wrenching social transfiguration away from its rural roots, and fundamental cultural crisis. In response, it formed a panoply of new social relations and institutions to help it cope, developed radically new ways of thinking and speaking about the world, and defended itself vigorously. The dizzying struggles among competing economic, class and political forces, projects and visions—the increasingly desperate remnants of the gentry and imperial state and the agrarian economy on which they rested, the rising but fragmented and politically weak bourgeoisie and despotic capitalism, and, in politics, the Guomindang, the Communist Party, warlords and the Japanese—buffeted the working class and propelled it into a complicated set of new social relationships and ways of thinking. But they also limited working class political formation in fundamental ways, producing a spasmodic, fragmented response in which the proletariat acted mainly at the local level but only rarely, when Communist Party leadership was available, on regional and national canvasses. By the time the Revolution triumphed, China's working class had developed a strong record of standing up for itself. But it had not been able to establish itself as a significant force within, or even, after 1927, at the popular base of the Communist Party. That contradictory legacy in turn set up the complex and tempestuous labor politics of the Maoist period, and, at its end, the defeat of the working class's exertions during both the Cultural Revolution and the structural reform that followed.

Economic Aspects of Class Formation

With the advent of industrialization in the first half of the twentieth century, China's newly forming working class was subjected to a particularly harsh capitalist labor régime. In the 1920s, wages were so low that Engel's Law, which postulates that as incomes rise the proportion of income spent on food will decline, operated in reverse. That is, Chinese workers and their families were so hungry that they spent any additional income that might come their way to eat a little more.[6] In many factories that housed workers, only two meals a day were

4 Throughout, this term will be reserved to refer to the working class under conditions of predatory wage labor. It will not, therefore, be used to refer to the working class during the Maoist period. In those decades, of course, workers were paid a wage. But there was no labor market to set wages in accord with supply and demand, and at levels calibrated to ensure the production and extraction of surplus value; nor were workers recruited and disciplined through the labor market. Living and working conditions and relations were often tough, but rarely despotic and cruel.

5 Jean Chesneaux, *The Chinese Labor Movement 1919–1927*, trans. H. M. Wright (Stanford, CA: Stanford University Press, 1968), 42.

6 Chesneaux, *The Chinese Labor Movement*, 99.

served. Their diet consisted primarily of cheap starches, producing serious malnutrition and vitamin deficiency. Housing was no better. In one survey, more than half of working class families did not even have a single room to themselves. Many rural migrants were too poor to keep their families in the city, so they lived in dormitories twelve or fifteen to a room—a precursor of sweatshop conditions under structural reform a century on. Yet significant proportions of workers—often over half—could not even afford such egregiously substandard food and housing, as indicated by their high rates of debt (for which they paid usurious interest, sometimes over 100 percent per year).[7]

While China lacked anything that could be called a "labor aristocracy" of well-off workers,[8] there were significant wage differentials within the working class. Large discrepancies prevailed from one industry to another and also within firms. For example, in silk factories, skilled reelers received over seven times the hourly wage of cocoon cleaners. In Japanese-owned firms, Chinese workers were often paid half as much as their Japanese counterparts. The gap between male and female workers was of a similar proportion, and it widened over time.[9]

Wage labor developed quickly, though pre-capitalist labor relations such as guilds and apprentice systems, while in steady decline, remained in place as well for a considerable period of time, even in parts of the modern industrial sector.[10] Moreover, the new capitalist wage labor remained embedded in a number of traditional, pre-capitalist social institutions.[11] Shopfloor management was ruthlessly despotic. Wages were often not paid in full (another problem that continues a century later) or on time; wage arrears were common. Bonuses—a not-so-hidden form of wage arrears—were also used to enforce discipline. Deductions for all manner of fines—for absenteeism, smoking, "poor quality work," or "damage"—were common. Workers sometimes had to present "gifts" and provide services to their supervisors, who could fire them at will. Frequently they were required to pay a share of their wages into self-funded insurance schemes as well. It was also customary in many firms for a portion of wages to be withheld until the managers were satisfied with the quality of work done. Workers were often subjected to forced overtime, in many cases with no pay increment. Sometimes they were even paid in kind rather than in cash. This often meant the provision of food and shelter, which, as already discussed, were minimal. Payment in kind increased workers' dependence on their employers, and, in terms of production relations, meant that workers were

7 Chesneaux, *The Chinese Labor Movement*, 97–105.

8 Ibid., 386.

9 Emily Honig, *Sisters and Strangers: Women in the Shanghai Cotton Mills, 1919–1949* (Stanford, CA: Stanford University Press, 1986), 55.

10 Chesneaux, *The Chinese Labor Movement*, 54, 118.

11 See p. 20.

actually part pre-capitalist apprentices and part capitalist wage laborers. While payment in kind was yet another way to fleece workers, at moments of roaring inflation—yet another profound threat to their incomes—they, sensibly enough, actually welcomed it.

Employment security and social services such as free housing and food were sometimes provided for skilled workers who were valuable and in short supply, but much less, if at all, for unskilled workers.[12] In many cases factories were not outfitted even with bathrooms and first-aid material.[13] Turnover rates were high, partly for this reason but mostly because managers were free to fire or lay off workers at will.[14] Unemployment was often astronomical, reaching to half the labor force at some junctures. In Chongqing over two-thirds of labor disputes in 1945–46 concerned firings.[15] China had a huge reserve army of the unemployed, which helped employers keep wages low and conditions of work miserable.

Finally, proletarianization involved a relentless process of deskilling. For example, in 1934, Chongqing Arsenal skilled workers outnumbered the semi-skilled and unskilled by two to one; by 1945, the proportions were roughly equal.[16] There, and in many other sectors, managers tried to increase profits by ramping up the rate of relative surplus value, seeking efficiency gains and increased shop floor control through mechanization, standardization, and Taylorization of the labor process.[17] And of course, unskilled workers could be paid much less than skilled ones.

In conclusion, China's working class that formed in the first half of the twentieth century suffered profoundly and in multifarious ways from the material effects of capitalist industrialization. Workers were exploited in the strictly analytical sense of providing a fount for the production and appropriation of a great deal of surplus value. They toiled long hours in horrific conditions for minuscule compensation. They lacked even a modicum of employment security and benefits. They were deprived of existing skills and any opportunity to learn new ones. This was a class whose material circumstances provided a great deal against which to inveigh. Whether, when and how workers would do so, however, depended on far more than their miserable material milieux.

12 Joshua Howard, "Workers at War: Labor in the Nationalist Arsenals of Chongqing, 1937–1949" (Ph.D. diss., University of California at Berkeley, 1998), 259–260, 268.

13 Chesneaux, *The Chinese Labor Movement*, 375.

14 Ibid., 90 *ff.*

15 Howard, "Workers at War," chap. 7.

16 Ibid., 170.

17 In China, as in other countries such as France and the U.S., skilled artisans had proven to be among the more active strata in early labor protests, so deskilling was a political as well as an economic benefit to capital.

Social Aspects of Class Formation

How China's workers reacted to all this turned in part on who they were in social terms. To begin with, they were, in the main, first-generation rural emigrants.[18] Less than one-fourth of Shanghai's population in 1930 had been born there or in another city.[19] In the Tianjin textile sector, the figure was more like 5 percent.[20] Another indication of the rural origins of the labor force is that absenteeism tended to rise during harvest periods, causing some factories to shut down entirely. Workers also spent up to 10 percent of their incomes on travel expenses—a significant proportion, given their low wages and the myriad deductions and expenses to which they were already subject.[21]

As outsiders to the city with little or no education, sophistication or familiarity with urban life, these villagers needed, and were readily attracted to, formal and informal institutions that would introduce and acclimate them to the city. Most important to them was the labor contractor (包工头, which could also be translated as "labor boss").[22] He generally recruited farmers from a specific locality in which he had contacts. Thus, workers usually came to the city as part of a group of fellow *landsleute*. Moreover, since the unit of the contracting process was generally such a group, workers tended to be assigned to particular workshops alongside people of similar origin. This produced a pattern of regional and even local segmentation on the shop floor. It also promoted the elaboration of particularistic institutions—native place groups, sisterhoods and brotherhoods and secret societies. Such origins and institutions complicated, but did not necessarily discourage, and in fact often encouraged working class solidarity and contentious collective action.[23] The networks and the brotherhoods and sisterhoods also focused workers' cultural and political horizons on the enterprise rather than their class or the state.

Skill levels marked out a significant cleavage in the working class, one that mapped onto place of origin.[24] In general, skilled workers originated from traditional artisans from southern China (江南). There they were fairly well grounded in urban life and organized and recruited into the industrial labor force through guilds. (Actually, the guild affiliation was more substantial and operative than the skill itself, since skills could be learned in much less than

18 Howard, "Workers at War," 180.
19 Smith, *Like Cattle and Horses*, 15.
20 Gail Hershatter, *The Workers of Tianjin, 1900–1949* (Stanford, CA: Stanford University Press, 1986), 49.
21 Chesneaux, *The Chinese Labor Movement*, 50–51.
22 Some of the flavor of the hierarchical, authoritarian relationship between workers and labor contractors or bosses can also be gleaned from the fact that they were also known as "*na-mo-wen*," pidgin for "number one."
23 Perry, *Shanghai on Strike*, 37 and *passim*.
24 Ibid., chaps. 2 and 3.

the three years of apprenticeship required by the guild.)[25] By contrast, workers from Northern China (苏北) were generally more semi-skilled and unskilled, remained more tied to their villages, and tended to be brought to and organized in the city by gang bosses.[26]

Both women and men numbered significantly in China's working class. They tended to be segregated by sector, with women predominating in the textile and other sweatshop trades, and men in other lines of modern factory production, such as arms production. Women were most concentrated among the unskilled,[27] and men in artisanal and handicraft fields and in non-factory work such as construction, transportation and the longshore. Thus, while the working class as a whole was more male than female, women actually outnumbered men by large margins in the Shanghai factory proletariat, both at the turn of the century and still in 1928.[28] Within factories, a gender-based division of labor prevailed, though as the decades rolled on, women came to be employed in lines of work that had previously been male preserves.[29]

Chinese and foreign capitalists, particularly those in the textile sector, employed child labor as well, though the practice declined over time.[30] Most workers were young, at least when they were first recruited, since it was easier for the callow and unmarried to leave their villages, and since labor bosses preferred the heartier and unencumbered. In late 1920s Tianjin, for example, 85 percent of cotton mill workers surveyed were under 30 years old. Most were, of course, poorly educated and unskilled.

Erik Olin Wright has distinguished between exploitation, in which, following Marx, the capitalist purchases labor power for a wage but actually depends on the worker to provide the labor that produces surplus value, and "nonexploitative oppression," in which a dominant power simply appropriates the assets of the subordinate.[31] Reflecting their position astride pre-capitalist and capitalist forms, Chinese workers were almost always recruited through non-market processes—guilds for the more skilled artisans, contractors for the semiskilled and unskilled, both of which trapped them in patron–client relationships that were

25 Ibid., 36.

26 Naturally, these tendencies did not apply everywhere. In Tianjin, in north China, artisans and unskilled workers' backgrounds were more similar. Hershatter, *Workers of Tianjin*, 49–63.

27 Perry, *Shanghai on Strike*, 55.

28 Smith, *Like Cattle and Horses*, 18.

29 Honig, *Sisters and Strangers*, 50.

30 Chesneaux, *The Chinese Labor Movement*, 65; Hershatter, *The Workers of Tianjin*, 53.

31 Erik Olin Wright, *Class Counts* (New York and Cambridge, UK, Cambridge University Press, 1997), 9 *ff.* This maps onto Marx's distinction between "expanded reproduction" and the "primitive accumulation" that got it up and running in the first place. And David Harvey has theorized the latter as an ongoing form of appropriation that he calls "accumulation by dispossession." See Karl Marx, *Capital* (New York: Penguin, 1992), chaps. 26–33; and David Harvey, *A Companion to Marx's* Capital (London: Verso, 2010), chap. 11.

both exploitative and oppressive. These gang bosses were men who had roots or strong connections in a rural area as well as in a city. They collected from the would-be workers sizable fees paid in advance or taken as a credit against future wages (which effectively turned the workers into indentured labor). The gang bosses often skinned the ox twice,[32] supplementing their incomes at workers' expense by providing them with housing and food at a significant profit. Sometimes there were even intermediaries between the recruits and the bosses, who also collected fees for providing the introduction or guaranteeing the performance and credit of the worker. Finally, secret societies and criminal gangs were involved as well. In Chongqing, the Green Gang (请帮) and the Society of Elders and Brothers (哥老会) were similarly active in channeling workers into industrial employment.[33] Shanghai's powerful and fearsome Green Gang controlled labor recruitment into the city's cotton mills. It did not so much contract female labor to factories as virtually come to own the young women, often selling them as housekeepers or sex workers and, of course, using them to satisfy their own sexual appetites. From the women's point of view, these criminal "contractors" were an even bigger problem than the factory managers, even though the latter were also known to harass female employees sexually.[34]

In this context, workplace social relations were, predictably, highly authoritarian and often downright abusive. Lacking any contractual or organizational protection, workers had little choice but to endure despotic shop floor régimes.[35] Atavistically, they often had to perform the traditional ritual of *kowtow* (口头), crouching on the floor and knocking their heads on the ground in front of managers to enact total submission. Visits to the toilet were regimented and timed. Workers were often searched at the factory gates and required to carry identification cards. Those who broke rules were publicly shamed and sometimes incarcerated in the plant for a week or more.[36] Indeed, many plants were militarized, making use of private guards or even local police.[37] Managers often meted out beatings to workers who broke factory rules.[38] In the Shanghai cotton mills, overseers prowled the aisles, rapping with a stick the knuckles of women whom they thought were underperforming.[39] Incidents in which fellow workers suffered some particularly egregious abuse often stimulated strikes.

32 The phrase is Lenin's, used to describe Krupp's practice of profiting both from loans and from profits on goods bought with the credit. See Vladimir Lenin, *Imperialism: The Highest Phase of Capitalism*, in Robert C. Tucker, ed., *The Lenin Anthology* (New York: Norton, 1975), 265.

33 Howard, "Workers at War," 178.

34 Honig, *Sisters and Strangers*, 121–131, 144, 247; Hershatter, *The Workers of Tianjin*, 160–161.

35 On the concept of factory "despotism," see Michael Burawoy, *The Politics of Production* (London: Verso, 1985), especially chap. 2.

36 Howard, "Workers at War," 275–276.

37 Hershatter, *The Workers of Tianjin*, 161 *ff.*

38 For example, see Hershatter, *The Workers of Tianjin*, 160.

39 Honig, *Sisters and Strangers*, 144.

Work was frequently dirty and dangerous. There were virtually no protections against pollution. Workers generally lived and worked in the same clothes. Showers or baths were sometimes provided, but often used communal water, and were generally filthy.[40] Factories often lacked the simplest first-aid facilities; or when they had them, workers were sometimes afraid to avail themselves of their services for fear of being sent home or fired. Mortality rates were far higher for factory workers than for their population cohorts in other urban settings.[41]

Residential patterns varied a great deal. Many workers lived in factory premises or working class precincts close to their plants.[42] Indeed, industrial zones with both factories and cheap housing were built in many cities. Yet elsewhere workers had to live at great distances from their plants because they could not afford accommodation closer to the industrial centers.[43] The social history of China's working class does not afford material with which to test the political effects of these different residential patterns. In general, though, China does not appear to correspond to the pattern analyzed by Katznelson in the U.S., where the separation of workplace and residence developed into a "city trench"[44] that undermined class-based politics. In the nineteenth and early twentieth centuries, American cities were possessed of "democratic" elaborate political institutions—parties, city governments, the franchise, and their concatenation within political machines—that were able to incorporate workers into local politics outside the workplace.[45] By contrast, China's cities lacked such institutions. As we shall see, this left workers and labor activists focused on workplace issues and undistracted by other, community-based agendas of urban politics.

In short, in the first half of the twentieth century, Chinese workers found themselves in a social milieu that constituted a radical break from their previous experience. As villagers, most found the city unfamiliar, difficult to navigate, frightening, and dangerous, or worse, both physically and spiritually. It must have been strange indeed, both for women and men, for so many women to be working outside their homes. The multiple radical novelties of social life in early industrial China gave rise to a variety of adaptive institutions—labor

40 Hershatter, *Workers of Tianjin*, 154.

41 Howard, "Workers at War," 227 *ff.*

42 Hershatter, *The Workers of Tianjin*, 44.

43 Chesneaux, *The Chinese Labor Movement*, 105.

44 The term derives from Gramsci: "The superstructures of civil society are like the trench systems of modern warfare." He also writes: "The massive structures of the modern democracies, both as state organizations, and as complexes of associations in civil society, constitute for the art of politics as it were the 'trenches' and the permanent fortifications of the front in the war of position." Antonio Gramsci, *Selections from the Prison Notebooks of Antonio Gramsci*, ed. and trans. Quintin Hoare and Geoffrey Nowell Smith (London: Lawrence & Wishart; New York: International Publishers, 1971), 235, 243.

45 Katznelson, *City Trenches*.

markets and formal and informal, legal and illegal social organizations—that subordinated and segmented the working class.[46] Workers' shared experience, their variegated backgrounds and institutional relationships, and the range of political leaders and institutions they encountered, some who encouraged them and some who obstructed them, combined in complex and locally contingent processes, explored further below, to shape their thinking and their politics.

Cultural Aspects of Class Formation

How did workers in these material conditions and social milieux understand their world? The universe of elements comprising working class culture includes understandings and dispositions relating to class, gender, nation, particularistic relationships (such as clientelism or affiliation with a formal or informal organization) and region.[47]

Class

The modern term "class" (阶级) has a long history dating back to the Chinese classics.[48] As early as 1905, fifteen years before the first organizations of the Communist Party, striking workers protested their "exploitation" (剥削).[49] In 1912, Shanghai artisans spoke of "laborers" *vs.* "capitalists," and in 1916 of "oppression of capitalists and the bitterness of workers' life."[50] From the earliest days of industrialization, then, Chinese workers—more frequently skilled, educated artisans than unskilled laborers[51]—could see themselves as sharing some work-related interests with at least some, if not all, fellow workers. What did they understand those interests to be? How did they understand those class-based interests in relation to other social interests such as nation, gender or particularistic loyalties? Did they conceive their class interests as bringing them into conflict with other social groups or classes (such as capital, other workers or the state)? And if so, what kinds and levels of conflict?

At various times and places, workers expressed their interests in various ways. They spoke of enlightenment to the potentiality of freely chosen human will and self-improvement, and liberation from fatalistic, slavish subservience to traditional norms. Education became a major theme in workers' movements, both as something leaders and donors would supply but also of which enthusiastic workers seeking self-betterment would avail themselves. The language of

46 Perry, *Shanghai on Strike*.
47 They are listed in alphabetical order, to avoid any implicit *a priori* analytical hierarchy.
48 Smith, *Like Cattle and Horses*, 129.
49 Ibid., 58–59.
50 Perry, *Shanghai on Strike*, 47.
51 Ibid., 60.

liberation was used to describe the process, but it had a decidedly collective or corporate dynamic rather than the individualistic, privatistic one associated in the West with "liberty."[52] The achievement of human dignity and a respected place in society—of no longer being beasts of burden "like cattle and horses"—was an oft-repeated goal, and it was to be achieved through concerted (rather than individual) action. In this connection, labor itself was increasingly seen as moral, noble and even sacred. Moreover, it could contribute to national development. Solidarity with fellow workers in living these values and in constructing a new world founded on them became a value in itself.

Even as workers developed this sense of their class's project, they often identified their interests as consistent—or at least not inconsistent—with those of other classes. Again and again, they tended to resist a concept of class as inherently antagonistic and conflictual. They often appealed to employers by reminding them of their duty to treat workers fairly and to care for their well-being.[53] A common term for class was *jie* (阶), which can be translated as level, rank or stratum; Steve Smith glosses it as "section of society," which, though a bit cumbersome, captures the idea that it was a corporate component of a unified whole.[54] Even the breadth of the boundaries of the "working class" (or "workers section of society" [工阶])—which could take in anyone who did physical work, including employers—expresses this non-antagonistic conceptualization of class relations. So it is not so surprising that even the Guomindang—China's broad, multi-class Nationalist Party committed to national unification, political reform and modernization—trafficked in the language of class to urge harmony between workers and employers.[55] As time wore on, workers, sometimes at the behest of Marxist leadership, but sometimes on their own as well, began to conceptualize class relations in more antagonistic terms. Yet the concept of *jie* never died out completely, as evidenced by the fact that the Communist Party/state itself returned to it after 1949 as it attempted to calm the fires of working class radicalism and establish its own hegemony.[56]

Nation

The tenacious cultural bonds linking workers with other classes were more than some holdover of Confucian cosmology emphasizing harmony, hierarchy and subservience to authority. They were also propelled by the novel, active principle of nationalism. Workers often conceptualized themselves and their class as

52 Smith, *Like Cattle and Horses*, 118.

53 For example, Smith, *Like Cattle and Horses*, 59.

54 Ibid., 52.

55 Michael Tsin, *Nation, Governance and Modernity in China: Canton, 1900–1927* (Stanford, CA: Stanford University Press, 1999), 82–83, 116.

56 Smith, *Like Cattle and Horses*, 251.

"creators of the nation's wealth, as the key to its economic modernization" that was necessary to triumph over the foreigners, and as "selfless fighters against imperialism." Not only conservative political leadership such as the post-1927 Guomindang, but many radical intellectuals as well, "interpellated [workers] as members of the Chinese nation rather than of a working class, urging them to organize in order to make their distinctive contribution to nation-building."[57] This message resonated with many workers. In Shanghai through the fatal year of 1927, when, in the infamous "White Terror," Chiang Kai-shek veered right-ward and crushed the city's radical labor movement, workers were much more inclined to struggle against foreign than Chinese employers.[58] Many singled out foreigners as particularly obnoxious and odious perpetrators of the indignities and inhumanity ruining their lives. In the words of one worker among a group who had beaten up their foreman: "The mill is owned by Japanese who look upon us as cattle and horses and treat us as pigs and dogs. They feel free to assault us whenever they please."[59] Striking postal workers referred to their foreign bosses as "presumptuous guests usurping the host's role (喧宾夺主)."[60] Common parlance came to include bitter insults for Chinese who helped run foreign plants, such as "foreigners' slaves," "running dogs," "foxes adopting the terror of the tiger," and "traitors to China."[61] Smith developed the concept of "class-inflected nationalism" to convey the idea that class and national consciousness were not opposed but complementary. Workers understood that they were exploited and oppressed as workers, but for many their main enemy was foreign: both individual foreign capitalists for whom they may have worked, but also imperialism more generally, which kept China weak, dependent and impoverished.

Gender

For women (though not men), gender was a necessary and potent part of working class self-understanding. Even before the collapse of the Qing dynasty, during the earliest days of China's industrialization, most strikers were women. They called themselves "women workers" (女工), reflecting their sense that gender and class were of a piece. They organized their own unions and strikes, though this was at least as much if not more a function of the division of labor by gender as of any specifically feminist consciousness. When they did so, they sometimes singled out issues such as sexual harassment or childcare. Yet

57 *Smith, Like Cattle and Horses*, 261.
58 Ibid., 209. Smith shows, moreover, that this finding is probably not an epiphenomenon of economic factors such as deeper pockets in foreign firms (210).
59 *North China Herald*, March 13, 1926, 475; cited in Smith, *Like Cattle and Horses*, 202.
60 Smith, *Like Cattle and Horses*, 205.
61 Ibid., 203–204.

women seem to have understood the indignities inflicted upon them as a particularly egregious effect of imperialism and capitalism more than of patriarchy *per se*.[62] Smith concludes that "the gendered marking of nationalist discourse was not especially prominent."[63]

Regional and Particularistic Affinities

Likewise, the social world of the Chinese proletariat was shot through with regional and particularistic ties that were absolutely crucial to workers' adaptation and survival in their strange and cruel new world, and that were prominent in their cognitive mapping thereof. As discussed below,[64] workers often organized and mobilized contentious collective action through such localistic or clientelist loyalties. Yet, as with gender, there is little evidence that workers enmeshed in such networks and organizations understood their interests as profoundly tied up with these specific social affinities. They rarely militated on behalf of specific interests as workers from a locality or secret society. Nor did such affinities undermine class formation by cutting across class lines and linking workers with capitalist owners. On the contrary, community solidarity often helped form meaningful bonds that promoted collective action.[65]

Such clientelism as there was linked workers to gang bosses who mediated between workers on the one hand and factory owners and managers on the other. Sometimes gang bosses did help management by enforcing labor discipline, but often they also stood up against factory bosses for the workers in their gang. While such particularistic cleavages did bring the occasional strike or protest to grief by undermining workers' class and nationalist solidarity, more often than not workers demonstrated the capacity to overcome these differences.[66]

Conclusion

In conclusion, class and nation were the dominant features of Chinese workers' cognitive map of their world and their self-understandings of their place in it. Moreover, these two affinities were closely intertwined and complementary rather than contradictory. Workers' *Weltanschauungen* also included loyalties to their home places, to various particularistic networks, and, for women, to their gender, though these did not appear to conflict with their class-based and nationalistic forms of consciousness or predispositions to act on them—to which we now turn.

62 Perry, *Shanghai on Strike*, 150, 158, 170, 199.
63 Smith, *Like Cattle and Horses*, 54–59, 206–207.
64 See p. 33 *ff.*
65 Perry, *Shanghai on Strike*, 37 and *passim*.
66 Smith, *Like Cattle and Horses*, 83, 263, 269.

Political Aspects of Class Formation

Organization

China's working class came together in a dizzying array of organizations formal and informal: particularistic ones such as *bang* (帮, usually translated as "gangs"), brotherhoods and sisterhoods, and native place networks and groups; philanthropic and self-help outfits; unions; criminal secret societies; militias; and parties.

Workers' overwhelmingly rural origins contributed to the elaboration of a congeries of particularistic organizations. One type was the regionally based, informal but organizationally complex *bang*. They had resonances with secret societies: one actually "joined" (rather than simply belonged by virtue of origin), and the process required recommendation by an existing member. They also functioned like guilds, cultivating, protecting and monopolizing particular trades. They were, however, less formally organized than guilds, were often clandestine, and tended to operate in less skilled trades, such as coolie transport, or semi-skilled or unskilled labor in particular sectors such as tanning, construction, ship fitting and the longshore. Internal social and micro-political relations were structured around patron–client norms. Externally, *bang* often fought with each other, sometimes literally, to secure labor market niches.

Brotherhoods and sisterhoods formed another kind of particularistic institution. They were minuscule groupings—generally numbering up to ten—of men or women who took simple, *ad hoc* oaths to protect and provide for each other in the event of misfortune. They often mapped onto shared native-place ties, and vicariated familial bonds in the alienated urban milieu: members addressed each other as sister or auntie, or brother or uncle.[67]

Shared native place was a powerful identity[68] and therefore source of organization—one, moreover, that often mapped onto other bases of association. For skilled workers, guilds (公所) often recruited artisans from the same home areas; for the semi-skilled and unskilled, home-place societies (会馆 or 同乡会) did so. Those with greater resources built temples and schools; and even the less well endowed variously provided credit, matchmaking, employment, housing, protection and burial.[69] In places like the Chongqing Arsenal, native place organizations' welfare functions declined by the 1940s as state provision expanded. Their political roles also varied widely. While some did

67 Smith, *Like Cattle and Horses*, 27; Honig, *Sisters and Strangers*, 212, 216.
68 Smith, *Like Cattle and Horses*, 20.
69 Ibid., 20–23; Perry, *Shanghai on Strike*, 19.

run left-wing study groups,[70] and guilds could even engage in radical politics as quasi-unions,[71] others remained apolitical.[72]

Liberal and developmental reformers, including some foreigners, established organizations to promote industrial upgrading and help workers subsist or advance in the labor market. The patriotic and modernizing fervor of the May 4 Movement—named for the 1919 demonstration protesting the formerly secret clauses of the Versailles Treaty that gave Japan special rights in China—spawned a panoply of political and social improvement, as well as academic organizations such as the Society for the Promotion of Industry, the All-China Society for Industrial Advancement, the Shanghai Workers and Merchants Friendly Society and the Society for Industrial Advance. Some were also trade-specific, such as the Electrical Industries Federation or the Guangzhou Mechanics' Union, both of which included employers as well as workers; they were modernizing versions of guilds. As part of their efforts to promote Chinese industrial growth to challenge the economic offensives of foreigners, these organizations developed education and training programs for workers. In the 1930s, the Young Women's Christian Association (YWCA) continued similar efforts, in its case in the context of a more philanthropic than developmentalist program. It proved to be an important training ground for labor movement activists, especially women.[73]

Labor unions proliferated throughout the first half of the twentieth century. Many were *ad hoc* outfits: informal organizations that developed out of the heat of a wildcat strike and disappeared once it was settled. Others grew up, especially in the radicalizing atmosphere of the May 4 period, as specifically working class alternatives to the cross-class industrial organizations. Most were rooted in particular trades, localities and/or native-place groups. Their regional character was a natural effect of China's geographic and political fragmentation. Trade union federations were established in key industrial provinces and cities, where they became involved not just in organizing drives but also, and often mainly, in political movements. For example, the powerful Shanghai General Labor Union grew out of and supplied leadership for the May 30 Movement.[74] By 1927, the All-China General Union, a trade union federation originally established in Guangzhou in 1925, had become a large organization whose reach extended to many other parts of the country. In February, it proved capable of organizing a one-hour general strike joined by two million workers in seven provinces.[75]

70 Howard, "Workers at War," 226.
71 Perry, *Shanghai on Strike*, 46, 53.
72 Howard, "Workers at War," 118.
73 Chesneaux, *The Chinese Labor Movement*, 158–161; Honig, *Sisters and Strangers*, 217–224.
74 See p. 33.
75 Chesneaux, *The Chinese Labor Movement*, 345–347.

Unions ran the gamut in terms of their militance and political complexion. Many were aggressive in promoting workers' interests, especially in the heady political atmosphere that prevailed from the 'teens through the White Terror of 1927. Their pugnacity was not always functional for the working class or the labor movement as a whole, though. More than once, rivalry among competing unions undermined important strikes.[76] Moreover, after 1927, the Guomindang, now under the hegemony of its rightist, militarist wing, and in collaboration with organized criminal gangs, established "yellow" unions and labor federations (which workers dubbed as "black") to help it control the working class and promote its collaboration with capital. Yet even some of these proved capable of becoming genuine labor organizations once the political atmosphere changed. The Chinese Association of Labor, established in 1935 as a state corporatist outfit, became "an outspoken representative for labor's independent interests" a decade later.[77]

Secret societies were yet another such organization. Organized criminal groups such as the Green Gang were central to the labor movement after 1927. They were the largest, most formally and organizationally developed particularistic groups, characterized by elaborate rules and strict hierarchy. They often dominated the labor market in specific sectors, such as the Green Gang's legendary monopoly of the Shanghai docks. All told, the Green Gang could probably count a constituency of one-fifth of the city's working class.[78] The Guomindang, whose Republican government suffered from very low state capacity, collaborated closely with them in order to stay in power. Du Yuesheng, the head of the Green Gang, was a brilliant political manipulator who developed a strong base within the working class that he could use to threaten the government and extort capitalists. The Green Gang's patronage networks within the labor movement also provided a valuable resource for its own nefarious activities.[79]

Chinese workers also formed militias. In some of the earliest strikes, years before the CCP was founded, they formed their own "worker patrols"[80] in several cities to prevent scabbing. In 1922, striking Hong Kong seamen, many inspired by the armed workers of the Russian Revolution, organized their own Worker Patrols Department to help enforce discipline, including intimidating and beating back scabs, eventually sending a party to Guangdong to enforce a port blockade there as well. In the May 30 Movement of 1925, they formed

76 Tsin, *Nation, Governance and Modernity in China*, 131–139.
77 Howard, "Workers at War," 467 *ff.*
78 Smith, *Like Cattle and Horses*, 31.
79 Perry, *Shanghai on Strike*, chap. 5.
80 The conventional translation of 工人纠察队 is "workers pickets." But they did a great deal more than picket. The literal translation of 纠察队 is "rectification and investigation team," and the second character (察) is a component of the word "police." "Patrol," therefore, seems closer to the actual meaning.

hundreds of patrols, including specialized women's outfits, organized into a complex hierarchy to provide coordination. Over the years, worker militias continued to form and re-form, sometimes organized spontaneously by workers, but more often by the Guomindang, their merchant allies, the Communists, warlords or secret societies. Even when workers joined militias established by others, though, they were not always loyal followers. The Communist Party often had trouble reining in their radicalism—in 1945, the patrols turned criticism sessions into bloodbaths—or preventing them from turning into gangs of self-serving thugs.[81]

Finally, there were political parties. In the flush of the 1911 Revolution, the Labor Party put in a brief appearance. Founded jointly by Xu Qiwen, a reformist intellectual, and Zhu Zhiyao, a progressive industrialist, it was a mélange: part society for promoting industrialization, part provider of social services for workers, part strike organizer and supporter, part political advocate and part revolutionary vanguard. It was dissolved in 1913 when Xu was arrested and executed for mobilizing workers to seize the Jiangnan Arsenal. A number of anarchist parties gained working class support throughout the 'teens. By the mid-1920s, they had succumbed both to warlord repression and to the exertions of the newly formed CCP. Until 1927, the Communists were allied in a "united front" with the Guomindang, which was content to leave labor organization mostly to them. The CCP became dominant in the wave of labor activism and strikes that broke out in the early 1920s in Hunan, and then in the mid-twenties as the Northern Expeditionary Armies, led by the still-progressive Guomindang, marched out from Guangzhou to wipe out warlordism and unify the country. The Communists lost their capacity to lead the labor movement after Chiang Kai-shek turned on them in 1927—a crucial moment with path-dependent effects a century on.[82] They attempted to return to that role after the CCP and the Guomindang patched up their differences in the "second united front" of 1937.[83]

While the CCP played a very significant role in mobilizing and leading the labor movement in the 1920s and again in the late 1940s, the working class also displayed its own capacity for spontaneous organizational virtuosity independent of the Party. The Guangzhou proletariat was organized and militant well in advance of any activities of the CCP.[84] As we have seen,[85] even after the Party's formation, workers frequently created unions on the fly in the heat of spontaneous strike and protest initiatives. These were connected to Communist Party

81 Elizabeth Perry, *Patrolling the Revolution: Worker Militias, Citizenship and the Modern Chinese State* (Lanham: Rowman & Littlefield, 2006), chaps. 1–3.

82 See pp. 9, 203 and *passim*.

83 See p. 34 *ff.*

84 Linda Shaffer, *Mao and the Workers* (Armonk, NY: M. E. Sharpe, 1982), 212.

85 See p. 29.

cells but were not their creatures or subjects. In the 1940s, workers elaborated what Joshua Howard terms a "subculture of opposition," including publications, mutual-aid societies, reading groups and night schools.[86]

Overall, then, China's working class elaborated a broad and complex set of organizations during the first half of the twentieth century. They reflected the full complexity of this rapidly forming class's economic conditions and social origins. Some of them, such as the clientelist and particularistic institutions of the labor market and social life, reflected the working class's novelty, its continuing roots in pre-industrial society and, thus, its weaknesses. That is, the economic and social aspects of class formation made themselves felt directly in the political. Yet even these organizations did not impede the rapid development of more modern forms of working class organization or, as we shall see directly, contentious collective action. Moreover, these organizational achievements cannot be chalked up solely to the initiatives of skilled and committed political leaders and entrepreneurs. For as we have seen, China's working class also evinced its own capacity for a great deal of self-organization.

Contentious Collective Action

Starting with the onset of industrialization in the later nineteenth century, Chinese workers engaged in a great deal of contentious collective action that took many forms. Though concentrated in Shanghai, it spanned the country from Chengdu in the west to Tieling in the northeast to the major cities in the lower Yangzi region to Fuzhou, Guangzhou and even Hong Kong in the southeast.[87] They struck, sometimes in a spontaneous, unorganized, wildcat manner, and sometimes in planned walkouts that were even concerted across enterprises, localities and regions. They participated in broad popular movements, such as the May 4 (1919) and May 30 (1925) Movements and the Three Armed Uprisings (1926–27). They undertook slowdowns and campaigns of industrial sabotage and theft. They joined boycotts. They beat up managers. They worked with the CCP for revolution. All this they directed against a wide range of targets: individual supervisors and managers, both Chinese and foreign; foreign governments operating in China; and reactionary or corrupt Chinese leaders and politicians. The issues that propelled them were just as numerous: wages, bonuses, profit-sharing, apprenticeships, internal labor markets, hours, vacations, arrears, sick pay, health benefits, working conditions, shop floor management, welfare (including factory meals, maternity leave, daycare and death

86 Howard, "Workers at War," 447 *ff.* Howard draws the term "subculture of opposition" from Richard Jules Oestreicher, *Solidarity and Fragmentation: Working People and Class Consciousness in Detroit, 1875–1900* (Urbana and Chicago: University of Illinois Press, 1986), xv.

87 Chesneaux, *The Chinese Labor Movement*, 125–131.

benefits), job security, severance pay, reinstatement of fired workers, physical abuse by managers, insurance, social recognition and respect, national humiliation, union recognition, the right to political expression such as permission to wear Sun Yat-sen style jackets or to celebrate May Day, political and economic corruption and simple human dignity. Finally, the participants in contentious collective action ran the full gamut of the working class: more and less skilled, female and male, old and young, inland and coast, employees of foreign and Chinese firms, members and non-members of secret societies and gangs, and workers from sectors and industrial branches of all kinds.

From 1895 to 1919, a year before the CCP was even founded, 152 strikes were recorded, and surely many more occurred. By the time the Party came into being in 1920, it found an already mobilized working class to try to lead. Even before the First Party Congress in 1921, it had begun publishing labor journals and organizing unions and workers' schools, especially in Shanghai, Guangzhou and Hunan. By 1922, it was active in the victorious Hong Kong Seamen's Strike, the first with "national significance and a well-defined class orientation," drawing in 100,000 strikers from as far as Shanghai. In 1923, the Party led 150,000 workers in over 100 strikes, including Shanghai textile mills, the Anyuan and Kailan coal mines and the Beijing-Hankou Railway.[88] This flurry of labor protest came to a screeching halt in the February 7 (1923) Massacre, when warlord Wu Peifu's forces slaughtered dozens and injured hundreds of railwaymen. Chen Duxiu, the Party's general secretary, abandoned labor-related work in favor of the united front with the Guomindang and its policy of mobilizing the working class for the nationalist and anti-warlord struggles.[89] But for the next two years, the Party also worked quietly to develop its own organizational capacity and create new unions, which soon paid off.

In 1925, the Party returned to active working class mobilization around labor issues, leading strikes in twenty-two Japanese-owned cotton mills in Shanghai and Qingdao from February to April. In May, it helped organize the Second National Labor Conference in Guangzhou, exerting considerable influence among the 166 participating unions which represented 540,000 workers—a threefold increase from the number of workers under the Party's self-claimed "influence" three years earlier. The Communist Party was very active in the May 30 Movement, which led a general strike involving several hundred thousand workers in Guangzhou and Hong Kong. The Hong Kong strike lasted sixteen months—the longest in Chinese history. While it was eventually dissolved, in deference to the united front with the Guomindang in connection with the Northern Expedition, without much in the way of material gains, it amounted to a huge political gain for the Communist Party, for the first time

88 Harrison, *The Long March to Power*, 37–38.
89 Ibid., 58.

convincing it of the revolutionary power of popular movements.[90] The high tide of the Party's labor activism continued for the next two years. It admitted hundreds of thousands of workers, who, for the only moment in its history, came to comprise more than half of its members by 1927.[91] Throughout the Northern Expedition starting in 1926, it organized workers' patrols to shut down railways and conduct economic sabotage.

All this came crashing down in the April 12, 1927, White Terror, when Chiang Kai-shek collaborated with the Green Gang to betray the Shanghai working class, which had mobilized to prepare for the Northern Expedition forces to take the city. Several hundred were slaughtered, including its leader Wang Shouhua. (Zhou Enlai, later China's renowned Premier, narrowly escaped.) The repression soon spread to Nanjing and Wuhan. In August, Communists were defeated in the Nanchang Uprising, their first pitched battle with Guomindang forces. The following month, they were defeated again in the Autumn Harvest Uprisings. At its November Plenum, the Party shifted its strategy to focus on the countryside. In December, the Guangzhou Commune uprising failed. By the end of the year, the Party's membership was decimated, dropping from 58,000 to 5,000.

Over the next ten years, though, the working class did not fold its cards even as the Communists were confined to the countryside. Its left radicalism transmogrified into a right corporatist pattern under the now-autocratic Republic. The CCP was crushed in the urban areas, and labor politics came to be dominated by organized criminals with whom the weak Guomindang was forced to ally in order to govern at all. Workers still struck from time to time, sometimes in spectacular fashion, as when a 1932 postal strike for higher wages spread from Shanghai to Beiping (as Beijing was then known), Tianjin and Nanjing. But most strikes were, variously, permitted, encouraged or even mobilized by gangsters and sometimes even state officials who could then extract money from employers in order to reach settlements or, in the case of strikes against government agencies, advance their own political positions. Nonetheless, workers connected to the criminal corporatist networks also benefited from winning strikes and from gang-based patronage networks.[92]

Working class politics were transformed again after 1937, as the Guomindang and the Communists formed a Second United Front against Japan. With the Japanese occupation of Shanghai and the retreat of the Guomindang to a new capital at inland Chongqing, the gangs began to work alongside the CCP to lead the labor movement. Throughout the Second World War, which, arguably, began with the Japanese offensive in China starting in 1937, contentious politics

90 Harrison, *The Long March to Power*, 63–64, 86.
91 Ibid., 64.
92 Perry, *Shanghai on Strike*, 97 and *passim*.

remained at a low ebb thanks to Japanese repression, generally unfavorable wartime economic and political conditions, and the CCP's shift from a failed radical policy after 1927 to a more moderate, broad-based one.[93]

Contentious working class collective action did not peak again until the second half of the 1940s, with the victory over Japan, the return to power of the exhausted Guomindang, and the renewal of revolutionary civil war between the Nationalists and the Communists. The latter began to go on the offensive in urban areas by organizing unions, recruiting workers into the Party, and ultimately organizing strikes in a number of cities, including Shanghai and Chongqing. By 1947, their radicalism concerned the Party, which condemned their "left adventurism" and urged them to focus on production in the interests of winning the civil war and promoting development.[94] The working class's left efflorescence may be related at least in part to specific economic factors such as the spike in inflation and the declining demand for labor with the end of wartime production. Yet earlier sharp economic downturns—the Great Depression, which struck China hard, and the economic collapse caused by the Japanese offensive of 1937—did not coincide with any upsurge in contentious collective action. Likewise, it is difficult to relate the ebb and flow of proletarian protest to shifts in the social aspects of class formation. Neither life on the shop floor nor the other social structures in which the working class was immersed underwent significant changes corresponding to anything like the rhythms of contentious collective action. Nor, it is safe to say, did workers' underlying cultural predispositions and cognitive maps of the world.

What did move in beat to the ebb and flow of labor activism was China's politics. In the mid-1920s, the Guomindang was a vibrant, progressive, populistic young movement party that had acquired a strong political base in Guangzhou, democratic aspirations, a military force capable of advancing its aspirations to unify the country under its reformist program, a social base in the progressive middle class, and an alliance with the energetic, up-and-coming Communist Party. It was, in short, China's most credible hegemonic project grounded in a potent hegemonic bloc.[95] But by the latter 1940s, the GMD had transformed utterly into an autocratic, corrupt, right-wing, militaristic and politically ineffectual party with little in the way of public support. By contrast, the CCP's counter-hegemonic project, with its own hegemonic bloc composed of most of the peasantry at its core and incipient alliances with parts of the working and middle classes, was on the move, ramping up its political and military struggles with the Guomindang now that the Japanese had been defeated.

93 Perry, *Shanghai on Strike*, 114 and *passim*.

94 Robert Cliver, "*Minzhu Guanli*: The Democratization of Factory Management in the Chinese Revolution," *Labor History* 50, no. 4 (November 2009): 413.

95 "Hegemonic bloc" refers to a group of social classes and groups assembled around and supporting a core hegemonic actor.

What, however, was the precise relationship of the political openings of the 1920s and 1940s to the development of labor contention? Of the many strands in social movement theory, the one most centered on politics and the state has been developed by Sidney Tarrow around "political opportunity structure." He defines "political opportunity" as "consistent—but not necessarily formal, permanent or national—dimensions of the political struggle that encourage people to engage in contentious politics." He goes on to define "political constraints" as "factors—including repression but also authorities' capacity to present a solid front to insurgents—that discourage contention." "Political opportunity structure" is the concatenation of the two. Tarrow's argument is that "contentious politics"—which "occurs when ordinary people, often in league with more influential citizens, join forces in confrontations with élites, authorities, and opponents"—is more likely to happen when "ordinary citizens, sometimes encouraged by counter élites or leaders, respond to opportunities that lower the costs of contentious collective action, reveal potential allies, show where élites and authorities are most vulnerable, and trigger social networks and collective identities into action around common themes."[96]

It is tempting to see the peak periods of contentious working class collective action before 1949 as corresponding to these openings in China's political opportunity structure. After all, from 1919 to 1927, and again in the latter half of the 1940s, China lacked a coherent, capacious national government, and was starting to generate credible revolutionary movements. On closer inspection, though, many aspects of the political opportunity structure were also decidedly unfavorable for working class contentious collective action during much of these periods. China may have undergone a great deal of development of new political ideas, organization and general ferment starting in May 1919, but the costs and risks of contentious collective action remained strong in ensuing years. Striking Hunan workers and their leaders learned as much, to their deadly cost, when provincial warlords suppressed their movement, killing thirty-five strikers in the infamous February 7 (1923) incident and the subsequent destruction in December of the Shuikoushan Workers' Club, which had led the last of the major strikes. The May 30 (1925) Movement occurred not at a moment of short-term political opening, but precisely in response to a violent fusillade against the labor movement. It and the Three Armed Uprisings were not so much results of a political opening as attempts to create the conditions for the Northern Expedition to establish one—which were ultimately betrayed in the White Terror, the bloodiest and most consequential defeat ever encountered by China's working class. In the years following the end of the Second World War, workers mobilized in cities that were still under the control of the proto-fascist Guomindang-run Republic, a state that could still muster the capacity,

96 Tarrow, *Power in Movement*, 2, 19–20.

however unevenly and fleetingly, to smash unions linked to the CCP and to arrest their leaders.

What these "moments of enthusiasm"[97]—the early and middle 1920s and the late 1940s—shared, however, was not just potential tipping-points in labor politics, but also rising activism and boldness by leadership associated with the Communist Party. In 1922, the young, energetic, committed activists of the CCP were involved in the victorious Anyuan strike and in the Hunan strikes for which they provided crucial leadership and coordination, both directly and through the Hunan Labor Secretariat. They led the May 30 Movement through the Shanghai General Labor Union. They played the key role in mobilizing workers for the Three Armed Uprisings. From 1945 to 1949, the CCP, now liberated from its preoccupation with the Anti-Japanese War and from the constraints imposed by its Second United Front with the Guomindang, began to divert some of its energies into revolutionary struggles in the cities. It was behind the revival of the labor movement in Shanghai, Chongqing and other cities. The effects of the Party's resurgence on working class contentious collective action were both direct but also structural and indirect. For example, in explaining the 1946 Chongqing strike wave, Howard writes that "ongoing negotiations between the Nationalists and Communists opened up political space for social movements, since the government did not want to appear too heavy handed."[98]

Yet it would obviously be too simplistic to argue that the CCP produced the Chinese labor movement or its most contentious moments of collective action. As we have seen, Chinese workers began to undertake meaningful contentious

97 "No class of civil society can play this role without arousing a moment of enthusiasm in itself and in the masses, a moment in which it fraternizes and merges with society in general, becomes confused with it and is perceived and acknowledged as its general representative, a moment in which its claims and rights are truly the claims and rights of society itself, a moment in which it is truly the social head and the social heart. Only in the name of the general rights of society can a particular class vindicate for itself general domination. For the storming of this emancipatory position, and hence for the political exploitation of all sections of society in the interests of its own section, revolutionary energy and spiritual self-feeling alone are not sufficient. For the revolution of a nation, and the emancipation of a particular class of civil society to coincide, for one estate to be acknowledged as the estate of the whole society, all the defects of society must conversely be concentrated in another class, a particular estate must be the estate of the general stumbling-block, the incorporation of the general limitation, a particular social sphere must be recognized as the notorious crime of the whole of society, so that liberation from that sphere appears as general self-liberation. For one estate to be par excellence the estate of liberation, another estate must conversely be the obvious estate of oppression. The negative general significance of the French nobility and the French clergy determined the positive general significance of the nearest neighboring and opposed class of the bourgeoisie." Karl Marx, "A Contribution to the Critique of Hegel's Philosophy of Right: Introduction," 1843, *Marxists Internet Archive*. https://www.marxists.org/archive/marx/works/1843/critique-hpr/intro.htm (accessed 24 September, 2025).

98 Howard, "Workers at War," 486.

collective action long before the formation of the CCP. And even after the Party's formation, workers often organized strikes and demonstrations without its help. Their activities were fostered and marked by other aspects of what Tarrow calls "mobilizing structures" of the social aspects of class formation. As we have also seen, the life of the Chinese proletariat may have been miserable, but it was anything but atomistic. Workers were knitted together in all manner of networks and institutions. In Shanghai, far from undermining their capacity for contentious collective action, the particularistic cleavages within China's working class actually promoted it.[99] Both there and in other cities, secret societies, gangs and even labor bosses and supervisors often helped organize strikes. Moreover, workers' rural roots meant that they had a ready escape route in the event that protest went badly, which helped them overcome aversion to risk.

Political opportunity structure, then, should be conceptualized as having micro- as well as macro-levels. At the macro level, China's political institutions did not offer particularly favorable conditions for the development of contentious collective action by the working class. Political fragmentation, warlord repression, imperialism and civil war were serious obstacles to regional and national organization and mobilization. This was true even at moments—such as the early and mid-1920s and the late 1940s—of detectable flux and destabilization. By contrast, at the micro level—in factories and cities—a more favorable political opportunity structure for contentious collective action often prevailed. Mobilizing structures were advantageous: workers came to the cities already bound up in corporate groups, they formed new corporate bonds while there, and they had corporate communities to which they could return when the going got too rough. Moreover, political opportunities were also more propitious: counterélites such as the CCP were often more organized and effective locally than nationally, and local political authorities often lacked either the capacity or the will to repress workers' attacks against employers. That is, the weakness of political institutions had opposite effects at the local level and the local and regional and at national ones, creating favorable conditions for proletarian contention in the former but undermining it in the latter. Moreover, this articulation of contradictory macro- and micro-level forces and structures helps explain China's pattern of proletarian politics before 1949, which consisted of significant localized activity over a protracted period that was nonetheless difficult to knit into a coherent and effective regional, much less national, movement.

Finally, the contradiction between micro- and macro-level political opportunity structures helps explain the peaks in contentious collective action in the 1920s and 1940s and the role of the Communist Party therein. Workers suffering in terms of the economic and social aspects of class formation from

99 Perry, *Shanghai on Strike*.

the depredations of unbridled, late developing and partly dependent capitalism could organize contentious collective action on their own, provided the macro-political opportunity structure was not too terribly unfavorable (as it was between 1927 and 1945). However, even then, it took the special resources provided by the Communists—their drive, organizational theory and acumen, and extensive organizational network across the country—to overcome the macro-level obstacles. Only then could the working class elaborate its myriad local struggles into regional or national movements at least at certain key moments. The fact that it could do so in the 1920s and again in the late 1940s but not in between was determined both by the generally unfavorable macro-level political opportunity structures throughout and by specific political conjunctures such as the rise of the Guomindang as a progressive force in the early 1920s, the repression of 1927, the invasion and subsequent defeat of Japan, and the return of political competition after the end of the Second World War. As Smith concludes: "...politics was essentially a contingent process of mobilization rather than one rooted in the social, and...labor politics are best understood as the result of competing political forces, overdetermined by the wider conjuncture."[100] That is, agency mattered more than structure or contingency.

In a different, more Gramscian conceptual lexicon, the absence of political hegemony created different effects at the national and local or regional levels. Where local and regional authorities were weak, and no national-level hegemony obtained, workers could mobilize, sometimes spectacularly, in their cities and occasionally link up regionally. Where municipal or provincial governments were strong enough and sufficiently anti-labor, the working class could be crushed—the most spectacular example was the White Terror of 1927. At the national level, the lack of effective repression by a political hegemon or more consent-based hegemony made it very difficult for the working class to coordinate politically across regions, and the only times it could do so were when the Communist Party was able to provide effective leadership.

Politicization

A key aspect of working class formation is the extent to which its contentious collective action had or lacked a political character and implications. Was it oriented mainly to economic or political demands? Was it directed against employers or political authorities (domestic or foreign)? Did it connect them, and if so, how? Did it result in integration or incorporation of the working class into the country's major competing political institutions and their hegemonic projects? What were its consequences for political change?

100 Smith, *Like Cattle and Horses*, 266–267.

In his scholarship on working class formation in the U.S., Katznelson has emphasized that class-based organization—primarily in unions—and political organization—primarily in parties and urban political machines—were distinct.

> American unions were, on the whole, disconnected from partisan electoral activity. Their domain came to be restricted largely to the workplace and to political demands that directly affected work or their right to organize. In reciprocal fashion, public officials tolerated strikes only when they were limited to workplace concerns, and the trade unions increasingly diminished the scope of their activity to bread-and-butter unionism.[101]

In China, by contrast, class-based and political organizations were more closely intertwined. Anarchist organizations worked closely with the labor movement in the 1910s and early 1920s. The Communist Party, and until 1927 the Guomindang as well, cultivated the labor movement. They not only deliberately created the political conditions for working class contentious collective action, but they actively encouraged the development of unions as well as slowdowns, strikes, boycotts and demonstrations. Nationalism, the dominant political ideology of the day, sank deep roots in the working class.

On the whole, however, Chinese workers were not incorporated in a significant way into either the Guomindang or the Communist Party. These disjunctures had institutional roots on each side. The Guomindang, focused on putting together a broad, cross-class nationalist coalition, did not make serious efforts to bind the working class to itself. Until 1927 it left working class organization and mobilization mostly to the CCP. After 1927, any efforts to link itself in a fascistic way to the working class were superficial and ineffective, due to the Republic's low capacity, high autonomy, its need to suppress the working class in the interests of the bourgeoisie and the war effort, and its distraction by its military conflicts against Japan and the Communists. For its part, the CCP was never a working class organization. For only the briefest moment, in 1926–27, did workers comprise half of the Party's membership, and almost none of them held important Party positions. One Central Committee member remarked that "workers cannot read, cannot write, cannot speak, and cannot understand anything." Driven into the countryside in 1927, the Party lost the capacity to engage effectively with the working class for its two profoundly formative decades. In 1930, only 8 percent of Party members hailed from the working class, and only 2 percent were factory workers. By 1949, less than 5 percent were.[102] In sharp contrast with the U.S., where the universal male franchise and the activity and

101 Katznelson, *Working-Class Formation*, 26. See also Katznelson, *City Trenches.*
102 Harrison, *The Long March to Power*, 99, 161.

proximity of urban political machines made for close ties between the working class and Party, at least locally,[103] in China, except for brief moments in the mid-1920s and the latter 1940s, workers experienced both the Guomindang Republic and the Communist Party as far more remote.

In general, then, working class contentious collective action, even when organized with CCP help, focused on workplaces and economic issues much more than politics. The major issues provoking slowdowns and strikes had to do with income, working conditions and livelihood. Union recognition—a political issue—was also often a prominent concern, but it is significant (if so obvious as to have been overlooked by the scholarship) that workers pursued it at the micro level mainly through strikes rather than at the macro level through legislative campaigns or other political avenues. Even workers' predisposition to nationalism played out in their contentious collective action as attacks on their own foreign bosses. This localistic focus, of course, reflects what Tarrow calls the mobilizing structures of the working class, which were, primarily, geographically specific and enterprise-based. The propinquitous horizon of those structures was itself a product of the economic, social and macro-political aspects of class formation. China's modern industrial sector was geographically fragmented, due to the specific splintered pattern of imperialism as well as the historically strong localism of Chinese artisanal manufacturing and regionalism of its economic networks.[104] The localistic nature of labor recruitment and of the division of labor reinforced that centrifugality. Finally, at the national level, there were no coherent, robust institutions (such as a legislature or corporatist peak associations and arrangements) to attract the interest, energy, organizational virtuosity or institutional affiliation of the working class. In short, there was no hegemonic political power into which the working class could be integrated, and there were significant obstacles to its incorporation even within the counter-hegemonic Communist Party, its most likely home.

Yet none of this precluded the workers' participation in political movements whether local, regional or trans-regional. It just means that when they did so—*e.g.*, during the May 4 or May 30 Movements—they were responding to mobilization by political leaders, to which they proved available and amenable. This is a pattern that would be repeated in the Maoist period and would also occur in reverse in the structural reform period, when workers responded surprisingly supinely to the state's program of working class demobilization. Willingness to join or abjure from political activity when so encouraged is,

103 Katznelson, *City Trenches*.

104 G. William Skinner expounded thus in a long career of important publications, including most seminally "Marketing and Social Structure in Rural China: Part I," *Journal of Asian Studies* 24, no. 1 (November 1964): 3–43; and "Marketing and Social Structure in Rural China: Part II," *Journal of Asian Studies*, 24, no. 2 (February 1965): 195–228.

however, fundamentally different from structural integration into hegemonic political institutions on an ongoing basis.

The medium-term effect of the low level of working class political incorporation and politicization was the well-known failure of the proletariat to amount to a significant force in the Chinese Revolution. In the longer term, it prefigured a pattern of working class politics in the Maoist and structural reform periods strongly shaped by the impulses and interpellation of what had by then become a hegemonic Party/state. When all is said and done, working class formation in China left the proletariat without significant experience or expectations of political self-determination nationally. Yet it also left the proletariat with a record of, and continuing penchant for, localized action, grounded in its specific economic and social life, which it also carried into the People's Republic during both the Maoist and structural reform periods.

Conclusion

During the first half of the twentieth century, a large, variegated and active working class formed in China. Like many of its fellow proletariats in late industrializing countries, in economic terms, it experienced deep immiseration and exploitation by China's late, rapidly developing, and imperialistically driven capitalism. Socially, it underwent a profound shock to its social life, as rural people found themselves adrift in a brave new urban world, thrown together in new and radically unfamiliar ways with members of the opposite sex and with people from different localities. It sought the protection of a range of particularistic relationships to cushion the blow. Culturally, the working class developed strong senses of class and nation, also novel and unfamiliar ideas, while retaining older ones of gender, locality and fellowship. Politically, it spawned a breathless pattern of organization, welcomed becoming a constituency of rising political parties, secret societies and organized criminal networks, and engaged in an impressive range and level of local contentious collective action that it could only periodically extend regionally and nationally when such leadership was available. In its organizational and contentious activities, it tended to keep its focus local and economic, reflecting the economic, social and even political aspects of its class formation within which it found itself. It was, therefore, unable to establish its own political foothold in the new national institutions—the Guomindang and its Republic, or the CCP and its provisional governments—that were forming amid the maelstrom of repeated wars and crises.

Of course, the Communist Party was intimately involved with the working class. But the Party was never primarily a party of the working class. It was not the creature of the labor movement (like the British Labour Party, for example); its leaders were not mainly of the working class economically, existentially, culturally or politically. Rather, it came, during its formative decades, to be as or more committed to rural constituencies, and its political programs generally reflected that.

Let us return to the two questions posed at the outset. First, using class formation as a noun, how fully and coherently developed did it become in China's first half-century of industrial capitalism? Economically, China had a large class of workers who were producing significant surplus value, who were not deeply divided into income- or skill-based strata, and who were broadly immiserated. Socially, workers were fragmented along geographic and gender lines, but again not in ways that set them profoundly at odds; on the contrary, such subdivisions often proved helpful to their mobilization, and they were often able to unify across the social cleavages that differentiated and separated them but did not set them against each other. Culturally, the working class developed coherent discourses that mixed class, nation and gender fairly seamlessly. And politically, the working class was able, thanks to its economic, social and cultural formations, to act both spontaneously at the local level and also in concert with wider political movements organized by the Communist Party and established unions. But the social cleavages within the working class, along with features of the wider political context such as the institutional weaknesses of its unions, the vanguard nature of the Communist Party, and Guomindang repression, and the general absence of any hegemonic power or bloc favorable to the working class, undermined its ability to exert itself or even participate meaningfully in the embryonic hegemonic projects of the era.

Second, how can we explain the historical ebb and flow of working class political formation? That it could organize and act, often autonomously and spontaneously, at the micro level as much and as effectively as it did in so unfavorable an environment depended on its shared economic misery, its complex pattern of social formation, its shared and eclectic yet coherent self-understanding, and a somewhat favorable micro-level political opportunity structure. The ebbs and flows of its ability to mobilize regionally and nationally are best explained by features of politics itself—specifically, the challenges posed by the macro-level political opportunity structure and, more important, the role and capacity of the Communist Party to enable the working class to act on a broad canvas at specific moments.

At bottom, then, the absence of any robust hegemony amid China's total economic, social, cultural and political crisis profoundly shaped working class formation. It left capital unrestrained in its exploitation, oppression and abuse of the proletariat, all of which produced a great deal of resistance. It shocked workers' worlds to the core, in response to which they became bound up in a panoply of nascent social relations and institutions through which they struggled to cope and fight back. It produced a cultural and discursive hybrid that mixed themes of class, nation and gender. And it ultimately produced two bitterly competing hegemonic political projects—the Guomindang and the Communists. When they first cooperated, working class politics achieved some of its greatest levels of mobilization. When they didn't, the Nationalists dealt a powerful and lasting blow to working class political formation, while the Communists eventually provided the leadership that proved necessary for its modest but ultimately limited development.

All this had major implications for working class politics in the Maoist and structural reform periods that followed. It emerged into the state socialist era as a class with a record and experience of considerable institutional virtuosity in social terms, strong senses of class and nation, and active political self-organization and mobilization. Decades of autocratic repression by the Guomindang Republic, isolation from the defeated Communists, and the absence of labor-oriented institutional development imparted a certain radicalism, a definite cynicism toward national authority, and a sense of the need for political self-reliance. All this played out in the subsequent three decades.

2

RADICALISM

The Apotheosis of China's Working Class

With the foundation of the People's Republic of China in 1949, the new Party/state began to reorganize the economy, society, culture and politics from top to bottom. It led a program of crash industrialization, which not only vastly expanded the working class but also induced the new government to improve and stabilize workers' material lives and elevate their social status to levels unimaginable just a few years earlier. It also promoted new cultural and political values and institutions that profoundly transformed the way workers conceived their world and battled for a bold new vision of it. Over three decades, the working class demanded and began to achieve not just a better material life but also a much more participatory and egalitarian one in their workplaces.

That it could do so was attributable in part to the legacy of its many decades of organization and struggle before 1949. But the ways it did so, and the victories it won as well as the ultimate failure it suffered, were also shaped profoundly by the specific institutions and political fault lines of the new hegemonic project of radical state socialism. That is, it benefited from and fought on a terrain not mainly of its own making. It became divided in various, often complex ways, not just by the normal cleavages of age, gender, locality, education, skill and sector, but also into new economic, social and political ones created by the Party/state—especially urban-resident and rural contract workers, but also those included in and excluded from factory patron–client networks, and ideological ones revolving around inclinations toward radical socialism and Party/state authority itself. The working class deployed tactics, strategies and outlooks of its own, but also those put forward variously by both radical and "conservative" Party/state leaders. It operated within political institutions established by the Party/state and was unable to establish its own. It got caught

DOI: 10.4324/9781003518228-3

up in the extraordinary, heady political movements of Maoist China, especially the Cultural Revolution. All this led to its ultimate defeat, as it could not defend itself when the Party/state's radical hegemonic project went down.

The historical patterning of working class politics in the Maoist decades bears some significant similarities with that of the revolutionary period, but also some differences. Changes in the political opportunity structure still mattered a great deal, though the relationship cannot be reified and is clearer in retrospect than in prospect. Workers still proved capable of a great deal of spontaneity and political virtuosity. And yet their capacity to act successfully, especially on a regional and national canvas, depended, as before, on the wider hegemonic and contingent forces beyond their making and control. Nonetheless, they proved highly consequential. And finally, in a break with the past, working class politics now focused not only on material questions but also heavily on issues of power itself.

Working class formation in Maoist-era China also presents, at least at first blush, something of a paradox. For this was a time not just of extraordinary gains for workers thanks to the new Party/state, but also of significant bouts of radical collective action within and against it. Why would the working class bite the hand that was finally feeding it? The answer has to do with the ways that the new Party/state not only delivered the goods but also posed new sorts of questions and vastly expanded the horizons that workers could glimpse, to which they could aspire, and for which they could struggle. As David Laitin has argued, following Thomas Metzger, hegemony involves not just the answers but, just as centrally, the dominant questions.[1] And as Gramsci insisted, it also sets up specific lines of conflict.[2] The hegemonic project of the Party/state induced the working class to struggle for a radically new world, and drew it into complex political battles that it won for a time but that ultimately consumed it because of its subordinate position in the Party/state and the ultimately dysfunctional, hyper-conflictual politics it unleashed.

Following the analytical scheme of the previous chapter, this one organizes the analysis around the intertwined economic, social, cultural and political aspects of China's working class as it re-formed under Maoist state socialism.

Economic Aspects of Class Re-formation

Initially, the three Maoist decades saw vast improvements in workers' economic lives. Wages rose, and benefits even more. Rapid growth in income and

1 Thomas Metzger, *Escape From Predicament: Neo-Confucianism and China's Evolving Political Culture* (New York: Columbia University Press, 1977), 14, cited in David Laitin, *Hegemony and Culture: Politics and Religious Change Among the Yoruba* (Chicago: University of Chicago Press, 1986), 29.

2 Gramsci, *Selections from the Prison Notebooks*, 349 and *passim*.

benefits in the first part of the 1950s was followed by the crisis of the Great Leap Forward and then stagnation thereafter. For urban-resident workers (but not rural contract workers),[3] employment became very secure. All workers found themselves employed by state or collective enterprises, in which shopfloor relations and payment systems cleaved toward socialist forms.

The revolutionary victory of 1949 took place in an atmosphere of economic crisis for China's working class. In Shanghai, only one-fourth of industrial enterprises were operating in mid-year, and less than two-thirds by the end of the year. Inflation too was a major problem. In Shanghai rice prices sextupled in the middle of the year despite the government's introduction of the *renminbi,* its new currency. The cost of living in Tianjin had gyrated wildly throughout the year, doubling in May due to severe food shortages, rising 170 percent in August due to floods and grain exports to newly liberated Shanghai, and 275 percent in November because of plague and the legacy of the Republican government's excessive resort to the printing press. The new government redoubled its attack on inflation, which by early 1950 had succeeded too well, producing deflation and, therefore, a wave of factory closures. Unemployment spiked to 1.7 million by mid-1950. Wage arrears had become epidemic, and one-eighth of Shanghai's private firms shut. In this context, managers revived the pre-1949 practice in economic downturns of payment in kind—in the form of housing and meals—because it was functional for both them and their workers as well as the new government's anti-inflationary policy.[4]

Yet if material conditions were worsening at the very outset, the new government was beginning to put in place structural changes that would transform workers' economic lives in coming years. The advent of state socialism brought about the opportunity to abolish the severe oppression, exploitation and immiseration that China's working class had experienced since its birth more than half a century earlier. The nearly 3,000 firms that had been owned by the Republic government, which employed a quarter of a million workers, were of course nationalized immediately. So were those abandoned by owners who fled to Taiwan or abroad. But other private firms were not. This change of ownership, of course, gave the new government the opportunity to institute radical improvements in workers' material lives. Overall, its approach to industry had

3 The material in this section refers to the urban-resident working class—*i.e.*, workers with urban (literally, "non-rural") household registrations (非农业户口). They are distinguished from rural contract workers—people with rural household registrations (农业户口) who had been brought into urban factories during the Great Leap Forward, and who managed to stay or return after most were extruded back home in the wake of its crisis. Their economic and employment conditions were significantly lower than urban-resident workers', though better than those of their neighbors who stayed in farming. See p. 54.

4 Mark W. Frazier, *The Making of the Chinese Industrial Workplace* (Cambridge: Cambridge University Press, 2002), chap. 4; Kenneth Lieberthal, *Revolution and Tradition in Tientsin, 1949–52* (Stanford, CA: Stanford University Press, 1980), 38–39.

moderated from radical policies that had prevailed in CCP-controlled cities in 1945–47, such as doubling of wages, subsidization of workers' medical care, and democratic procedures for firings. The Party leadership now criticized such breakthroughs as "leftist," and the new government, concerned about restoring production, emphasized labor–management cooperation. Nonetheless, new regulations covering workers in both state and private firms enforced widely ignored Republic laws restricting managers' power to fire workers. The new government also issued policies of its own limiting overtime and entitling workers who had left their factories in the closing days of the Nationalist régime to their jobs back. Many companies were forced to convert part-time workers to full-time work.[5] In 1952, with inflation brought under control and daily commodities less scarce, the government standardized wages in state-owned firms, linking them to regional differences in the cost of living. Starting in 1951 it also developed a labor insurance scheme that provided medical and disability benefits and pensions. On average, real wages rose 17 percent from 1950 to 1952.[6]

The First Five-Year Plan (1953–57), a program of crash industrial expansion and the creation of a Soviet-style system of state ownership and planning, involved deepened structural changes that profoundly reshaped working class economic life. The state-owned sector became predominant. The government now converted formerly private firms, in many of which it had taken minority stakes in the early 1950s, into majority or fully state-owned enterprises. It also built 90,000 new factories.[7] While the First Five-Year Plan consolidated and extended the gains workers had already received in the areas of economic security, regularization of employment, and freedom from factory despotism, workers did not get everything they wanted from a government focused also on rapid development. The 1952 state enterprise wage reform was extended to all enterprises in 1956. Chinese workers were put on a standard eight-grade wage scale, formally ending a predominantly seniority-based system that, according to the new government, had been an engine for significant exploitation of younger and more skilled workers. But the government's real goal was to emphasize skill differentials as part of its overriding concern with industrial modernization: grade one workers received an 8 percent raise, but grade eight got 18 percent, and in some places double that. This met resistance from older, less skilled workers as well as management that did not want to provoke problems by dividing the workforce. And when implementation was, necessarily, left to factories, most managers tended to assign workers to different grades more by seniority than by skill or assiduity. As early as 1952, the government

5 For example, Jardine Matheson executives involved in negotiations with the new government over the Shanghai docks complained bitterly about this. Interviews, Hong Kong, 1975.

6 Frazier, *The Making of the Chinese Industrial Workplace*, chaps. 4 and 5.

7 Andrew Walder, "The Remaking of the Chinese Working Class, 1949–1981," *Modern China* 10, 1 (January 1984): 18.

also promoted piece rates, and by the mid-1950s nearly half of all wages were paid this way. Managers and technicians, whose work could not be evaluated by piece-rates, received time rates and bonuses, though. Piece rates too proved controversial, and by 1957 they began to be abandoned.[8]

Overall, though, wages were significantly improved compared with pre-1949 days, and total compensation even more. Under the First Five-Year Plan, real wages rose 22 percent from 1952 to 1957.[9] With the onset of the Great Leap Forward in 1958, real wages fell back to 6 percent below the 1952 level as the government sought to maximize state socialist accumulation in the service of its developmental program. When the economic crisis caused by the Leap bottomed out, 1961 wages dropped to 85 percent of the 1952 level. They recovered by 1965 to 96 percent of the 1956 all-time high but then went into a slow secular decline through the end of the Maoist period.[10] When all was said and done, Chinese workers had not had a raise since 1956.[11]

But wages were only around half of urban-resident workers' total incomes, another 82 percent of which on average came in the form of benefits.[12] The government compensated by expanding the supply of collective goods. Firms began to provide their workers with an "iron rice bowl" (铁饭碗)—a guarantee of lifetime economic security, including employment, income, food, housing, medical care, education for their children, pensions and, finally, funeral expenses. All these involved considerable costs for the government, which saw budgets for "non-productive investment" skyrocket.[13] But compensating workers in this way rather than wages made macroeconomic sense by improving the labor force, as well as microeconomic sense by focusing the reduced pool of wages on incentive-based distribution. It also made political sense: workers valued their non-wage income deeply.[14]

The political roots of the marked initial improvements in wages and benefits lay in the activist legacy of the working class movement before 1949. They

8 Frazier, *The Making of the Chinese Industrial Workplace*, chap. 5; Peter N. S. Lee, *Industrial Management and Economic Reform in China, 1949–1984* (Hong Kong: Oxford University Press, 1987), chap. 2.

9 国家统计局 (State Statistical Bureau), 中国统计年鉴1981 (*China Statistical Yearbook 1981*). 香港, 香港经济导报社 (Hong Kong: Hong Kong Economic Report), 1982, 403 and 426; cited in Walder, "The Remaking": 43.

10 *China Statistical Yearbook 1981*, 403 and 426. These figures do not include wages of temporary state workers, collective workers, or rural contract workers, of whom more on p. 53 *ff.*

11 Andrew Walder, *Communist Neo-traditionalism: Work and Authority in Chinese Industry* (Berkeley: University of California Press, 1988), chap. 5; 庄启东, 袁伦渠, 李建立 (Zhuang, Qidong, Yuan Lunqu, and Li Jianli), 新中国工资史稿 (*On Wages in New China*), 北京:中国财政经济才不是 (Beijing: China Finance and Economics Press, 1986), 117, 142.

12 Walder, "The Remaking": 37.

13 Frazier, *The Making of the Chinese Industrial Workplace*, 139.

14 Huaiyin Li, "Worker Performance in State-Owned Factories in Maoist China: A Reinterpretation," *Modern China* 42, no. 4 (July 2016): 395 and *passim*.

were spearheaded in the early 1950s by Li Lisan, the Party's main labor leader in the 1920s, its chair from 1928–30, and the head of the new government's trade union federation until 1951 and the Minister of Labor through 1954.[15] Thus, the vast improvements in workers' livelihoods were not just gifts *from* the revolutionary government; they were very much the products of working class activism over many decades, which could now be realized at last *through* that government.

Yet the new state socialist political economy probably did involve significant appropriation of surplus product by the state, since wage growth did not keep pace at all with rising labor productivity. It fueled the rapid growth in industrial output, which averaged 18 percent annually during the First Five-Year Plan. Real wages grew only 4 percent from 1952 to 1957—less than a quarter the 1950–52 rate.[16] Nonetheless, in the 1950s workers saw a distinct rise in their incomes, standards of living and economic security compared with the former capitalist economy.

During the Great Leap Forward, workers scored gains in how they were paid, but losses on how much they were paid and what they did for their pay. Workers who had been disadvantaged by piece rates were emboldened by Maoist attacks under the broad theme of "politics in command." Together radical leaders and workers managed to stop the practice almost completely—by 1960, only 5 percent of workers were receiving piece rates—or to take the bite out by replacing it with above-quota bonus evaluation that took into account not just output quantity but also quality and attitude. Their success in banishing piece rates was costly, though, as workers' incomes dropped as much as 30 percent. Real wages in state enterprises plummeted to 1.5 percent below their 1952 levels. Moreover, workers were subjected to demands for superhuman Stakhanovite exertion just at the time that the economy began to collapse. As the Leap wore on, malnourished, overworked laborers began to develop tuberculosis, hepatitis and hypertension, to name just a few. Managers tried to relieve the situation with expanded social welfare spending, various temporary payments and offers of employment to family members. Factory cadres took smaller food rations than workers.[17] But in the context of the economic crisis brought about by the Leap and the fact that the industrial labor force had expanded by over twenty million under the decentralization of 1957 and the subsequent Leap starting in 1958,

15 Elizabeth J. Perry, "From Native Place to Workplace: Labor Origins and Outcomes of China's *Danwei* System." In *Danwei: The Changing Chinese Workplace in Historical and Comparative Perspective*, ed. Xiaobo Lü and Elizabeth J. Perry (Armonk: M. E. Sharpe, 1997), 42–59; Patrick Lescot, *Before Mao: The Untold Story of Li Lisan and the Creation of Communist China*, trans. Steven Rendall (New York: HarperCollins, 2004), 283.

16 State Statistical Bureau, *Statistical Yearbook of China 1987* (Hong Kong: Longman, 1988), 609.

17 Interview, June 8, 1999.

the costs had ballooned, and management's resources were too meager to be able to make a dent in the working class's suffering.[18] The deep retrenchment in industrial employment in the wake of the Leap—discussed below—produced massive layoffs that only added to the economic woes of a significant swath of the working class.

Through the rest of the 1960s and 1970s, real wages in state enterprises recovered, but actually remained well below the 1957 level; by the mid-1970s they averaged only around 10 percent higher than 1952.[19] Wage adjustments were undertaken every few years, but their main beneficiaries were older workers, for moral reasons—they had larger families to support—but also political ones: in the context of the Cultural Revolution, seniority proved a less controversial basis for wage differentials than skill or assiduity, both for managers but also for workers involved in participatory methods of wage setting. Some workers who received promotions through the eight-grade wage scale saw their own incomes rise more than this, though on the whole the system, originally meant to combat seniority-based wage-setting, actually came to reinforce it for the same reasons as the national wage adjustments. Workers also continued to benefit from their welfare guarantees, however minimal, and from ironclad employment security. Indeed, job guarantees extended even beyond retirement, as workers could often pass their jobs on to their children. If under capitalism labor is commodified as private property, under Chinese radical state socialism employment itself came to be "owned" by the workers.[20]

...

In short, China's working class's economic life improved radically for almost the first decade of the radical socialist period, plummeted vertiginously during the Great Leap Forward, and then stabilized within a few years to a level at which it stagnated until the end of the era. The working class experienced new levels of economic security and welfare provision. Its material conditions also fragmented between the urban-resident workers and growing substrata rural contract workers employed on less favorable terms.

18 Frazier, *The Making of the Chinese Industrial Workplace*, chap. 7; Lee, *Industrial Management*, chap. 3. Nonetheless, workers fared better than farmers, as the urban–rural ratio of consumption in 1959 and 1960 climbed to its highest level in the Maoist period—over 3:1—since figures began to be kept after 1949. See Dennis Tao Yang and Cai Fang, "The Political Economy of China's Rural-Urban Divide," *Stanford Center for International Development Working Paper* no. 62, 1999 (Stanford, CA: Stanford University, 1999).

19 *Statistical Yearbook of China 1987*, 592, 609.

20 One might also add that they actually had it better than tenured professors and teachers!

Social Aspects of Class Re-formation

In social terms, radical state socialism profoundly re-formed China's working class, in ways that differed sharply over time and space. It expanded, contracted and expanded again sharply. Its composition diversified and fragmented. Workers came to live, eat, shop, meet, socialize, educate their children, and receive medical care together in factory-provided communities. Within their enterprises, urban-resident workers experienced a world of significantly flattened social hierarchy with each other and with factory officials (especially on the shop floor), though a significant gap opened up between them and rural contract workers who worked alongside them in many factories.

Size, Composition and Residence

The industrial factory working class[21] expanded and contracted dramatically. During the First Five-Year Plan of 1953–57, it grew by 2,400,000, a 50 percent increase.[22] It ballooned by ten times as much during the 1957 decentralization, as provinces and localities rushed to expand their industrial bases.[23] The Great Leap Forward, beginning immediately thereafter, produced another spurt of industrial exertion and proletarian expansion. Nationally, from 1958 to 1960 factories added 30 million workers, a 150 percent increase.[24] The lion's share took place outside the major industrial centers of Shanghai, Guangzhou and Manchuria.[25] Most of the recruits during the Leap were farmers fleeing harsh conditions in the countryside. With the industrial retrenchment that marked the latter years of the Leap, the working class contracted sharply as most of them were sent back to their villages. For the remainder of the Maoist period, the government hardened the administrative boundary between urban and rural areas. Nonetheless, the working class continued to expand: from 1962 to 1978, it added 142,000,000—a 55 percent increase—as the urban population grew and as some rural people were reabsorbed as temporary contract workers.[26]

21 These figures exclude artisans who were self-employed or worked in small workshops, who in 1949 vastly outnumbered factory workers. See Walder, "The Remaking": 5–9.

22 国家统计局 (State Statistical Bureau), *中国劳动工资统计资料 1949–1985* (*China Labor and Wage Statistical Materials, 1949–1985*), 北京: 中国统计出版社 (Beijing: China Statistics Press), 1987, 83; cited in Frazier, *The Making of the Chinese Industrial Workplace*, 132.

23 Frazier, *The Making of the Chinese Industrial Workplace*, 205.

24 Walder, "The Remaking", 17.

25 From 1957–1960, Shanghai added 700,000 workers—a 20 percent increase. Over the same period, the employment rolls of Guangdong Province's state enterprises "only" doubled, adding over a million workers. Frazier, *The Making of the Chinese Industrial Workplace*, 206.

26 国家统计局人口社会科技统计司 (National Bureau of Statistics Department of Population, Social Science and Technology Statistics) and 劳动和社会保障规划财务司 (Ministry of Labor and Social Security Department of Planning and Finance), *中国劳动统计年鉴2001* (*China*

It was a class that mixed older workers well experienced in factory life and politics with an ever-expanding phalanx of younger recruits for whom industrial employment was strange and novel. Moreover, the new cohort was itself divided among ordinary line workers and those who, as beneficiaries of China's blossoming educational development, were more skilled. Data on the percentage of women in the industrial working class is fragmentary and inexact: in one small sample around 25–30 percent in 1966, in another around 55 percent in 1977–78.[27] In short, the Maoist-era working class was more diverse in sociological, generational and educational terms than it had been before 1949.

The tendency of factories occasionally to pay workers in kind during the first half of the century took on a new and more thoroughgoing form in the Maoist period, as residence and workplace were literally merged in most industrial enterprises. Workers almost always lived with their fellow workers in the same "work unit" (*danwei* [单位]), in flats or dormitories provided by the plant, often on its premises. They took some of their meals in communal dining halls. Factories ran clinics and recreation facilities as well; larger ones were cities in their own right, operating schools, hospitals, theaters, parks and social halls. Chinese enterprises were not just workplaces, but virtual social microcosms, a fact that was only accentuated by the way they were, by and large, walled off, often literally, from the outside. This produced close-knit social networks grounded in myriad quotidian interactions. They ran the gamut, from asymmetrical power between leaders and ordinary workers that produced patronage and conflict, to quotidian friction, to more communitarian relationships.[28] Working class formation surely involves the full range. That is, the work unit intensified the "classness" of the working class, with all the attendant tensions and harmonies that is bound to bring in tow.

Stratification

China's working class was divided into several strata differentiated by rural *vs.* urban residence, factory ownership and by employment terms. The vast majority were urban-resident workers employed on a permanent basis in state-owned factories. They held urban household registrations, which entitled them to the

Labour Statistical Yearbook 2001) (北京：总过统计出版社 [Beijing: China Statistics Press], 2001), 8.

27 Barry M. Richman, *Industrial Society in Communist China* (New York: Random House, 1969), 305; Martin King Whyte and William L. Parish, *Urban Life in Contemporary China* (Chicago: University of Chicago Press, 1983), 204.

28 Walder emphasizes patronage: Walder, *Communist Neo-Traditionalism*. Womack takes issue: "Transfigured Community: Neo-Traditionalism and Work Unit Socialism in China," *China Quarterly* 126 (June, 1991): 313–332. Bjorklund too emphasizes social solidarity: "The Danwei: Socio-Spatial Characteristics of Work Units in China's Urban Society," *Economic Geography* 62, no. 1 (January 1986): 19–29.

full range of urban government benefits beyond those provided by their enterprises. In addition, there were temporary state workers, who also held urban household registrations but were employed only for renewable terms of up to a year. They did not receive the full complement of benefits from their enterprises that the permanent workers did. But because they had urban household registrations, they could live in their cities legally, and take advantage of educational, medical and residential services provided by their municipal government. A third category were workers employed in collective firms owned by urban or other local governments rather than by a state ministry. Wages and benefits varied with the size of the enterprise; in large ones, they were similar to those of permanent state enterprise workers, but smaller ones did not provide the full complement of benefits that state factories did. They too could live legally in their cities and use municipal schools and services. They tended to be younger and more heavily female than the permanent state workers.[29] Fourth were a small number of urban-resident workers who were reassigned in the wake of the Great Leap Forward to work in rural factories or development projects. Despite the differences among these four strata, though, the cleavage between these urban-resident workers on the one hand and the rural contract workers on the other was far deeper and more significant. Thus it will guide most of the analysis that follows.

Rural contract workers were farmers who obtained employment either on their own or through arrangements between factories that needed labor and rural communes that could supply it.[30] In the former case, they were paid less—often 25 percent less—than urban-resident workers, though this was often much higher than their rural incomes. In the latter case, the factory paid these workers' wages to the commune, which in turn awarded them work points—the shares of collective income received by farmers as their main income—and perhaps a small living allowance, some of which they could salt away as additional net income. The communes retained what was usually a significant difference as a contribution to collective coffers. Whether paid directly or through their communes, contract workers lacked job security, wage subsidies, pensions, labor insurance, and entitlement to housing, education for their children, and other such benefits from their enterprises or the governments of the cities in which they worked (since they were not formal residents there). Unless they commuted home on a daily basis, they were housed in minimal factory dormitories, returning home at various intervals depending on the distances. They also were generally allocated the worst jobs on the shop floor. The gap between

29 Walder, *The Remaking*: 32–36.

30 Marc Blecher, "Peasant Labour for Urban Industry: Temporary Contract Labour, Urban-Rural Balance and Class Relations in a Chinese County," *World Development* 9, no. 8 (August 1983): 731–746.

urban-resident and rural contract workers would create serious political frictions during the Cultural Revolution.

Social relations within enterprises involved a contradictory combination of equality and hierarchy. On the one hand, overall the socio-economic structure among urban-resident workers, and especially within the substratum of permanent state enterprise workers who made up the bulk of the labor force, was fairly flat. Differentials in wages, total compensation and standard of living were small. There is no evidence that a clear status hierarchy developed around seniority or skill, due in part to ongoing political debates about their relative value, but also to many workers' own sense that skills should be rewarded.

> Some older, skilled workers who had had high pay in the days when the plant was still private received up to ¥360/month [at a time when most older workers received around ¥100]. The other workers didn't resent this, since they knew these people were highly skilled (有本事) — one fellow had done his apprenticeship in Germany, after all — and had worked for a long time.[31]

Moreover, the socio-economic gap between these workers and factory officials—and not just those on the shop floor—was relatively small.[32] They lived in similar quarters and dressed and ate similarly as well.

> In the late 1950s and the 1960s, there was relative equality of the workers and the management in my plant, including even the factory Party secretary. At that time, we had the "3 togethernesses" [三同]: eating, living and working [同吃,同住,同劳动]. Wages were pretty equal too.[33]
>
> There was real economic equality. For example, while many level 8 workers got ¥96–100, many shop floor cadres only got ¥60–70… The workers and managers were so equal that many people did not want to be cadres.[34]

In fact, during the food shortages of the Great Leap Forward, factory cadres took smaller grain quotas and worked the longest hours.

> In the 1950s and 1960s the Party members worked harder than others. They really did. During the three hard years [of the Great Leap Forward {1958–61}], the cadres got less grain than the workers. Cadres got 28–29 *jin* (斤 [= 14 kg.])/month, while workers like me got 41 *jin* [20 kg.], and other workers doing hardest work got 47 *jin* [23 kg.]. My wife, who did light work, got 35

31 Interview, June 8, 1999.

32 Wang Shaoguang, *Failure of Charisma: The Cultural Revolution in Wuhan* (Hong Kong: Oxford University Press, 1995), 42.

33 Interview, June 29, 1996.

34 Interview, June 8, 1999.

> *jin* [17 kg]. More cadres had swollen bellies from malnutrition. At that time few people wanted to be cadres.[35]

In the wake of the Leap, cadres developed edema at three times the rate of workers.

On the other hand, though, the disparity between urban-resident workers and the rural contract workers could be significant. To be sure, the latter had definite advantages over their fellow farmers. Their incomes were a good deal higher. They also generally found factory work and city life much more to their liking than their previous rural existence.[36] This was especially true of women, who found patriarchy, though surely still present in the cities, less oppressive there. In one Shanghai plant, recent rural female hires threatened with dismissal during the post-Leap retrenchment were willing to accept wage arrears for two to three years rather than return to their villages.[37] However, rural contract workers tended to compare themselves more to the urban-resident workers alongside whom they toiled day in day out. If this "social" aspect of class is, for Katznelson, "experience-near" compared with the cold, objective facts of the economic level,[38] many rural contract workers also experienced their economic lives as profoundly unjust, even as some of these same people were also grateful to have the jobs they had.[39] Not only were they paid less and more insecure, but they also suffered in the division of labor. In status terms, they were looked down upon by managers and fellow workers as country bumpkins. This social cleavage would become deeply politicized during the Cultural Revolution.

In short, the social aspects of working class formation during China's radical state socialist decades involved complex, tumultuous change. The former proletariat of heavily exploited and oppressed wage workers benefited from the end of labor commodification and the abolition of capitalist employment markets both within firms and in recruitment into them. The working class expanded, contracted and diversified abruptly and repeatedly. Its core stratum of urban-resident permanent state enterprise workers came to live in new social communities bounded by their factories, where they received a range of benefits and developed new solidaristic and patronage relationships. Other urban-resident workers benefited from less of all this, and rural contract workers none of it. These strata also differed in terms of employment security, remuneration and the division of labor. All these transformations of workers' lived experiences

35 Interview, June 8, 1999.

36 Huaiyin Li, "Worker Performance": 13.

37 Frazier, *The Making of the Chinese Industrial Workplace*, 218–219.

38 Katznelson, *City Trenches*, 202. He derived the concept from Clifford Geertz, "On the Nature of Anthropological Understanding," *American Scientist* 63, no. 1 (1975): 47. Geertz himself credits the psychoanalyst Heinz Kohut with inventing it.

39 Li, "Worker Performance:" 13.

reshaped their understandings of themselves and their places in the world as well as their political responses to it.

Cultural Aspects of Class Re-formation

Two new, radical and radically different forms of working class self-conception emerged during China's three decades of radical state socialism. Earliest out of the gate, many workers put forward aggressively a newfound "workerist"[40] sense of the moral centrality and even superiority of labor and the working class over both other classes and even the state. Almost two decades later, during the heat of the Cultural Revolution, rural temporary contract workers let out a more defensive but no less radical and confrontational "cry for justice" against the mistreatment they had endured at the hands of their factories and the urban-biased government.

"Workerism"

With the dispatch of the Guomindang and much of the national bourgeoisie to Taiwan, and with foreign capital now on the defensive, many in the Chinese proletariat began to evince a stark new confidence and assertiveness. They proclaimed loudly that legitimate political power rested in the hands of the working class. This opened up a sharp cleavage between the working class and the revolutionary leadership and forces, grounded in the mutual alienation of the Party and the working class during the formative decades of both.

For example, in the fall of 1949, even before the proclamation of the People's Republic of China, Shanghai workers told soldiers of the People's Liberation Army (PLA), who were entering the city, and whom they viewed as country bumpkins, to "go back to your farms!" so the workers could run the plants that they now claimed as theirs. For their part, the revolutionary cadres and military officers liberating the cities of North China condescended to the workers, whom they felt had not contributed to the revolutionary victory, and also resented their relatively privileged position as urbanites.[41] Officers insulted them as "stinking" and worse.[42] Workers mocked the soldiers as "Texaco" because of the resemblance of the stars on their caps to the oil company's logo (Figure 2.1)—a particularly harsh taunt since the company was, of course, a major foreign capitalist. Showing off their verbal dexterity, workers condemned the Party for reducing the dignity of industrial work (工) to dirt (土), a similar-looking character that

40 The term is mine, *i.e.*, I have never found it in the discursive world of China labor politics. It developed particular significance (as *operaismo*) in Italian working class politics.

41 William Brugger, *Democracy and Organisation in the Chinese Industrial Enterprise, 1948–1953* (Cambridge: Cambridge University Press, 1976), 71–2.

42 Frazier, *The Making of the Chinese Industrial Workplace*, 108.

FIGURE 2.1 Dueling logos.

also means (rural) land. When the new government tried to establish its own labor unions, workers accused their officials of "kowtowing" to the capitalists. Where workers had often feared what they called the "black unions" established by the Guomindang (though, as we have seen, they also managed to make use of them for their own ends),[43] they viewed the new CCP-sponsored union as powerless and freely ignored it. They booed Mao and army commander Zhu De even as they themselves declared in good communist lingo that their factories belonged to the working class—clearly implying that they were truer Marxists than the Party leadership.[44] In what would become a repeated pattern, they spontaneously asserted themselves through the radical ideological and political lenses of the hegemonic project aspects they opposed.

In the early and mid-1950s, workerist sentiments continued to percolate, often taking substantively contradictory forms depending on the shifting political and economic contexts. Many workers remained skeptical even about the benefits of their factories coming under partial state ownership. Sensing the new government's strong developmentalism, they actually—and presciently—feared wage cuts and a stepped up pace of work. Most—in particular, older, less skilled workers—also consistently opposed piece rates and other incentive pay schemes, discussed above and below,[45] regarding them as not just contrary to their economic interests but also as an insult to the working class and a threat to its unity. They once again deployed the Party's own lingo to denounce such wage forms, coining a cutting pun to condemn fellow workers who advocated incentive pay as "serving the people's currency (人民币 [*renmin bi*])" rather than "serving the people (*renmin* [人民])." They also made up ditties

43 See p. 30.
44 Frazier, *The Making of the Chinese Industrial Workplace*, 101–112.
45 See pp. 49, 50, 60 and 73 *ff.*

claiming the credit for imparting the skills from which fellow workers were now benefiting.

> The one who started first was me,
> the one with better luck is thee;
> I taught you how to work a day,
> but you're the one with better pay.[46]

Even some skilled workers who would benefit from pay differentials evinced such workerist sentiments, declaring their unwillingness to receive the highest pay grades because that would require them to supervise their fellow workers. On the other hand, workers were much more favorable about policies that brought management and political officials into working posts on the shop floor. Many also welcomed the practice of setting wages at work group meetings.[47]

The strike wave of 1957 and the Great Leap Forward brought out this same sense of self-confident working class consciousness. Workers had the temerity to threaten the state with a Hungarian-style uprising. Yet their position was not anti-communist. On the contrary, they declared their intention to take their complaints to the Comintern and to Nikita Khrushchev himself on his impending visit, implying again that China's workers were truer communists than the CCP.[48] And they continued in other ways to throw socialist principles and slogans back in the Party's face: workers declared ironically that unless they got raises they would "work according to pay" (按酬付劳), inverting the basic socialist principle of "pay according to work" (按劳分配). When during the Great Leap the Party called for superhuman storming and voluntary extensions of the working day and week, in some cases to sixteen hours a day, workers demanded instead to be paid for it. Yet they also continued to denounce incentive pay, proclaiming—once again, using the Party's own tropes—that it violated the Great Leap principle by substituting cash for "politics in command" and by fostering individualism.[49] Demands to be paid for all their work did not, in their minds, contradict critiques of "cash in command," since the remuneration was to be distributed relatively equally to all workers. Their critique was not, then, of material remuneration *per se* but of individual differentials in such remuneration that undermined working class solidarity and dignity. As one older worker looked back on it in the 1990s:

46 Frazier, *The Making of the Chinese Industrial Workplace*, 170–171.
47 Ibid., 170–186.
48 Elizabeth J. Perry, "Shanghai's Strike Wave of 1957," *China Quarterly* 137 (March 1994): 11.
49 Frazier, *The Making of the Chinese Industrial Workplace*, chap. 7.

> Workers did work hard in those days despite the iron rice bowl. That's because there was some genuine competition: among wage grades and for bonuses, both of which were limited. In addition, people really were enthusiastic (有精神力量) about building up the plant and the country. There was lots of propaganda about this, and on the whole it fit people's life experiences. People looked down on slackers.[50]

Workers also caught management in a contradiction by arguing that piece rates actually undermined managerial power (of which they were no fans, of course), since workers would ignore instructions that interfered with meeting their quotas. They attacked elaborate work rules that interfered with their own control of the labor process, and demanded that the technical experts who had developed them instead come down to the shop floor themselves and do some real work.[51] All this has definite resonances with the syndicalist view that the factory does best when left to workers.

The Cultural Revolution produced an unprecedented outpouring of working class political expression. While the available sources reveal much about what various groups of workers wanted and the extraordinary tenacity with which they acted, they don't always bring us closer to the underlying cultural values, sensibilities and assumptions of the working class. Political expression during the Cultural Revolution had to be couched in the highly charged polemical rhetoric of the day—"capitalist roaders," "reactionaries," "running dogs," "stinking ninth category," and so on. Moreover, Cultural Revolution participants generally attempted to apply such abstract generalizations to highly specific targets and personal conflicts. While some of these were individuals whom rebel workers accused of doing wrong in terms of socialist "line" and policy, most of those targeted seem to have been supervisors whom workers thought had wronged them in various ways, accusing them of being "backward" in their political attitudes and their work and on that basis victimizing them in job assignments, pay decisions, distribution of public goods and political campaigns.[52] None of this provides particularly fertile ground for digging down to the social and political consciousness that lay beneath the surface.

That said, the major strands of the Cultural Revolution were broadly consistent with the syndicalistic or "workerist" forms of working class ideation focused on the most basic-level shopfloor politics that were in evidence since 1949. Interestingly, they appeared on both sides of the ubiquitous divide

50 Interview, June 8, 1999. Also see Li, "Worker Performance."

51 Frazier, *The Making of the Chinese Industrial Workplace*, 206–7, 214.

52 Wang, *Failure of Charisma*, 37, 98. Also see Marc Blecher and Gordon White, *Micropolitics in Contemporary China: A Technical Unit During and After the Cultural Revolution* (Armonk, N.Y.: M.E. Sharpe, 1979).

between "rebels" and "conservatives" that characterized most cities.[53] For example, workers in the renegade rebel faction of the Shanghai Diesel Engine Plant tended to focus their ire not on the higher levels of factory leadership so much as their immediate superiors, who had victimized many of them for their "bad" class backgrounds[54] or political peccadilloes. Moreover, they opposed the efforts of shop floor officials to organize their own "conservative" political outfits to attack the higher levels of factory leadership in order to take the spotlight off themselves.[55] Workers in "conservative" factions in Wuhan were equally assertive in defending basic-level factory Party officials, whom they viewed with definite respect for having adopted a frugal lifestyle not very different from that of ordinary workers, and with whom they had made common cause against technical experts and managerial professionals who had promoted incentive pay and one-man management.[56] No matter which side they were on, then, in evidence here is workers' bumptious, workerist preoccupation with shop floor authority and their own power both in the labor process and also around distributive issues.

"Economism"

Another, very different posture emerged in the Cultural Revolution, oriented mainly to economic inequalities rather than shopfloor political power and authority. Perry and Li term it a "cry for justice,"[57] though it came to be branded "economistic" by its critics. In Shanghai and elsewhere it was grounded mainly among rural contract workers, although Wang Shaoguang notes that in Wuhan a number of urban-resident workers also took up the cause.[58] It focused on the structural gap in pay, benefits and security between the villagers who had flocked to factory work in the late 1950s and the more entitled urban-resident workers. As such, this worldview lacked "workerism's" self-confidence, evincing instead feelings born of inequality, subordination and relative powerlessness. Nonetheless, the "economistics," like the urban-resident workers to whom they counterposed themselves, proved equally adept at summoning up the temerity to toss the Party's own claims and values back in its face. "Labor insurance was given to us by the Communist Party and Chairman Mao," rural

53 Who they were and what their specific positions were are discussed in the subsequent section on political aspects of class formation, see p. 63 *ff.*

54 For example, bourgeois, petit-bourgeois, overseas Chinese, rich peasants and landlords.

55 Elizabeth J. Perry and Li Xun, *Proletarian Power: Shanghai in the Cultural Revolution* (Boulder: Westview, 1997, chap. 4).

56 Wang, *Failure of Charisma*, 96. "One-man management" was a system of autocratic, non-participatory factory authority based on Soviet practice and in connection with the First Five-Year Plan (FFYP) beginning in 1953.

57 Perry and Li, *Proletarian Power*, chap. 4.

58 Wang, *Failure of Charisma*, 168.

contract workers reminded the factory officials who were dismissing them, in effect accusing them of betraying the highest authorities in the country. Some attacked the supreme leader himself. "Chairman Mao has problems? I've got problems too." And like the more self-confident urban workers, "economism" too partook of acerbic irony. The Chinese characters for "proletariat" are, literally, "the class without property." One bitter laid-off worker from the countryside screamed out: "You Communists...have taken away all property, and now there's no food to eat..."[59] At rebel rallies, contract workers refused to listen to denunciations of "capitalist roaders" in the Shanghai Party Committee, bellowing instead, "We want to become permanent workers," and, "We want a pay raise." They focused also on the wide range of benefits that urban-resident workers received but which were denied to them. Rural contract workers who had been laid off roared, "We want to return to work," and, in a precursor to the incantations of laid-off workers in China's northeast three decades hence, "We want to eat."[60] Some even demanded political and economic rights for private entrepreneurs—an extraordinarily bold claim in the heat of the Cultural Revolution. While their protests were among the most vociferous, aggressive and even violent of the Cultural Revolution,[61] the rural temporary contract workers seem to have lacked the cocky self-confidence of the rebel factions. In fact, they complained bitterly about the powerlessness that flowed from management's ability to fire them at will. Their sense of their own weakness may also have had to do with the fact that the "economistic" protesters were much more heavily female than the rebels. Their outcry was loud and bold but, in substantive terms, plaintive, unlike the rebels' demand for positive radical change. This innate sense of relative weakness may have helped contribute to the fact that their movement was snuffed out within a month.[62]

...

In conclusion, throughout the ups and downs of the Maoist period, and across the sharp political battles it stimulated, two distinct forms of working class consciousness developed. The sizable minority of rural Chinese who had recently migrated to temporary contract industrial work focused on their inequality and subordination in relation to the urban-resident stratum of the working class. In doing so, they evinced profound anger born of a sense of powerlessness.

59 Frazier, *The Making of the Chinese Industrial Workplace*, 219–220.

60 In China, food and eating carry an existential, humanistic meaning that goes beyond mere nutrition. A common greeting is "Have you eaten?", which evinces concern for the other person's general welfare.

61 See p. 61 *ff.*

62 Perry and Li, *Proletarian Power*, chap. 4; Hong Yung Lee, *The Politics of the Chinese Cultural Revolution* (Berkeley: University of California Press, 1978), 130–132; Wang, *Failure of Charisma*, chap. 6.

By contrast, the urban-resident workers became conscious of their power as both rightful and real. In this world view, management's legitimate role is to coordinate and administer but not to order or command. The labor done by workers was central. Management is not a superior class that deserves privilege or power. Of course how prevalent such a sensibility was, how unevenly it was distributed over time and space, and how it coexisted with other, more traditional or capitalistic ones (in which bosses are there to boss and workers just to work), is impossible to research. But the important point is that this sense of workers' power—and of the fact that China really was taking definite steps on the road to becoming a workers' state—was significant within China's urban working class.

Workerism had definite resonances with Communist Party discourse, especially its powerful Maoist strand. Both "rebel" and "conservative" workers derived inspiration from ideals of popular participation in production, of radical socialism, and eventually of "class struggle" against "capitalist roaders" in factories, even as they applied them differently in political practice. They expected officials to work on the shop floor. They strove to become "masters of their enterprises" (主人翁), to win "labor competitions," to be dubbed "labor models" and "iron girls." Yet they also developed their own syncretic variations on those themes, demanding, for example, to be paid for the exceptional exertions demanded of them, and even calling out the Chairman himself. As such, their thinking grew directly out of and sat squarely within the Party/state's hegemonic discourse and values, which they took so genuinely to heart that they extended them beyond their original limits. That is, workerism was the working class's way of thinking about and expressing themselves in terms broadly given by the Party, even when they criticized it—a core indication of ideological hegemony. As such, when radical state socialism ultimately lost out, China's working class too lost the core of its ways of thinking and understanding itself and its world. So in discursive terms it was left helpless to stand up against the onslaught of structural reform.

Political Aspects of Working Class Re-formation

But the real roots of the working class's ultimate defeat lay less in the way they understood the world and their place in it than in the way they acted and reacted politically to defend and advance that position. In the Maoist period, sections of the working class engaged in significant, often radical activism that transcended its previous preoccupations with compensation, labor conditions and abusive shopfloor authority.[63] They struggled, rather, for real power to

63 These issues would return to the center stage of labor politics during the structural reform period that followed.

remake their factories in the mold of revolutionary state socialism. In doing so, they took their cues from the Maoist strand of the Party/state, sometimes even exceeding it. That had two major implications. First, it helps explain why much working class politics was at its most radical during the historical period when workers were also most privileged relative to their own past and to other classes and strata of the day. Second, it provides an important reason for the working class's ultimate defeat at the end of the Cultural Revolution decade, and for its surprising passivity as structural reform dissolved its Maoist-era gains and subjected it to capitalistic labor markets, exploitation, and often sweated depredations of factory authority.

As in Chapter 1, the discussion here proceeds under three broad rubrics: in the political realm—specifically, the institutions within which the working class developed, the policies that shaped it and the politics that bore down on it and in which it participated.

Institutions

During the Maoist era, working class political formation took place almost completely within the increasingly hegemonic institutions of the Party/state. Workers were not particularly intimidated by this context; on the contrary, they repeatedly tried to use it to go on the offensive, including against it. In the end, though, this institutional setting undermined political class formation.

Workplace Organizations

In the early 1950s, the Party/state established new participatory institutions in industrial enterprises. In private firms, it created labor-capital consultative conferences (LCCCs; 劳资协商会议) "to discuss topics related to labor, including production, worker training and safety, workers' wages and promotion, and administrative rules affecting employees." "Committees to Increase Production and Economy" were soon added to the mix. Composed of Party and union officials—who were coopted from among politically active workers—and the owner, managers and engineers, they served as much to control labor as capital. For example, they urged striking workers to get back to work and pursue their grievances through these newly established institutional channels as well as the factory management committees (FMCs) and the unions. That said, the LCCCs also pressured owners and managers to keep factories operating even at a loss, rehire laid-off workers, and pay them their full wages.[64] They were disbanded with the completion of full socialization of ownership in 1956.

64 Joel Andreas, *Disenfranchised: The Rise and Fall of Industrial Citizenship in China* (Oxford: Oxford University Press, 2019), 29–30, 34, 38.

In state-owned firms the Party/state established "factory management committees" (FMCs; 工厂管理委员会). They grew directly out of the policy of "democratic management" (民主管理) that it had promulgated from 1948 to 1951.[65] FMCs were composed of "the factory director, the deputy director, the chief engineer, the party secretary, the union chair, and a number of worker representatives who were elected by employees for six-month terms." They were "charged with deciding major questions relating to production and management such as administrative regulations, the organization of production, personnel assignments, as well as wages and welfare policies." Their major purpose was to "gain Chinese workers' support for the implementation of 'scientific management' in state enterprises"—and specifically, to "master… and disseminate… [the workers'] skills and knowledge vital to the state's developmental goals."[66] With the rise of "one-man management," the FMCs quickly atrophied. General meetings were increasingly replaced with those of executive committees.

> If you only look at…the documents, it would seem that the FMC had great power, but in reality, in terms of implementation, power was completely concentrated in the hands of the factory director. Moreover, at meetings it mostly discussed issues raised by higher levels or by the enterprise administration and seldom discussed issues raised by the masses. As a result, the masses gradually lost interest in the FMC, and the administrative leadership cadres began to feel there was no need for it, and so it could not but degenerate into formalism.[67]

In both private and state-owned firms, the Party/state organized "staff and workers congresses" (SWCs; 职工代表大会) responsible for "supervising the FMC and the factory leadership, which meant that factory leaders were to present reports to the congress, accounting for their activities and offering self-criticisms for problems, and then invite discussion and criticism."[68] In some places Party members could comprise no more than one-third of SWC delegates, and

65 Cliver, *Minzhu Guanli.*

66 Ibid., 414. Cliver invokes the radical American labor leader "Big" Bill Haywood, who said "The manager's brains are under the workman's cap." One could also turn to Karl Marx, who, in Chapter 15 of *Das Kapital*, laid bare the complex processes by which machines are built by engineers who closely observed workers' skills in the labor process and then appropriated them when designing machines. "The machine, therefore, is a mechanism that… performs with its tools the same operations that the worker formerly did with similar tools," Karl Marx, *Capital: A Critique of Political Economy* (New York: Vintage, 1977), 495.

67 Su Ke (苏克), "从我国工人群众参与企业管理的历史经验来看当前合营企业的民主管理问题" ("Current problems with democratic management in joint enterprises from the perspective of our country's historical experience with workers' participation in enterprise management,") *工人日报* (*Workers' Daily*), January 5, 1957, cited in Andreas, *Disenfranchised*, 39.

68 Andreas, *Disenfranchised*, 29–30.

60 percent of delegates and half of their *presidia* had to be "frontline workers." Yet they were more about Party-regulated participation than actual worker democracy. Though a minority on the SWC, cadres were nonetheless overrepresented compared with their proportion of factory employees. Elections for ordinary worker representatives were "carefully orchestrated" to include those most loyal to the leadership, and Party-approved nomination lists were barely larger than the number of seats to be filled. They served to mobilize workers to participate in the Three- and Five-Anti Campaigns of 1951 and 1952.[69] "Although workers participated, these top-down campaigns did not leave much room for initiative or autonomy on the workers' part."[70] The SWCs were further undermined by the First Five-Year Plan and its emphasis on "one-man management," which became a flashpoint of the 1957 strike wave.[71]

But in the context of the Maoist Hundred Flowers movement, with its call for critique of state socialist ossification, they were revived in 1956 by Lai Ruoyu, the Chair of the All-China Federation of Trade Unions. He had found them too atrophic and wanted them to serve as the "highest administrative organ" of the factory and even to appoint and dismiss the leadership. They should enable workers to "freely criticize the work of the enterprise in all its aspects and actively put forward proposals so that they may fully play their role of supervision over the leadership." Workers quickly took up the new latitude and official *imprimatur*. Pushing back against the orchestration of elections, in one factory workers "organized elections for congress representatives on their own, which factory union leaders refused to recognize." They were known to spend weeks preparing for meetings. Factory and Party leaders soon complained that the SWCs had become "too democratic." Discussions were often substantive and lively.[72]

SWCs continued to wax and wane as the wider political and economic contexts shifted. Though they declined in the wake of the Great Leap Forward crisis, the Four Cleans movement to rein in overweening forces of economic and political rationalization revived them in 1965 and 1966. The Cultural Revolution that followed, full of radicalized conflict, eclipsed them for the remainder of the Maoist period.[73]

To sum up, the new workplace institutions attracted considerable working class interest in standing up for itself. But they could only do so at times and places when the political conditions set by the Party/state were favorable

69 The "Three-Antis" opposed bureaucratism, corruption and waste in state enterprises; the "Five-Anti" attacked bribery, tax evasion, theft of state property, cheating on government contracts and stealing government economic information in state enterprises.

70 Andreas, *Disenfranchised*, 33.

71 See p. 75.

72 Andreas, *Disenfranchised*, 45–46.

73 Ibid., 45–46, 75–79, 93.

and those afforded by the ebb and flow of radical changes in economic organization and performance allowed. Here again, working class formation took place squarely within hegemonic bounds. Mobilizing themselves inside those trenches, however ardently, ultimately set the working class up for defeat.

Unions

Before 1949, workers had often striven to form labor unions. They demanded the right to organize during strikes and showed considerable virtuosity in forming unions in their factories, specific industries and localities. They even managed to turn some state corporatist unions organized under the Nationalists into meaningful and potent labor organizations.[74] With the collapse of the Republic, union organization began to flourish anew. Some were put together by the workers themselves, and some by the Communist Party.[75] For the first few years of the People's Republic, even the unions that had been organized by the Party retained a considerable degree of operational and political autonomy both locally and at the centers of power. In the words of one local union official in the Chongqing Arsenal: "The [union's] staff-worker representative council had a lot of power. Everything had to pass through the council."[76] In Beijing, the All-China Federation of Trade Unions (ACFTU), established by the CCP in 1925, was now charged with overseeing and developing China's organized labor movement. While this was of course to take place under the Party's supervision, the ACFTU leader, the veteran and former Communist Party chair Li Lisan, strove to carve out a definite sphere of autonomy for the Federation within the new Party/state. Sensing the workers' hesitation about the Party, he argued that the unions rather than the Party should be the main force in the relationship between the working class and the new state. The 1951 Trade Union Law, with which Li was closely identified, did not mention rallying workers to support the Party as one of the ACFTU's responsibilities.[77]

Tension between the unions and the Party grew more pointed. Many workers, while happy at the opportunity afforded by the victory of the revolution, nonetheless did not warm to the Party. Some had had their fill of political parties from their experience with the Guomindang. And most knew little or nothing about the CCP, which had generally been unable to operate in China's cities. Many did not believe that the Party would hold power; and if it did not, they feared recriminations. But more important than their views of the Party was their greater enthusiasm about unions, which were, after all, institutions that

74 See p. 30.

75 Howard, "Workers at War," 330 *ff.*; Lee Lai To, *Trade Unions in China* (Singapore: Singapore University Press, 1986), 41; Lieberthal, *Revolution and Tradition in Tientsin*, 82.

76 Howard, "Workers at War," 334.

77 Lee, *Trade Unions*, 80–81.

felt much more like their own (and often were) and with which they often had a considerable history. And the Party's program—promoting industrial peace to help development and mobilizing support for the Korean War—was a great deal less appealing to workers than the income and welfare issues that they could pursue through their unions. As discussed below, they did so with a great deal of enthusiasm and spontaneity.[78]

Partly for that reason, but also in line with the Party's deep Leninist reflexes, it did not take long for the Party to bring the union movement to heel. On the ground, the Party did try to revive flagging worker interest in unions by holding struggle meetings (at which workers welcomed the opportunity to denounce the worst managers and Guomindang officials). They held elections to union posts, made a dent initially in severe wage inequalities, tried to solve the worst housing problems, established cooperative stores selling necessities at discounts, and worked on literacy and education.[79] While workers welcomed much of this, it all reflected and reinforced the Party's new control of the unions. At the national level, Li Lisan was removed in 1951, though his ouster was not announced publicly for two years. He was replaced by Lai Ruoyu, an important Party official not previously known for union work (though he would stand up for strengthening workers' role and autonomy in workplace institutions).[80] The ACFTU Constitution was amended in 1953 to stress Party leadership.[81] Having led the union for several years, though, Lai and his deputies began, during the propitious moment of the "Hundred Flowers" in 1956, to seek some operational, though not political, autonomy. This meant little more than that lower-level union offices should be subject to higher-level union rather than Party ones. This would, they argued, increase the credibility of the union with the workers, who continued to believe that the union was under the thumb of the Party and, therefore, of the management of the now socialized firms. But with the coming of the 1957 Anti-Rightist Campaign and the 1958 Great Leap, with its strong message of "politics in command," the union advocates lost out, their efforts criticized as "syndicalist." Until the onset of the Cultural Revolution, in factories the ACFTU had become essentially an arm of management. More widely, from the localities to the center, it was now a powerless "mass organization" in the Leninist mold, under the full control of the Communist Party.[82] When the Party came under radical attack during the Cultural Revolution, the ACFTU

78 Frazier, *The Making of the Chinese Industrial Workplace*, 110–114; Howard, "Workers at War," 334 and *passim*.
79 Howard, "Workers at War," 333 *ff.*
80 See p. 66.
81 Lee, *Trade Unions*, 81–82.
82 Lee, *Trade Unions*, chap. 4; Ng Sek Hong and Malcolm Warner, *China's Trade Unions and Management* (Houndmills: Macmillan, 1998).

was not spared. In January 1967, Premier Zhou Enlai denounced its "bureaucratism," its headquarters were seized by the left, and it became defunct.[83]

Militias

Workers' militias were involved in consolidation of power during the early days of the People's Republic. By and large they were successors of pre-1949 armed outfits. But whereas in those years workers organized their own militias while also being recruited into those organized by the parties,[84] now they were the creatures of the new organs of political power: the unions, the Party and the army. A complex politics developed among them over the militias' role and control, with workers themselves playing the role only of recruits mobilized into service rather than the organizers themselves. But even so, some continued to act on their own initiative—*e.g.,* by resisting orders to disarm. If anything, the wider working class's own political role in 1949 and the early 1950s was to resist these state-run militias, which often proved ineffective in their assigned role of bringing working class radicalism under control. In fact, their ham-fisted efforts to purge alleged "reactionaries" and Guomindang agents in the factories often alienated workers.[85]

But workers did organize their own patrols during the strike wave of 1957.[86] Operating as a branch of the workers' own United Command Headquarters, they not only enforced workers' participation in the strike, but also had the temerity to put up resistance to cadres of the Party and the labor union who tried to quell the protests. This frightened the state enough to help provoke a stern crackdown leading to the harsh Anti-Rightist Campaign.[87] For the next ten years, militias were a strictly and closely supervised state-run affair.

During the Cultural Revolution decade, militias flowered on both the rebel and conservative sides, and they were responsible for some of the worst factional violence. While workers were recruited into them, and many participated with great enthusiasm, these outfits were very much creatures of faction leaderships rather than the spontaneous creations of the working class. For just one example, of the ten original leaders of the rebel Shanghai "Attack with Words—Defend with Weapons," which eventually became the Shanghai Militia, only one was a worker, and he was the only one of the ten who was not a Party member.[88]

83 Lee, *Trade Unions*, 113.
84 See p. 30.
85 Perry, *Patrolling the Revolution*, chap. 4.
86 See p. 75.
87 Perry, *Patrolling the Revolution*, 180–81.
88 Ibid., 222.

Cultural Revolution Red Guards

Even less were the main red guard organizations that emerged during the Cultural Revolution the working class's own creations. On both the rebel and conservative sides, most of the leaders were officials and cadres. Even those who had originally hailed from working class backgrounds were no longer recognizable as Chinese workers, having switched to political careers many years earlier. The rebel leader most closely identified in the popular imagination with the working class was Wang Hongwen. Born into a peasant family, in 1956 he was sent to a Shanghai cotton mill after his demobilization from the army. But by 1960 he was assigned to full-time militia work, whence he began his meteoric rise—his nickname became "helicopter"—to the national Cultural Revolution Small Group, where he was one of the "Gang of Four" top rebels in the country. He certainly was not a serious or consistent advocate for specifically working class interests. In heavily industrial Wuhan, workers comprised only a tiny minority of the rebel groups. Most conservative red guard leaders were also lower- and middle-level officials. The workers among them were that tiny minority of the working class who had been dubbed "activists" (积极分子), "backbones" (骨干分子) or "labor models" (劳动模范), or who had in quieter ways become clients of patrons in their factory leadership. Most of these people were viewed with suspicion by the bulk of their fellow workers.

The most authentically working class organizations during the Cultural Revolution were the "economistic" outfits formed spontaneously at the end of 1966, after Beijing issued a November directive permitting workers to participate in the Cultural Revolution. In contrast to the main rebel and conservative groups, which were developed by political élites, these were *ad hoc* organizations put together, apparently, by workers themselves. Their leaders were not known political figures before or after the Cultural Revolution. The participants were rural contract workers, urban workers who had been sent to the villages or rural construction projects in the post-Leap retrenchment, rusticated urban students, and even private entrepreneurs. Moreover, while the rebels and conservatives focused on the question of political power from the shop floor to the halls of power in Beijing, and were implicated heavily in national, regional and local-level political battles within the Party/state, the "economistic" organizations directed their ire at the structural inequalities between their members and constituencies on the one hand and the urban-resident workers on the other. They did attract support for a brief month in December 1966 from rebel groups, including top leaders in the Cultural Revolution Small Group, who saw in them a bludgeon with which to attack the Party leaders they were seeking to topple. But when orders by their élite supporters that factories should compensate them and give them their jobs back caused financial crisis, the rebels had to back off. At the start of January 1967, just weeks after these groups had appeared, the Party center attacked "economism" as individualistic and, therefore, reactionary, and the "economistic" organizations representing the most vulnerable strata of the working class were summarily criticized and shut down. Another wave of "economistic" demands came to the fore in July 1967, but this time they were put forward, almost anarchistically, not even by *ad hoc* groups, but by unorganized mobs.[89]

The Party

The Communist Party was, by any measure, not a working class organization, even though it claimed to be. In 1949 fewer than 5 percent of members were workers. It did make a major effort to expand worker representation, doubling that percentage to 7.2 percent in just three years, and doubling it again to 14 percent by 1957. Moreover, in that year 18 percent of workers were Party members. In 1956, seven of the eighty-one members of the Party Central Committee chosen at the Eighth Congress were workers. By 1961, working class membership in the Party had not grown significantly. In 1969 the Ninth Congress Central Committee members included one-fourth farmers and workers, so we can surmise little change from the Eighth. By and large, throughout the Maoist period, the Communist Party was comprised predominantly of petit-bourgeois intellectuals; and an astonishing two-thirds of the latter were Party members.[90]

...

When it came to organization, the Maoist-era working class was enmeshed almost completely within the hegemonic institutions of the state. During the Maoist era, China's working class lacked sustained organizations of its own. In the 1950s it made sporadic attempts to carve out some autonomous space within the unions that were being incorporated into the ACFTU. During the 1957 strike wave, workers even went so far as to ban ACFTU cadres from their wildcat unions,[91] and also formed militias to patrol and enforce their strikes. Mainly, though, the working class expressed itself in *unorganized* resistance to the efforts of the new state to bring workers into its own new organizations — in, of course, the subordinate position prescribed by Leninist "democratic centralism." The only authentically working class organizations that appeared in the Cultural Revolution were snuffed out within a month. In contrast to the lively organizational virtuosity evinced by the working class in the first half of the century, when the political opportunity structure was more favorable, Maoist China, with its Leninist principle of Party/state monopoly of all political space, was a definite setback to the political aspects of working class formation.

89 Perry and Li, *Proletarian Power*, chap. 4; Wang, *Failure of Charisma*, 168–9.
90 Harrison, *The Long March to Power*, 458–9.
91 See p. 29.

And in turn, the working class's low level of political institutionalization, which drove so much of its political activism, however radical, inside the institutions of the Party/state, constituted powerful hegemonic entrenchments that undermined it.

Contentious Collective Action

Working class contentious politics went through several phases: wildcat opposition against managerial rationalization in the early 1950s, critique of any sort of incentive pay in the mid- and late-1950s, radical attacks on managers during the height of the Cultural Revolution, and participation in top-down ideological and political campaigns for the remainder of the Cultural Revolution decade through 1976.

1949–1952: Recovery and Consolidation

The fall of the Republic, the concomitant decampment of much of the industrial bourgeoisie, and their replacement by the Communists amounted, of course, to a massive transformation of the political opportunity structure[92] for China's working class. Workers began very quickly to take matters into their own hands. Despite orders from the CCP not to do so, radical Tianjin workers organized industrial coops, which soon went bankrupt. Particularly in the industrial northeast, workers and grassroots communist cadres attacked capitalists and managers. The largest wave of strikes and protests Shanghai had ever seen broke out in 1949, as workers demanded enforcement of pro-labor policies, payment and cessation of wage arrears, and restoration of jobs from which they had been laid off. Yet deflationary policies of the new government created an economic downturn that made it difficult for owners and managers to meet workers' demands. When managers in the machine tools and shipbuilding sectors failed to rehire laid-off workers, they found themselves encircled and taunted. Workers gorged themselves at "eat-ins" (坐吃), going to the homes of factory directors as well as their plant refectories and devouring everything in sight. They ostentatiously napped on the job. As noted above,[93] they even went so far as to attack the new Party/state itself, denouncing and battling soldiers and officers—dozens were killed—and jeering the central leadership including Chairman Mao himself.[94]

In 1951, the state began to arrest "counterrevolutionaries" among shop floor officials and even in the working class itself. Workers responded with demands

92 See p. 58.
93 See p. 58 *ff.*
94 Brugger, *Democracy*, 73; Frazier, *The Making of the Chinese Industrial Workplace*, 96–108.

that the misdeeds of "number ones" ("*na-mo-wen*" in pidgin)—*i.e.,* shop floor supervisors—be investigated. Those in private firms called for their dismissal, as had happened in state-owned firms. Some even demanded radical management reforms to eliminate "number one" positions altogether. Women workers were particularly forceful in demanding that these petty despots be brought to account for their various depredations. Many workers responded to Party-led calls to "speak bitterness" (诉苦) about the past. Some of those accused were hauled in front of workers' meetings to undertake "self-criticism."[95]

In 1952, the CCP mobilized the country for the Five-Anti Movement.[96] As the size and illegal sources of their employers' fortunes came to light, workers, particularly those in smaller firms, responded by going on strike and in some cases beating their bosses. Once again, they demanded rehiring laid-off workers, an end to further dismissals and increased worker involvement in management. Some employers offered bonuses and benefits to mollify angry employees.[97] Such wage increases undermined the state's interest in wage restraint in connection with its efforts to stem inflation. Workers may not have made much headway in their demands to participate in running the plants, but they did manage to undermine managers' shop floor power. This too ran counter to the state's wish to maintain and increase industrial production.[98]

1952–1957: Battles over Incentive Pay and Factory Management

The First Five-Year Plan emphasized nationalization of private firms, rapid development, bureaucratic planning, technocratic management and industrial discipline. It therefore brought in tow piece rates, other incentive pay schemes, wage cuts that could run to 50 percent or more (especially for workers in newly nationalized firms) and efforts to expand welfare benefits to make up for workers' declining incomes.

Piece rates were unpopular with workers unaccustomed to a rapid pace of work and self-imposed labor discipline, especially at a moment when they had just begun to experience the shop floor pleasures of plummeting managerial power. Those workers also objected to piece rates in an environment that lacked regular supplies of inputs and spare parts, which could make it impossible for even the most assiduous among them to meet quotas. Conflicts broke out as well between rate busters and the workers who resented them. Some factory Party committees suddenly found themselves having to mediate disputes between

95 Frazier, *The Making of the Chinese Industrial Workplace*, 117 *ff.*

96 See p. 66, note 69.

97 Frazier, *The Making of the Chinese Industrial Workplace*, 115–117; Stephen Andors, *China's Industrial Revolution: Politics, Planning and Management, 1949 to the Present* (Oxford: Wiley-Blackwell, 1977), 52.

98 Frazier, *The Making of the Chinese Industrial Workplace*, 126–130.

shop floor managers who set piece rates too high, due to their inexperience, lack of technical expertise, or zeal in trying to increase production, and frustrated, angry workers—in particular, older and less skilled workers who stood to lose out from piece rates. Conflicts also broke out among rate setters, accountants and supervisors over the administrative difficulties caused by piece rates. Other dysfunctions appeared, such as piece rates' negative effect on equipment maintenance and on innovation, as workers were unhappy about taking time out to service their machines or learn about new equipment or processes. Toward the end of the First Five-Year Plan, Mao and his allies in the leadership began to criticize piece rates as encouraging individual rather than collective striving, as part of a general attack on the Soviet model of industrial management. Yet those critiques were themselves rooted in part in the objections workers had already been leveling on the shop floor. The result of these myriad conflicts and problems fatally undermined the use of piece rates in China. In a departure from the standard practice in state socialist planned economies, they were abolished by the late 1950s.[99]

Bonuses were also tried as another incentive pay scheme. State officials concerned with promoting wage restraint and labor incentives wanted them to be carefully targeted and used sparingly. However, like piece rates, they proved administratively complex. They also rankled workers for many of the same reasons as piece rates: bonus targets could not be met simply by greater labor effort. Workers responded by slowing down work once the basic quotas or the limits of output set by available supplies, equipment and technology had been reached. Factory managers preferred, therefore, to distribute bonuses across the board to all workers, to simplify their own work while also mollifying shop-floor critics. They developed a range of creative ruses—safety bonuses, holiday bonuses and even "salting and tasting" bonuses for cooks (!) to accomplish this.[100]

The government sought to mollify workers' unhappiness over often drastic wage cuts by expanding welfare provision—labor insurance, pensions, food, childcare, education, housing and recreation—at the factory level. This policy was continuous with past practice: as discussed earlier,[101] in the Republican period, especially at moments of shortage or inflation, many firms provided a range of such benefits to their workers, who preferred goods to wages. Now again, expanding factory welfare would be a relatively inexpensive way of compensating workers who experienced wage and cash income cuts. It would also resonate with socialist values while binding workers ever more tightly to

99 Frazier, *The Making of the Chinese Industrial Workplace*, 154, 213, 238; Walder, *Communist Neo-Traditionalism*, 118–120.
100 Frazier, *The Making of the Chinese Industrial Workplace*, 153–154.
101 See p. 18.

their firms. Yet structural inequalities in the distribution of welfare too proved a catalyst of worker protest. Nationalized firms had much larger budgets to fund welfare than did private firms and small collective firms. In 1955 and 1956, Shanghai and Guangzhou workers in private and collective firms protested actively, often choosing as their method the symbolically appropriate "eat-in" as well as encircling leaders and staging slowdowns. They justified the latter by mocking the state's socialist rhetoric, declaring, as mentioned above,[102] that they were "working according to pay."[103]

More spectacular than these protests was the strike wave of 1957, which involved more than three times the number of firms that had been involved in the historic May 30 Movement of 1925, and more than twice as many as in the high tide of 1946. Workers in newly socialized small and medium-sized firms, apprentices and younger, more educated workers were particularly active. Fundamentally, this was a conflict over various cuts in wages and economic security visited on the working class by socialization. Apprentices protested aggressively, often violently, against the extension of their training terms, which policymakers had done as part of their effort to keep wage bills down. Workers also protested firings and demotions from permanent to temporary status. Wage arrears became yet another focus of protest. Welfare remained an irritant, both for the inequalities in provision and because of moves in some plants to divert wage arrears to fund welfare. Workers who had been transferred out of Shanghai "temporarily" were outraged when the state reneged on its promises of an early return. Explicitly political issues also surfaced. Workers protested against the proliferation of bureaucracy and their loss of the opportunity to participate in plant affairs following the adoption of Soviet-style "one-man management." Recent rural migrants expressed prescient fears that the emerging household registration system would permanently relegate them to a lower status of welfare entitlement.[104]

The 1957 strike wave demonstrated workers' capacity to deploy a highly variegated, aggressive and creative protest repertoire. Continuing the culinary theme that ran through earlier outbursts, they staged hunger strikes, but also held eat-ins at factory refectories and had the audacity to order festival meals from restaurants, billing them to their factory. Workers encircled, seized and even tortured factory managers. When their allotments of free toilet paper were cut, they used factory letterheads to clean themselves and send a contemptuous message in the same gesture. All this accompanied more prosaic forms of protest such as legal appeals, big character posters, handbills, marches, sit-ins, petitions and pickets. Workers also evinced impressive organizational

102 See p. 59.
103 Frazier, *The Making of the Chinese Industrial Workplace*, 141–2, 198–199.
104 Ibid., 198; Elizabeth Perry, "Shanghai's Strike Wave": 8–16.

virtuosity, despite the virtual absence of leadership by intellectuals who are often (and inaccurately) thought necessary to transform spontaneous into concerted action. They organized strike committees, liaisons and "united command headquarters" to coordinate protests among different plants, and formed autonomous unions (评难会 [literally, societies for critiquing hardship]) and a Democratic Party (民主党派). In doing so, they shrewdly decided specifically to exclude cadres of the state-run unions. Their rhetoric went so far as to invoke, ominously, the 1956 Hungarian protests.[105] While some older workers tried to mediate the disputes in their plants, the state's response was basically repressive. During the Anti-Rightist Campaign of 1957, strikers and other protesters were either arrested, sent to the countryside, or, if they were in staff positions, relegated to the production lines.[106]

The Great Leap Forward and Its Aftermath

Stern measures such as these did not silence China's workers, though. With the onset of the Great Leap Forward, the Party went on the offensive against the technocratic, bureaucratic and authoritarian bents of the First Five-Year Plan. Party secretaries replaced managers and engineers in day-to-day operations. In some cases they actually suspended management altogether, granting individual workers the latitude to set their own quotas, arrange their own inputs, and even do their own quality control and accounting. Workers joined in, remaining free with their criticisms of the politics of the shop floor, including the Party. As early as 1958, they wrote millions of big-character posters criticizing the First Five-Year Plan and calling on their plants' skilled experts to come down to the shop floor and pitch in. Where incentive pay schemes still operated, workers demanded their abolition, denouncing them as individualistic and citing the Great Leap Forward slogan of putting "politics in command." They also expressed their unhappiness on other economic matters, including inequities in compensation between workers and management that occurred through subsidies, bonuses, welfare payments and expense reimbursement. As pay became determined by public evaluations, workers proved hardest on members of the Communist Party and its Youth League.[107]

With the collapse of the economy due to the Great Leap, the inevitable retrenchments of industrial employment led to more protest in 1962. Older workers and women, who bore the brunt of the cuts, were particularly vociferous. They resorted to screaming matches, encirclements and physical attacks

105 Perry, "Shanghai's Strike Wave": 8–15.
106 Frazier, *The Making of the Chinese Industrial Workplace*, 199–200.
107 Ibid., 212–214.

against officials, and eat-ins at cadres' homes and food shops.[108] Meanwhile, factory management was re-rationalized. At the micro level, "The Seventy Articles" of 1961 restored the power of management and Party committees within plants, which in some places included the return of piece rates and bonuses. In macro terms, various new kinds of linkages among firms were tried to help streamline coordination, leading most grandly to the creation of enormous vertically integrated industrial combines known as "trusts." While the working class, politically and physically exhausted and frightened of further layoffs, did not react immediately in a significant way, all of these changes in labor allocation and industrial organization provided ready targets for radical criticism during the stunning Cultural Revolution.

The Cultural Revolution

Social Bases and Political Programs

Industrial workers were very active in the Cultural Revolution. The three distinct strands mentioned above—rebel, conservative and economist—had disparate political programs and definite if not always fully discrete social and political bases.

The Rebels The rebels tended to draw from a range of social groups and strata, including temporary and contract workers, part-study/part work program participants, apprentices, unskilled workers, those in smaller plants, younger workers, those who had been labeled as "backward" in their work performance or their political expression, and people with a range of formal class backgrounds, including the "bad" ones.[109] They sometimes received tacit support from more skilled workers and even former élites, who also had reasons to resent the political officials and their supporters targeted by the rebels. What all these constituencies had in common was that they had often come in for abuse in China's revolutionary society. Their leaders tended to be workers rather than cadres, younger (generally around 30), more educated, and, of course, more politically inclined.[110]

Rebels attacked the post-Leap rationalizations. They criticized the dominance of organizational rules and middle managers who enforced them, incentive pay, and bureaucracy and technocracy. They argued that the trusts were premised on factories being only sites of production when in fact they were and

108 Ibid., 219–220.

109 See note 54.

110 Andors, *China's Industrial Revolution*, 167; Lee, *The Politics of the Chinese Cultural Revolution*, 134–137; Perry and Li, *Proletarian Power*, 39–41, 58, 83; Wang, *Failure of Charisma*, 33 *ff.*

ought to be social and political communities as well. They asserted that such organization, combined with the educational background and political attitudes of technicians, made the trusts and the factories that comprised them into breeding grounds for new, retrograde class formations. This found expression both in factory political officials' work style as well as the distributive effects of the industrial structure (*e.g.,* between urban and rural areas and among regions), they expostulated.[111]

Though they couched their critique in radical political terms, it was often grounded in personal grievances against officials they regarded as high-handed. In many cases, the personal was, in fact, the level at which the political made itself manifest. Temporary and contract workers had received systematically lower compensation (including benefits) and more unfavorable working and employment conditions. It was not unreasonable for many to interpret such inferior treatment as having political roots, implications and remedies. Others with purely parochial gripes against officials used the radicalized political atmosphere, rhetoric and repertoire of the day to legitimate their revenge to others and to themselves.[112]

The Conservatives Conservative factions tended to attract Communist Party and Youth League members, middle- and lower-level factory officials, those with ties to factory and government leadership, including their friends, relatives and protégés, and others who had benefited under the industrial régime of the First Five-Year Plan and the post-Leap period. While most of them tended to hail from "good" class backgrounds, workers with "bad" class backgrounds sometimes gravitated to conservative factions in order to find political cover. Faction leaders hailed from among Party and Youth League members, model workers, "activists," and lower and mid-level factory staff (since higher-level plant officials were more frequently under attack).[113]

The conservatives were, naturally enough, concerned with defending the *status quo.* In ideological terms that were doubtless genuinely felt in many cases, they believed in the values of shop floor autonomy and even power for the working class. Less abstractly, they feared the corrosive effect of economic, social and political inequalities on workers' morale, industrial production and factory infrastructure (which was in danger of being run down under piece rates). Many conservatives were revolutionary cadres who had put their lives on the line to build a better world on the ruins of China's experience with imperialism and capitalist authoritarianism. They thought of themselves as a new and different breed of political official who served the people, and they could not

111 Andors, *China's Industrial Revolution,* 192 *ff.*
112 Ibid., 167, 187–191 *ff.*; Blecher and White, *Micropolitics*; Lee, *The Politics of the Chinese Cultural Revolution,* 136–137; Perry and Li, *Proletarian Power,* 64, 83.
113 Perry and Li, *Proletarian Power,* 39–41, 58, 83.

imagine themselves as having anything in common with the exploitive, oppressive élites whom they had dispatched. They were also loyal Communists who believed in the value and importance of Leninist discipline, especially at a time when the Chinese Revolution was still under threat from a well-armed opposition in Taiwan that maintained links to underground and latent supporters on the mainland and was backed by the military might of the United States. It was natural, then, that when the rebels began attacking them, they were not just bewildered and unable to recognize themselves as "capitalist roaders," but also alarmed if not surprised by the fact that many of their attackers came from "bad" class backgrounds. Thus they felt that they had to re-fight the revolution, and they acted accordingly.[114]

The conservatives were also motivated, of course, by personal factors. Many felt loyal to Party leaders whom they respected for their personal frugality, their advocacy of ordinary workers' interests on piece rates and one-man management, or the clientelist links that had developed.[115] And of course conservatives were also protecting their own material and political interests in the *status quo*.[116]

Economistic Protest The third strand of protest focused on economic grievances—in particular, those of temporary and contract workers, most hailing from the countryside, who worked alongside urban-resident workers, often in less desirable jobs, with less pay, benefits and employment security. They included a disproportionate number of women, apprentices, many workers who had been laid off during the post-Leap retrenchment, construction workers, youth who had been "sent down" to the countryside, and even former individual entrepreneurs. Their demands focused on compensation, welfare, subsidies, the right to join the state labor union (a requirement for receiving welfare), housing, reemployment after dismissals that had been touted as temporary, labor insurance, and obtaining urban household registrations.[117]

Collective Contention

Like most ordinary Chinese, workers did not participate in the early phases of the Cultural Revolution. Through October 1966, the movement was primarily the affair of political élites, academics, cultural professionals and students. The Party did not yet permit workers to join in, urging them instead to attend to production. Yet, over the summer, a small number of workers who had suffered discrimination over the years because of their "bad" class backgrounds

114 Perry and Li, *Proletarian Power*, 82–85.
115 Walder, *Communist Neo-Traditionalism*.
116 Perry and Li, *Proletarian Power*, 82–85; Blecher and White, *Micropolitics*.
117 Ibid., 98 *ff.*

or "backward" political expression began to stick their necks out, putting up "big character posters" denouncing factory leaders they held responsible. But these workers comprised a tiny minority of the labor force, and their positions were easily characterized by the leadership as springing from personal gripes, which was often true. At a moment when workers were not yet permitted by the Party to participate in the Cultural Revolution, factory officials felt in a strong position, and they once again branded the early proletarian protesters with political labels such as "rightist." Moreover, as we shall see, they had the support of many workers who had benefited from Chinese state socialism and who had good relations with factory officials. In fact, most workers were horrified when radical students started parading factory leaders around their cities in dunce caps.[118]

In light of the prohibitions against joining the radical movement, the small group of discontented workers who did could only respond by beginning to make quiet contacts with radical students who had suffered in similar ways, and who naturally welcomed and encouraged them. As the political situation shifted in the radicals' favor in October and early November, these workers felt confident enough to form their own rebel organizations and begin to hold rallies and sit-ins and attack "capitalist roaders" in the Party and government. In Shanghai radical workers tied up all railway traffic for thirty-one hours.[119] As the rebel workers movement gathered steam in many cities, Mao and his radical supporters in Beijing finally changed their position, allowing and encouraging worker participation in the Cultural Revolution. In this sense, workers, taking advantage of emerging political opportunities, acted spontaneously and autonomously to force themselves onto the political stage and induce the highest political leadership to reverse its position.

Moreover, the workers' initiative opened the floodgates for other social groups to activate themselves. Soon, "artists, contract workers, apprentices, cooks, [army] veterans, …teachers…, policemen, judges, prosecutors, street cleaners, doctors, militias…blind persons" and many others were forming rebel groups to protest their mistreatment at the hands of Party and government élites.[120] Thanks to the space opened up by audacious workers acting initially against Party directives, most of Chinese society was activated. A rebel offensive swept over the country through January 1967.

No sooner had rebellious workers pushed through the door than they began to engage in political and organizational mitosis. For example, in Wuhan, five "palace coups" took place within the Workers' Headquarters over the next few months. Meanwhile, three other large outfits—the Workers' Rebel

118 Wang, *Failure of Charisma*, 87 *ff.*
119 Perry and Li, *Proletarian Power*, 34 *ff.*
120 Wang, *Failure of Charisma*, 89.

Headquarters, the 17 August Corps, and the 13 September Corps—also came into being, along with myriad smaller groups. All this energetic organizational virtuosity lent the workers' movement tremendous attack strength and destructive power. In Shanghai, the Workers' General Headquarters became little more than a "loose amalgam" of five different "regiments."[121]

A key part of the fissiparous working class movement was the "economistic" "cry for justice" sent up by outraged rural contract workers and by urban-resident workers who had been ejected from their factories. In late December, representatives of the hastily organized "National Revolutionary Rebel Delegation of Red Workers" landed an audience with the leaders of the central Cultural Revolution Small Group, including Jiang Qing (Mao's wife). For five hours these second-class workers poured out their stories, and the assembled radical élites responded by pouring scorn on the "capitalistic" and "reactionary" officials who had allowed and benefited from the inequalities. "The contract workers must revolt!" the radical leadership thundered. They summarily issued orders to all the country's factories that the dismissed workers be rehired and paid back wages. This set off a nationwide scramble for financial gain that officials could not resist. Apprentices received payments worth many months' wages to compensate for previous wage differentials that were now deemed excessive and unjustifiable. Workers in private and collective factories and teachers in private schools, where pay scales were lower, demanded and achieved the conversion of their enterprises to the coveted ranks of the state sector, with its vaunted higher wages and welfare guarantees. They also demanded admission to the state-run labor union, not for any political reasons—they knew it represented the state and management rather than them—but because membership would qualify them for medical insurance. Some workers forcibly occupied unallocated apartments.[122]

As all this frenetic grasping for money eventually wrought economic havoc, the rebel leadership had little choice but to reverse itself and ring down the "economism" it had encouraged just weeks earlier. In early January, they issued a proclamation demanding that workers "raise the banner of politics, not the banner of economics!" A few days later the Party leadership denounced economism, blaming the very financial and bank officials and clerks on whom they had placed inexorable pressure to pay out just weeks earlier.[123] While the lower strata of the working class were the clear losers, they had also, unintentionally, inflicted considerable damage on the rebel side, which now had turned on much of its working class base and contradicted itself so palpably and publicly.

121 Ibid., 89–90; Perry and Li, *Proletarian Power*, 120 *ff.*
122 Perry and Li, *Proletarian Power*, 107–111.
123 Ibid., 111–2.

But that damage would not become apparent for a few more weeks. During the rest of January, rebel groups, including the discontented workers, held the high ground. They conducted some spectacular maneuvers, such as blocking rail lines. Following general instructions from Chairman Mao, they planned and executed "power seizures" in their factories, city halls and Party headquarters. Rebels chucked out factory leaders and staff, ministry and bureau officials, and city government cadres, mayors and Party secretaries, accused them of being capitalist roaders, dressed them in dunce caps, hung signs full of epithets around their necks, paraded them around town in open carts, forced them to stand for hours in the painful "airplane position" (bent forward with their hands tied behind their backs), and publicly humiliated them at massive rallies. Rebel worker groups occupied the vacant offices, busying themselves with burrowing through the files for evidence to substantiate their charges, and actually taking the reins of power to run things themselves. Naturally, the prospect of holding power only exacerbated the fissiparous tendencies among the rebels, who began to attack each other openly at the end of the month. At one juncture reminiscent of the absurd scene in *Monty Python's Life of Brian*, in which the handful of members of the People's Front of Judea would have no truck with the one-man Judean People's Front, in Wuhan the Workers' Headquarters attacked the Workers' Rebel Headquarters. But this wasn't at all funny: China was on the brink of anarchy and civil war.

The political tide shifted in February, as even Mao and the radicals around him in Beijing became worried that the Cultural Revolution was getting out of hand. They mobilized the armed forces to restore order, emphasized the rectitude and importance of most veteran cadres, and chastised the rebels, forcing them to share power with the armed forces and the Party. This provided an opportunity for the majority of urban-resident workers, who were loyal to their factory officials and had disapproved of the "January revolution." The core of China's working class had, after all, benefited significantly from the revolution. While many of them had disliked and resisted the industrial rationalizations of the First Five-Year Plan such as one-man management and incentive pay, they had also been relatively successful at turning that back. They had benefited from the rise of Party officials and politically oriented decision making *vis-à-vis* technical and managerial specialists—in communist shorthand, of "reds" over "experts." These workers found most factory-level Party officials honest, modest, serious and self-sacrificing. Thus they could not recognize the epithets—"capitalist roaders," "reactionaries" and the like—that rebels were hurling at their factory cadres. Now they rose to defend their leaders against rebel assaults, in what Wang Shaoguang has termed "the most spontaneous workers' movement during the Cultural Revolution."[124] In Shanghai, workers formed groups

124 Wang, *Failure of Charisma*, 50, 90–91, 96; Perry and Li, *Proletarian Power*, 31.

such as the redder-than-red "Scarlet Guards," the "Workers Patrols Defending Mao Zedong Thought," and the "February 7 Warriors." Within just days of their foundation, at a key confrontation at the #24 Yarn Dyeing Plant, the Scarlet Guards were able to muster 200,000 supporters to the rebels' 65,000. They even detained Wang Hongwen, the key rebel leader (and, later, Vice-Premier of China and third in the Party hierarchy). Moreover, unlike the highly factionalized rebels, the various "conservative" outfits that formed spontaneously were far more disciplined internally, and also they evinced a strong centripetal tendency to unite with each other.[125] After all, they consisted of many people with extensive experience in the Party, which provided them with ready networks of political trust and an innate sense of Leninist discipline. It also helped that they were not trying to seize power—which promoted competition—but only to defend themselves and their leaders.

The Cultural Revolution developed in spiral-like fashion over the rest of the spring and summer of 1967: the political initiative shifted back and forth between the rebels and conservatives, but with each turn the struggle grew fiercer. Rebel groups audaciously confronted military units sent to subdue them. It was perhaps no accident that in Wuhan the first use of physical force took place in a factory. At the end of April, the city's first punch-up broke out at a small textile mill, which opened the floodgates to a wave of major violent confrontations. Both sides took up arms, and pitched battles broke out.[126] In July the Wuhan rebels gained the upper hand, and the workers among them, having achieved their main goal of wreaking vengeance on their enemies, quickly turned to a more prosaic theme: money. "Economism" rebounded, supported by rebel state industry workers as well as the same temporary contract workers and rusticated workers who had seized the initiative the previous December. Urban-resident permanent workers in state enterprises militated for promotions and improved wages and benefits, temporary state factory workers demanded parity, and collective factory workers once again declared that their firms were now state industries, which entitled them to big pay increases, welfare benefits and job security. Some even began producing outside the plan for black and gray markets, generating big profits. The less ambitious took up individual occupations to earn a modest living.[127] The Cultural Revolution worker rebel mass movement, which came in with a stupendous bang in late 1966, went out with a pathetic whimper a year later.

Worker rebel organizations of course continued to function. They managed to gain some fleeting representation in the Party, the unions, the militia and the revolutionary committees that were established as new units of governance.

125 Perry and Li, *Proletarian Power*, chap. 3.
126 Wang, *Failure of Charisma*, 141 *ff.*
127 Ibid., 167–9.

But worker rebel leaders also suffered significant losses. They committed many acts that would normally be considered crimes—murder, assault, theft and the like. Campaigns to "clean class ranks" spearheaded by conservatives organized a movement to "strike at one [counterrevolutionaries] and oppose three [graft, profiteering and extravagance]" (一打三反) to ferret out the perpetrators. In Shanghai alone tens of thousands of worker rebels were punished, some with fines and public criticism, but many with beatings and imprisonment. The worker rebel organizations continued to function and, indeed, remained prominent. But what influence they had was directed at political rather than economic objectives. In the 1970s they mainly engaged in top-down mobilization during subsequent campaigns to "Criticize Lin Biao and Confucius" and the like, while doing next to nothing about workers' material grievances around issues such as income and the sorry condition of housing and social services. Little surprise, then, that most of China's working class tuned out.

...

Taking advantage of but also reflecting the political direction and discourse of the newly hegemonic Maoist Party/state, working class political formation took a decidedly radical turn. Workers took advantage of the new institutions, many of which were designed to coopt workers and canalize their politics, to press their own agendas, nonetheless, often attacking the Party/state from within its own institutional terrain. They also mobilized outside it, though, prosecuting the largest strike wave in Chinese history and, a decade later, plunging into the Cultural Revolution with extraordinary power and radical zest. They scored significant victories along the way. In the end, though, the working class's politics succumbed to the institutional and political hegemony of the Party/state, the chaotic politics it unleashed, and the working class fissiparousness—both structural and political—it induced.

Conclusion

Working Class Formation: The Economic, Social, Cultural and Political

1949 marked a moment of *path independence.* The establishment of the People's Republic remade China's working class. While of course in the early years most of the workers were the selfsame people they had been just a few years earlier, and while many practices and cultural understandings carried forward, the structural changes in the economics, social relations, self-understandings and politics of production in which they found themselves were profound.

The victory of the revolution brought tremendous economic gains for urban-resident workers in pay, a range of benefits and job security. Even though these proved to be a one-off boost, with stagnation after the Great Leap a decade in, the security they provided induced workers (with the exception of rural contractors) to put bread-and-butter issues on the back burner and focus instead on factory politics. In a broader sense, the material aspects of working class formation under Chinese state socialism enabled the working class seriously to take up the historic challenge Marx posited for it of building socialist society, culture and politics—in terms of this book, the world it lost.

Socially, working class formation did begin to move palpably in this as well. The working class expanded significantly. The Party/state undertook systematic efforts to elevate and propagate the highest social prestige for the working class. In many ways its homogeneity increased. Workers' lives were reorganized around close-knit "work unit" communities defined by factory-provided housing, and social, welfare, commercial and community services. While Andrew Walder argued that they provided the material and social basis of clientelism, vassalage and passivity under the watchful eye of the factory authorities,[128] it is also clear, as Elizabeth Perry and Li Xun have argued, "[t]he institution of the *danwei* produced not only dependency, but also defiance."[129] Overall, the working class's increased size, status and institutional concentration in work units raised its social capacities, which under the right circumstances could provide fertile grounds for militance.

Yet the working class also became divided and subdivided in a complex tessellation, which fueled political activity but also undermined the prospects for a unified political project. The first cut separated the stratum of urban-resident workers from a second tier of rural contract workers who landed employment in urban factories on much less favorable terms as well as urban workers who had been laid off and reassigned to rural enterprises. The urban-resident workers were subdivided into those with permanent employment, those on temporary contracts, and those employed in collective rather than state-owned firms. All these strata were in turn divided along several further cleavages including age and generation, education, skill, gender, birthplace, household registration, historical class background, social and political relations with supervisors and officials, and ideological proclivities. These divisions helped fuel sensational levels and forms of political conflict, within the working class and also between workers and the Party/state, during the 1957 strike wave and especially during the Cultural Revolution.

128 Walder, *Communist Neo-Traditionalism*; Gail Henderson and Myron Cohen, *The Chinese Hospital: A Socialist Work Unit* (New Haven: Yale University Press, 1984). For a Soviet case, see Stephen Crowley, *Hot Coal, Cold Steel: Russian and Ukrainian Workers From the End of the Soviet Union to the Post-Communist Transformations* (Ann Arbor: University of Michigan Press, 1997).

129 Perry and Li, *Proletarian Power*, 194.

Culturally, however, many workers across these subgroups of the urban-resident stratum of the working class evinced a similarly confident, assertive, almost syndicalistic self-understanding and set of values (which itself helped fuel the political conflict). In the early years, many clearly believed that they rather than the Communist Party or the Red Army should take over the factories. In the mid-1950s, a significant group strongly resented the state's industrial rationalizations, believing instead that socialist factories should be run, and would be run best, according to broadly participatory procedures and in the interest of distributive equality. And the Cultural Revolution brought out pronounced syndicalist values and discourses on both the rebel and conservative sides.

Finally, in political terms, many in the urban-resident stratum of the working class acted strenuously, repeatedly and often effectively to realize these values. At the outset, they had the temerity to denounce and resist the efforts of the Party and armed forces to consolidate the power of the new Party/state in the factories. In the mid-1950s, they staged the largest strike wave in Chinese history, successfully reversing one-man management and incentive pay. And during the Cultural Revolution, they stunningly disrupted the entire edifice of state socialist industry—the rebels seizing factory power in the name of the working class, and the conservatives defending what they understood to be a structure of shop floor power and factory management that was already grounded in and favored the working class.

The rural contract workers surely became better off materially than they had been before 1949, or they would have been had they stayed in the countryside afterward. Yet they did suffer tremendous inequalities with the urban-resident workers. And these inequalities were made palpable by the otherwise flat social structure of the shop floor, which often placed them right alongside urban-resident workers and had them doing the same or very similar work. Urban-resident workers who were sent to factories or construction projects in the countryside were still better off than in pre-1949 days, but again what they experienced in quotidian terms was a significant decline in their livelihoods compared with their more immediately previous urban factory lives and, of course, with those still living those lives in the cities. Culturally, their "cry for justice" was loud and heartfelt. But it was defensive and redistributive in demanding equal treatment rather than the urban-resident workers' offensive and reconstitutive call for yet another new world. And it was unable to avoid the persistent sense, which they shared with the urban-resident workers, of the superiority of the urban over the rural (a major reversal of traditional Chinese cosmology).

Politically, the rural contract workers and their allies among exiled and informally employed urbanites proved as capable as the urban-resident workers of autonomous, spontaneous, potent political action, at least during the Cultural Revolution. (They hadn't really been present in factories in large numbers before then.) But they proved much more vulnerable. They were a distinct minority of the working class. They had difficulty forming even *ad hoc* organizations of their own, for several reasons: they did not live together in factory housing; they lacked the organizational networks that the urban-resident workers could build out of existing social and political structures and relations; they were outsiders in the city; and they hailed from a wide range of different locales. For all these same reasons, of course, they had even more difficulty forming political linkages with the Cultural Revolution left. Thus, they remained allied with urban-resident rebel groups only until those groups dropped them summarily when the top leadership denounced the economic havoc their demands had set in train. And lacking clear, effective organization, they could not act in a disciplined, restrained way that might have prevented or stanched that economic crisis. Organization aside, the "economistic" protest leaders lacked political sophistication; theirs was an energetic, heartfelt "cry for justice," but not much more. And finally, they had no resources, even implicit ones, to bring to bear to prosecute their struggle or threaten their opponents. The government had, after all, been trying to get them out of industry in the first place.

Overall, then, working class formation in the Maoist period was marked by radical expansion, material improvement, complex stratification, and newly radical forms of thinking and collective action.

Temporality, Spontaneity, Efficacy, Politicization

At the dawn of the People's Republic, the Party/state was in a much better position than the working class to structure and fill political space. Victorious Leninist parties are "early arrivers" on steroids. The Chinese party, having spent decades in the countryside not just fighting for national power but also wielding it in local and regional governments, was even more fit to dominate the political landscape than most. All this, combined with the Party's historically attenuated relationship with the working class, put the latter at a serious disadvantage.

Nonetheless, the working class was anything but quiescent, even at the outset, despite its lower social and institutional capacity. The rhythms of its political class formation over the state socialist decades bore some broad similarities to that of the revolutionary period, but also very significant differences. As before, Chinese workers demonstrated a great deal of energy and virtuosity in engaging in political contention at several key moments, each associated with an apparent *apertura* in the political opportunity structure. In 1949 and 1950, the proto-fascist Republic was gone, and the political situation was in flux. In 1956, Mao had issued a general call for "a hundred flowers" to "bloom," and had expressed doubts about the bureaucratic and authoritarian aspects of the centrally planned industrial system based on the Soviet model that was emerging in China. The Cultural Revolution was induced by a call from Mao Zedong and his fellow radical leaders for a popular rebellion against "capitalist roaders."

Yet, as in revolutionary days, at each of these moments countervailing forces continued to lurk for anyone, visible to anyone who cared to look. In 1949–50, Party/state power was fortified by an army that had helped drive out Japan a few years before and had just beaten the U.S.-backed Guomindang; it soon grew stronger thanks to the victory in the Korean War and the prosecution of the "Three-" and "Five-Anti" Campaigns. The "Hundred Flowers" was soon followed by the Anti-Rightist Campaign. And in the Cultural Revolution potent, strident opponents of popular radicalism fought hard against it at each turn, ultimately triumphing. So while changes in the political opportunity structure may be important, then, they are often clearer in retrospect, so their role should not be overstated. Or perhaps what matters just as much is not whether an apparent political opportunity is real, but rather simply whether people believe one exists. Twentieth-century Chinese history is littered with the remains of fearless political activists who saw political opportunities that did not really or fully exist, and therefore who did not take full account of the forces arrayed against them. For many others who were too deeply committed or caught up in the maelstrom to care whether the time was ripe or not, political opportunity did not really matter much, if at all.

Second, and unlike the first half of the century, the working class's ability to act in a coordinated fashion on a broad national canvas was not always premised on a necessary role for political leadership from outside the working class. The protestations of workers against the Party and Army in 1949 and 1950 in cities across China emerged spontaneously, not as the result of any nationally organized political leadership—not even from the retreating Guomindang, secret societies, or organized criminals, all of whom had had significant ties to the working class. Likewise, the 1957 strike wave, though facilitated or even solicited by the Party/state's call for a "hundred flowers" to "bloom," was in practice a spontaneous outpouring that spread across many cities without any leadership to speak of, not the product of some organized Maoist initiative playing the role that the CCP played in the mid-1920s or the late 1940s, or that a radical faction in the Party would soon come to play in the Cultural Revolution. The Cultural Revolution itself was a more extreme example of this same dynamic: Mao and the radicals opened up a political opportunity by calling for rebellion against "capitalist roaders," but workers themselves helped push it open in the first place, forcing the radical leadership to allow them to join the movement in full. And once they jumped in, they also operated with a great deal of spontaneity and organizational virtuosity that repeatedly caught their leaders, including some of the most powerful people in the country, off guard, unable to control them, and sometimes under their arrest.

Third, though, as in pre-1949 days, if workers' contentious politics was more able than before 1949 to metastasize on a national scale on its own, the outcomes of their interventions—whether and how they succeeded or failed—were, as before 1949, heavily dependent on wider hegemonic political processes and constellations. In 1949–50 and 1957, workers' contentious collective action was soon beaten back by the Party/state's draconian deployment of political force. Yet workers at the latter moment could win significant concessions on factory power and incentive pay, but only with the backing of Mao and his followers at the center. In the Cultural Revolution, each twist and turn in the mass movements—*e.g.*, the economistic advance in December 1966, its defeat by a rebel political offensive in January 1967, and in turn the rebels' supersession by the conservatives in February—had as much to do with shifting élite politics as with developments on the ground. The rebels' defeat in late 1967 had everything to do with Mao's own second thoughts about the uprising, and their final destruction in 1976 with the radical élites' being outmaneuvered in the run-up to and the wake of Mao's death.

Fourth, and also similar to the revolutionary decades, it would be a serious mistake to say that working class politics were inconsequential. They may not have been able to bring about a victory for the East China system in the early 1950s, but their syndicalistic impulses and actions at that time surely encouraged Mao to believe that he would find popular support just a few years later for his critique of one-man management and incentive pay. Certainly, the strike wave of 1957 did so. As for the Cultural Revolution, the rebels did not just go down in defeat, but they also scored a pyrrhic victory. The Party/state leaders who put paid to the rebel movement and returned to their offices were, as the rebels so ardently hoped, unable for quite some time to wield power in anything like the way they had before. As discussed in Chapter 3,[130] in the 1980s factory managers were afraid to try to ratchet up labor discipline, as reformers were demanding. And the fact that the vast economic bureaucracy was profoundly wounded by the rebels' vituperative attacks helped smooth the way for the structural reforms to displace many of their previous functions. In a supreme irony, the rebel movement itself helped pave the "capitalist" road, which would really bring China's working class *qua* class to grief.

Fifth, in another discontinuity with the revolutionary past, China's working class politics, now taking its cue from radical state socialism, focused on fundamental issues of power rather than primarily on material matters. Workers contested head-on the nature of factory institutions and authority, the question of class struggle, the focus and nature of the Communist Party and its leadership, and the meaning of socialism itself. Even the "economistic" rural contract workers seeking equal treatment with urban-resident workers couched their demands in political as well as material terms. China's working class was at its most radical during the Maoist era—and it did as much to produce that period's radicalism as it was produced by it.

130 See p. 163.

Ascent and Radicalism

This chapter began with a puzzle. How can the apotheosis of the working class be reconciled with its pronounced radicalism? The answer lies in the quadruple effect of its exaltation. First, the elevation of the urban-resident working class helped embolden it. Material comforts and economic security cleared the way for many workers to focus on their political goals of economic equality and democratic or at least participatory management. Yet second, that same material advantage proved a profound irritant to rural contract workers and their allies in less formal industrial employment, who fueled some of the most radical and fissiparous politics of the Cultural Revolution. Third, alliances after 1957–58 in factories between relatively contented urban-resident workers and the factory political leadership (the "reds") fueled an often strident politics of resentment by workers left out of the game. And fourth, repeated support for radical change from Mao and his supporters at the very top of the Party provided many (though not all) of the ideas for working class radicalism as well as the political space and license for enraged workers to militate for them.

Party/State Hegemony and the Working Class

In the end, then, working class formation in Maoist China had everything to do with the newly triumphant hegemony of the Party/state. The expansion and the material and social elevation of the formerly immiserated and exploited proletariat into a large state socialist labor force, though driven by the legacy of workers' politics in revolutionary days, was implemented by the Party/state. Many of the most significant cleavages rending the new working class resulted from the industrial structures and policies it adopted and categories it created. The Party/state also established the institutions and ideologies within which the working class fought, even when it fought radically against officials of the Party/state itself. To put it more pointedly, when some workers took up their "class struggle" against "capitalist roaders" in the Party/state, they could only do so on political and ideological terrain established by that very same Party/state. And the Party/state, though most assuredly driven by Marxism and overarching commitments to socialism, was not itself an historical creature of the working class or much beholden to it.

That is why, when the left wing of the Party/state was ultimately defeated at the end of the Cultural Revolution decade, due in part to the fissiparousness and radicalism of working class politics produced under the hegemony of its target, China's working class was left defenseless. China's workers may have been promised a world to win, and for a time it may have looked like some of them were achieving it. But in the fullness of time, the way they sought it, shaped as it was by, and interacting with, the political hegemony of the radical Party/state, meant that the chance for such a world was lost.

3

STRUCTURAL REFORM

The Fall of China's Working Class

The structural reforms that began in 1979, and which in industry went into high gear in the early 1990s, have profoundly remade China's working class into its third incarnation since its birth just over a century ago. *Economically*, many workers have seen their incomes and standards of living rise, but many others—especially those who have become unemployed or have had to find new work due to industrial restructuring and the rise of the labor market—have not. Sweatshops, wage arrears and forced overtime have become endemic. Most, including those who remain employed in state industry, have lost the benefits that came with their jobs in state-owned firms. The employment security of Maoist days is gone. *Socially*, the working class has undergone massive expansion and contraction as well as diversification. Residence patterns have shifted away from factory communities. Workplaces have become far more authoritarian. The working class no longer holds the preeminent, highly prestigious position it occupied in the Maoist decades. *Culturally*, radical "workerism" is gone, replaced by a set of new sensibilities: atavism for the Maoist past, acceptance of market and state hegemony, and an admixture of attraction and repulsion among rural migrants to urban life and industrial work. *Politically*, workers have remained as active as ever in standing up for themselves but they have almost completely lost their radical edge and politicized focus and are mainly oriented instead to the basics of material life.

Why has the working class deradicalized precisely in an era when it has lost so much power? Why, after rebelling so ardently against bureaucratic and "capitalistic" relations and institutions in the Maoist era of radical state socialism, has it depoliticized precisely at the time when its previous political targets have become full-blown realities? As in revolutionary and state socialist days, the

DOI: 10.4324/9781003518228-4

answers have to do with the complex ways in which China's working class has been made and remade: the complex interrelationships among the economic, social, cultural and political aspects of working class formation, the sequencing of change, and the hegemonic forces that have shaped workers' responses, including their resistance, to those selfsame forces.

…

One fundamental driver of working class re-formation has been the structural disintegration (or at least dis-integration) of the new proletariat. As a first-order division, four categories of workers and attendant economic, social, cultural and political life can be distinguished.

- *Workers employed in government-owned enterprises* (formally, state, collective and cooperative firms). Over the years many enterprises in this sector have undergone profound restructuring, including full or partial privatization, absorption by other state, joint-state private, or private firms. In 1994, there were 1,908,300 state and collective industrial enterprises; by 2014, just 11,648 remained.[1] There have also been massive layoffs.
- *Workers employed in private or joint government-private industrial enterprises* of various kinds. In 2020 Chinese statistics distinguished twenty-seven categories, by criteria such as sole or joint ownership, foreign or domestic, and whether they are limited liability companies or not.[2] The number of such firms has flourished since the start of industrial restructuring, going from just 44,500 in 1994 to 331,342 in 2014.[3]
- *Rural migrants*, who generally work in private enterprises and lack the legal right to live in the city in which they work.
- China's *unemployed workers* including:
  - *Urban-resident workers who have been "laid off"* (下岗, literally, off-post). Formally, the laid-off continue to maintain an employment relationship with their firms, which are, in theory, meant to call them back to work if the firm's fortunes improve.
  - *Urban-resident workers who are unemployed* (失业) in the sense of having lost all ties to and claims on their former enterprises, and having been unable to find other work, including self-employment.
  - *Rural migrants who have lost their jobs.*

These categories have significant implications for various aspects of working class formation discussed in the rest of this chapter.

1 *China Statistical Yearbook 1995* [*中国统计年鉴1995*] (Beijing: China Statistical Yearbook Press, 1995), Table 12-1; *China Statistical Yearbook 2014*, Table 13-1.
2 *China Statistical Yearbook 2019*, Table 13-1.
3 *China Statistical Yearbook 1995*, Table 12-1; *China Statistical Yearbook 2014*, Table 13-1.

Economic Aspects of the Fall of the Working Class

Wages and Hours

In economic terms, under structural reform the overall economic position of China's working class improved absolutely, declined relatively, and became much more uneven. Both urban-based workers and rural migrants have experienced considerable improvements in their incomes and standards of living. Average real wages rose at an average annual rate of 8 percent between 1978 and 2017.[4] These figures include some professionals and low-level managers, so the figures for actual blue-collar workers were probably a bit lower; but since workers comprised the vast majority of employees, probably not significantly so. Fifty-seven percent of workers responding to a trade union survey in 1997 said that their incomes had risen in recent years.[5]

But the increases have been distributed very unevenly over time and space. Real wage rises in the 4-8 percent range through 1999 (Figure 3.1) were very significant compared with the overall stagnation of the last two Maoist decades; those in the 10-15 percent range in the first decade of the new century were extraordinary. Yet the rate of increase has been slowing significantly since 2009. In spatial terms (Figure 3.2), on the one hand, average real wages in 2017[6]

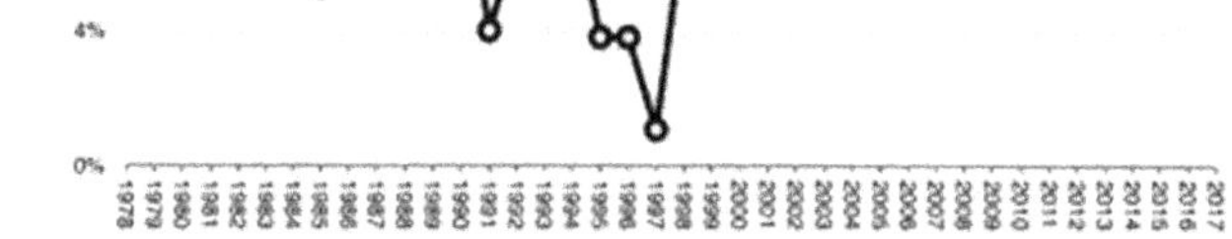

FIGURE 3.1 Average annual industrial real wage increases, 1978–2017.
Source: Calculated from *China Statistical Yearbook 2007*, Table 5-22, *China Statistical Yearbook 2014*, Table 4-11, and *China Statistical Yearbook 2018*, Table 4-11.

4 Calculated from *China Statistical Yearbook 2007*, Table 5-22, *China Statistical Yearbook 2014*, Table 4-11, and *China Statistical Yearbook 2018*, Table 4-11. See also Henry H. McVey, "China in Transition," *Insights: Global Macro Trends*, 3.3 (New York: KKR, April 2013), 10.

5 全国总工会政策研究室 (All-China Federation of Trade Unions Policy Research Office), *中国职工状况调查,数据卷* (*A Survey of the Condition of Chinese Workers and Staff*) (北京:西苑出版社,1999), 1337.

6 This series cannot be updated due to subsequent changes in the categories of aggregation.

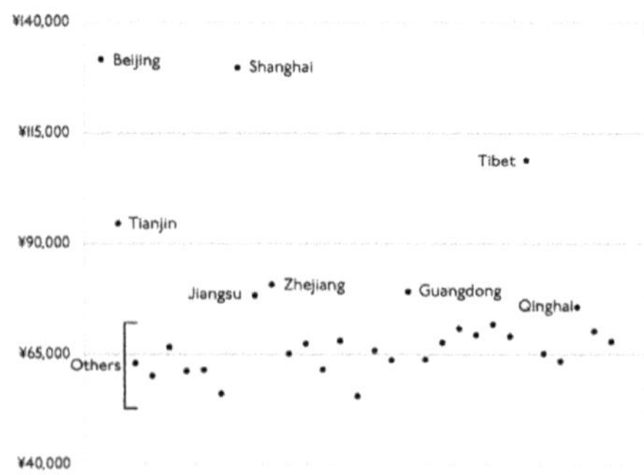

FIGURE 3.2 Average annual industrial wages by province, 2017.
Source: *China Statistical Yearbook 2018*, Table 4-11.

in twenty-two of China's thirty-one provinces and provincial-level municipalities clustered in a relatively narrow band between ¥55,000 and ¥72,000 per year. But on the other hand, five out of eight of the highest average wages were found in China's two greatest cities of Beijing and Shanghai and their environs (Tianjin [increasingly part of a conurbation with Beijing] and Zhejiang and Jiangsu [both in the Shanghai hinterland]). Guangdong, home to China's major export platforms, was another high-wage case. Yet given Guangdong's extraordinary importance to the national and, indeed, international economies, it may at first blush seem surprising that wages there were not still higher. The answer, of course, has everything to do with the fact that so much labor in Guangdong's Pearl River Delta is sweated.[7]

As neoliberal analysts of sweatshops have pointed out, migrants who flock to these firms do earn higher incomes than they would in the depressed (or at least relatively poorer) rural areas from which they flee, where their marginal productivity and opportunities to earn any income at all are sometimes near zero. That, of course, is why they join the working class. As one worker who lost her arm in an industrial accident put it, "I graduated from junior high at age 14, and went to work in a factory, because there was no point farming. No, I didn't know that it was illegal for children that age to work in factories."[8] Conditions were so bad in her home village that she said she didn't regret migrating despite her injury. But as critics point out, that is a very low bar which can be cleared even by the generally atrocious labor conditions of Chinese sweatshops. Wages can be as low as a few dollars a day. Often workers are not even told what the

7 The last case was Tibet, where high wages are required to attract needed workers to so remote and, in many ways, culturally foreign area.
8 Interview, September 23, 2002.

wage is at the time they are hired.[9] They have risen since the middle of the first decade of the new century due to a labor shortage produced by a confluence of ever-rising export demand and the long-term demographic effects of the one-child policy. But they plummeted again with the onset of the depression of 2008. Whatever their level at a given time, moreover, wages are subject to various deductions for dormitory and hiring fees—from the factory, intermediaries or both—as well as all manner of fines for infractions of elaborate, draconian labor rules. This, in conjunction with complex piece rates where used, makes it hard for workers to know what they will find in their wage packets at the end of the month.[10] Then there are the fees or deposits that are charged just to get a job, which can run into thousands of *yuan*.[11]

Incredibly, even these paltry wages often go unpaid. Arrears have prompted an epidemic of suicide attempts that has often peaked around the Spring Festival, when terrified young people face the prospect of returning home empty-handed to confront disappointed families, including, especially dangerously for women, enraged fathers.[12] Three-quarters of migrant construction workers have experienced arrears.[13] Already in 1997, over eleven million migrant and urban-resident workers nationally were subject to wage arrears averaging ¥1,900 per worker.[14] Almost 20 percent of those responding to the ACFTU 1997 survey reported experiencing wage arrears, and 46 percent of those said that they were due three months' pay or more.[15] In the late 1990s, a quarter of employed workers in Shenyang, the Liaoning provincial capital, reported wage arrears.[16] In Guangdong, 7 percent of workers reported wage arrears in 2009.[17] In January 2015, two protests against wage arrears running as high as ¥900,000 resulted

9 Interview, November 2002.
10 See p. 128.
11 May Wong, ed., *Voices From Below: China's Accession to WTO and Chinese Workers* (Hong Kong: Asia Monitor Resource Centre, 2008), 103.
12 "Tis the Season for Protests Over Unpaid Wages in China," *The Economist*, December 14, 2017. https://www.economist.com/china/2017/12/14/tis-the-season-for-protests-over-unpaid-wages-in-china (accessed 24 September, 2025); "Migrant Workers Struggling to Be Paid Ahead of Spring Festival," *China Daily* January 22, 2015. https://www.chinadaily.com.cn/china/2015-01/22/content_19374926.htm (accessed September 24, 2025).
13 China Labor News Translations, "Migrant Workers and the Chronic Problem of Owed Wages," February 2008.
14 *中国工会统计年鉴* (*Chinese Trade Unions Statistics Yearbook*) (北京: 中国统计出版社 [China Statistics Press], 1999), 147.
15 全国总工会政策研究室(All-China Federation of Trade Unions Policy Research Office), *中国职工状况调查,数据卷1997* (*1997 Survey of the Condition of Chinese Workers and Staff*), 1239.
16 Lee, *Against the Law*, 76, 77.
17 Cheng Zhiming, Ingrid Nielsen and Russell Smyth, "Determinants of Wage Arrears and their Implications for the Socioeconomic Wellbeing of China's Migrant Workers: Evidence from Guangdong Province," Monash University Department of Economics Discussion Paper 50/13, 2013.

in two deaths.[18] In 2018, 98 percent of protests in the construction sector, and most of those in retail were related to wage arrears.[19] In September 2020, the State Council ordered the Dafang County government to pay its teachers ¥470 million in wage arrears.[20] And at the end of the year, two workers were sentenced to a year in prison after defending themselves against thugs hired by their bosses to bat down their protest against arrears.[21] Even professional footballers have suffered and complained collectively, prompting the state-run Xinhua News Agency to call for unionization.[22] Though the issue has drawn criticism from China's state media, arrears nonetheless continue. In some cases, no doubt, private firms facing bankruptcy due to intense competitive pressure in the export sector actually lack the funds. No such excuse could be made in government-owned firms. And in both sectors, employers' stubborn refusal to pay their workers often stems not from budgetary incapacity but rather from employers' desire to discourage workers from quitting when conditions become unbearable because they would lose the unpaid wages due them.[23]

Workers also suffer from arrears in their pensions and employer insurance contributions. Four million retirees' benefits were in arrears in 2000—an issue that provoked a massive wave of protests and strikes in the Manchurian rustbelt.[24] In April 2014, the biggest strike at a single enterprise in Chinese history broke out at the Yue Yuen Shoe Factory in Dongguan, Guangzhou, when workers learned that the company had not been making its required pension contributions.[25]

Forced overtime in violation of China's labor legislation has been endemic. At the turn of the century, 20–30 hours of overtime a week was not uncommon.[26] Eighty percent of Chinese workers put in at least ten hours daily, nearly half reported regular seven-day weeks, around a dozen died annually of overwork in Shenzhen alone, and many thousands more suffered serious, life-changing

18 "Contractor's Teenage Daughter Falls to Her Death in Wage Arrears Protest," *China Labour Bulletin* January 21, 2015, http://www.clb.org.hk/en/content/contractor%E2%80%99s-teenage-daughter-falls-her-death-wage-arrears-protest (accessed 16 September 2025).

19 "The State of Labour Relations in China, 2018," *China Labour Bulletin*, January 9, 2019, https://clb.org.hk/content/state-labour-relations-china-2018 (accessed March 29, 2019).

20 Interview, November 2002; "关于贵州省毕节市大方县拖欠教师工资补贴 挤占挪用教育经费等问题的督查情况通报," http://www.gov.cn/hudong/ducha/2020-09/04/content_5540680.htm.

21 "Migrant Workers Beaten and Jailed After Claiming Wages in Arrears," *China Labour Bulletin*, April 26, 2021.

22 "Wage Arrears Threaten the Livelihoods of China's Workers," *China Labour Bulletin*, December 2021.

23 Interview, November 2002.

24 See p. 165 *ff.*

25 See p. 175 *ff.* and Marc Blecher, "The Yue Yuen Strike," in Ivan Franceschini and Christian Sorace, eds., *Proletarian China: A Century of Chinese Labor* (London: Verso, 2022), 622–630.

26 Interviews, 7C/T113–, September 2002; October 29, 2002; January 12, 2003.

injury.[27] In 2009, 41 percent of workers worked overtime (much of it presumably forced), and 29 percent were unpaid for it.[28] Foxconn, the maker of the iPhone and other popular brands, has been a particularly flagrant employer; at a Taiyuan plant, forced overtime ran to 130 hours per month in 2012.[29] Wages are so low—¥10 [$1.25] per day—that many workers actually prefer the overtime despite the punishing schedule they also report.[30]

Pushing wage levels to their lowest limit of zero, even slavery has returned.

> [In 1994] Guangdong officials, acting on reports in the local press, uncovered a vast network of 20 stone quarries in the province where slave labour was the norm. At a quarry near the town of Qingyuan, 39 workers had been locked in sheds at night and kept under guard in the pit for up to a year with no pay. A provincial official, interviewed on local radio at the time, said that forced labour was "common across the province." In 1996 another quarry in Guangdong's Zhanjiang was found to be employing 80 workers in what was described as "a concentration camp."...
>
> In May 2000... 90 farmers who had been displaced from the massive Three Gorges Dam project on the Yangtze River had ended up as slaves in brick factories in the northeastern city of Shenyang.[31]

In June 2007, Chinese journalists in Shanxi Province uncovered that

> ...32 migrants had been duped into believing that they were being offered paid jobs, but once inside the brickworks in Caosheng village of Shanxi province, they were forced to work under the watch of guards and dogs for 18 hours a day. None received any money for the whole time of their enslavement, and they survived only on water and steamed rolls of bread.
>
> When a police raid freed the migrants late last month it was discovered that one man had been beaten to death with a hammer. Among the others, eight were so traumatized that they could only remember their names. All had burns on their hands and bodies from having to carry the hot bricks without protection. Their clothes had been reduced to rags, and "the grime on their bodies was so thick it could be scraped off with a knife", said the report in the *Shanxi Evening News*.[32]

27 Lee, *Against the Law*, 163–64.

28 Linxiang Ye, T. H. Gindling and Shi Li, "Compliance with Legal Minimum Wages and Overtime Pay Regulations In China," *IZA Journal of Labor & Development* 4, no. 16 (2015): 14.

29 Jenny Chan, Mark Selden and Pun Ngai, *Dying for an iPhone: Apple, Foxconn, and the Lives of China's Workers* (Chicago: Haymarket, 2020), 191 and *passim*.

30 Interviews, November 2002, January 12, 2003.

31 Bruce Gilley, "Toil and Trouble," *Far Eastern Economic Review*, August 16, 2001.

32 Antoaneta Bezlova, "Lessons from China's Slavery Scandal," *Asia Times*, June 20, 2007, http://www.atimes.com/atimes/China_Business/IF20Cb02.html (accessed September 10, 2015).

Worse yet, Caosheng was not an isolated case, and children were being enslaved.

> It is reported that a crackdown campaign was launched to strike 11 cities of Shanxi Province. Coal mines, brick kilns, private contractors and small-sized enterprises will be under scrutiny after media reports revealed that hundreds of children had been kidnapped and forced to work in kilns in Shanxi.[33]

In all, 550 slaves were rescued. Adding injustice to injury, the traffickers got off with a fine,[34] and the police had been involved in the ring.[35] A subsequent investigation by the National People's Congress found that "53 thousand workers in Shanxi alone… were exploited in over two thousand brick kilns."[36] Four years later, slavery was still happening.

> Police have freed 30 disabled workers, used as slaves in illegal brick factories in Henan. China has failed to curb the exploitation of minors and disabled people in heavy labour, even though it announced zero tolerance and strict controls years ago.
>
> The workers, released Sept. 5 [2011], have severe learning difficulties and some can not (*sic*) even form whole sentences. They were forced to work long shifts without being paid, some for more than 7 years, frequently beaten… for any disobedience and error.[37]

In 2016, over three million Chinese were estimated to be enslaved, though it is impossible to specify how many were industrial or mine workers.[38] In 2017, students were assigned to forced labor in Foxconn factories to gain "work experience" unrelated to their studies—not exactly slavery but certainly forced labor.[39]

Benefits

Beginning in the mid-1990s, state and collective firms began to dismantle the "iron rice bowl" benefits they had guaranteed workers starting with the First

33 Kang Yi, "Some Human Traffickers May Walk Away in 'Slave' Case," *China Daily*, June 15, 2007, http://www.chinadaily.com.cn/china/2007-06/15/content_895414.htm.

34 "China 'Will Catch Slave Owners,'" *BBC*, June 16, 2007, http://news.bbc.co.uk/go/pr/fr/-/1/hi/world/asia-pacific/6759399.stm (accessed April 6, 2025).

35 "Officials, Police Implicated in China Slavery Ring," *Agence France Presse*, June 15, 2007.

36 "Police Free 30 Slaves from Henan Brick Kilns," *Asianews.it*, September 8, 2011.

37 "Police Free 30 Slaves," *Asianews.it*, September 8, 2011.

38 "Modern Slavery in China" *Walk Free Global Slavery Index*, https://www.globalslaveryindex.org/country/china (accessed March 29, 2025).

39 Yuan Yang, "Apple's iPhone X Assembled By Illegal Student Labour," https://www.ft.com/content/7cb56786-cda1-11e7-b781-794ce08b24dc (accessed March 10, 2018).

Five-Year Plan of the mid-1950s. Private employers never offered them in the first place. Health care and education are now provided on a fee basis, and the charges can be significant. In 1993, the 20 percent of urban Chinese with the lowest incomes were spending 14 percent of their annual income on health care, and in 2003, 11 percent. For the second lowest quintile, the figure was 8 percent in both years.[40] Many workers are no longer getting necessary medical help because they cannot afford it, and many others are bankrupted when they are forced by serious illness or injury to seek care they cannot afford. In 2003, 57 percent of urban Chinese did not seek outpatient care when they needed it (and over a third chalked the reason up to costs), 28 percent did not seek inpatient care (with over half citing costs), and 35 percent asked for early discharge from the hospital (with 53 percent citing costs).[41] More recent figures are hard to come by, but high health care costs for the urban poor remain a serious problem.[42]

Education had also been virtually free during the Maoist era. By 2004–05 the average urban household spent ¥3,522 to send one child to school. This figure amounted to almost a third of average urban total household income.[43] The percentage for workers was much higher: a migrant worker in Shenzhen earning ¥3,000 per year in 2002 reported middle school fees of ¥2,000 per semester.[44] In the late 1990s, when market-based school fees were developing, the value of the subsidy (in the form of discounted pricing) that some state and collective enterprises still provided was enough for one chemical plant worker to give up much higher-paying work he had found.

> I worked there for 13 years, though I was laid off twice—once for two years and once for three. I liked being laid off, actually, since then I could take a job at an American car radio factory in the open zone as a cook, where I made a lot more money. Here in the Chemical Factory I make just ¥700 per month. But when the factory called me back, I had to go. After all, I live in their housing, and they provide inexpensive schooling for my daughter.[45]

40 Center for Health Statistics and Information of MOH, An Analysis Report of National Health Services Survey in 2003 (Beijing: China Xiehe Medical University Press, 2004), pp. 83–85; cited in Wang Shaoguang, "State Extractive Capacity, Policy Orientation, and Inequity in the Financing and Delivery of Health Care in Urban China," *Social Sciences in China* 29, no. 1 (2008): 75.

41 卫生部, *第一次国家卫生服务调查, 第二次国家卫生服务调查, 第三次国家卫生服务调查*, cited in Wang, "State Extractive Capacity", 81.

42 Adam Jourdan and Ben Hirschler, "China Healthcare Costs Forcing Patients into Crippling Debt," *Reuters*, July 9, 2016, https://www.reuters.com/article/us-china-healthcare-debt/china-healthcare-costs-forcing-patients-into-crippling-debt-idUSKCN0ZQ03A.

43 "Survey: Education Costs One Third of Family Income in China," *China Daily*, August 22, 2006.

44 Interview, November 2002.

45 Interview, May 25, 1999.

Factory-provided housing has been a significant benefit to state sector workers, despite both marketization and the deterioration of old factory-built apartment blocks. In 1988, 80 percent of urban housing costs were paid by public subsidy, and even in 1995 it still came to 41 percent. The subsidy comprised 18 percent of urban income in 1988, and 10 percent in 1995—and, in all likelihood, much more for workers (who had relatively lower incomes).[46] Quite a few state and collective sector workers were able to live in surprisingly ample and decently maintained properties.[47]

As early as 1979, urban-resident workers began to be allowed to purchase their government-owned apartments at highly subsidized prices—often 10 or 20 percent of their market value once a market had been established by the 1990s.[48] Many workers were happy to become homeowners at a low price, especially as rents began to climb in the 1980s under a policy designed to generate funds to help maintain the often run-down buildings. Quite a few made windfall profits as prices skyrocketed starting in the 1990s.[49] But the policy was not the political success that it was in Thatcher's Britain. Sales sometimes could not be completed because firms failed to ante up their required share of housing provident funds used to supply mortgages.[50] In China, workers were often forced to purchase their flats, and many found it a bad deal. "We used to pay only ¥28 per month as rent. Then they made us pay ¥8,000 for the same apartment. What's the advantage to us?"[51] Moreover, what workers bought was not an unencumbered property right, but possession hemmed in by various restrictions on sub-leasing or inheritance; or it was merely a use right that remained conditional on continued employment in the firm.[52] And many had difficulty selling these increasingly dilapidated properties.[53]

State factories continued to allocate their housing until 1998. But as with government-owned apartments, in the 1980s and 1990s rents frequently rose to unaffordable levels, prompting a wave of non-payment.

> My factory pays me only ¥110, and rent costs ¥60 per month. How can I afford it? If I pay rent, how am I supposed to buy enough food to stay alive?

46 Azizur Rahman Khan and Carl Riskin, *Inequality and Poverty in China in the Age of Globalization* (Oxford: Oxford University Press, 2001), 21, 35.
47 Interview, December 4, 1995; Lee, *Against the Law*, 125.
48 Interviews, July 5, 1996; July 3, 1996.
49 Lee, *Against the Law*, 126; Deborah Davis, "From Welfare Benefits to Capitalized Asset: The Re-commodification of Residential Space in Urban China," in Ray Forrest and James Lee, eds., *Housing and Social Change: East-West Perspectives* (New York: Routledge, 2003).
50 Interview, May 28, 1999.
51 Lee, *Against the Law*, 127.
52 Interview, December 7, 2005; Lee, *Against the Law*, 126–127.
53 Mun Young Cho, *The Specter of "the People": Urban Poverty in Northeast China* (Ithaca: Cornell University Press, 2013), 42.

> I would say 80% of all tenants in this building refuse to pay rent and the Housing Bureau has stopped asking for payment. I have stopped paying rent for several years.[54]

A 1998 policy forbade any further allocations in an effort to get housing costs off enterprises' books as part of the state enterprise "reform" that was going into high gear at the time. The housing "reform" was also intended to smooth the process of layoffs by delinking employment from housing provision. It absolved the firms of the responsibility for the buildings, which then deteriorated further. In the new, partially marketized real estate environment, government plans to develop "affordable" and "low-income" housing generally failed to produce buildings that workers could afford. Many workers remained trapped in their old, increasingly squalid quarters. Where the land under these worthless buildings was subsequently sold to real estate developers, workers generally received at best only a pittance in compensation and usually faced no alternative but to move to remote locations that were little or no better than their previous digs. Little wonder, then, that some state and collective sector workers have looked back wistfully on the Maoist days when their firms provided them modest but secure housing.

> Some workers pine away for the old socialist days when everyone had housing. This is especially the case for those who don't have housing, such as those who want to marry but can't because they have no place for a couple to live.[55]

For rural migrant workers, housing is a different matter altogether. Many live in crowded factory-provided dormitories and eat in factory canteens run by their employers-*cum*-landlords, who are, as Lenin put it in a different context, "skinning the ox twice."[56] Their living costs can consume most of their wages.[57] Some rent much more expensive off-site housing, for which they are meant to receive subsidies on which employers frequently renege.[58] Construction workers often have no housing at all, sleeping in the open on the work site.

54 Lee, *Against the Law*, 127.

55 Interview, June 29, 1996.

56 Vladimir Lenin, *Imperialism, the Highest Stage of Capitalism*, https://www.marxists.org/archive/lenin/works/1916/imp-hsc/ch09.htm (accessed March 11, 2018).

57 Jay Greene, "Riots, Suicides, and Other Issues in Foxconn's iPhone Factories," CNET, September 25, 2012, http://www.cnet.com/news/riots-suicides-and-other-issues-in-foxconns-iphone-factories/ (accessed June 6, 2015).

58 For just one example, see Wong, Chun Han, "China Factory Workers Strike Over Housing Benefits," *Wall Street Journal*, March 11, 2015, http://www.wsj.com/articles/china-factory-workers-strike-over-housing-benefits-1426054854 (accessed June 6, 2015).

Nonetheless, whether owned or rented, and whether rent is paid or not, the fact that almost all workers in China, including the unemployed, have had and continue to have a place to live is highly prized and very significant. As Ching Kwan Lee has pointed out, there is little or no homelessness in China's working class, even among the most destitute.[59] An apartment, no matter how dismal or remote, is a social and economic lifeline for many workers. Some who have a room or even just a bed they don't absolutely need rent it out to generate a bit of sorely needed income. For others, it is a place to house grown children who are unable to get their own place in the newly marketized environment.[60] A tragic indicator of the importance of housing to Chinese workers is the fact that disputes over allocation and ownership between workers on the one hand and employers or housing authorities on the other, or even within families, are often bitter and have sometimes turned violent, including suicide.[61]

Rural migrants were never entitled to any of the benefits that were provided for a time to many urban workers, most prominently medical services and education for their children.

> It costs me three hundred *yuan* for an injection and some medicine! If we were Shenzhen locals or state-owned enterprise workers, we would not have to pay that outrageous amount... We get no welfare from the government even though we contribute our labor.[62]

What they are entitled to receive, though, is the dreaded "dibao" (低保), short for "minimum livelihood guarantee," mainly a subsidy to both urban and rural resident unemployed. It is not just minuscule but also plagued, as a program, by corruption, poor targeting, and shaming, and it has made only a negligible dent at best in urban poverty.[63]

Employment Insecurity

In the Maoist period, layoffs mainly hit rural migrants who had flocked to industrial employment in the mid-1950s boom and were then extruded back to their villages during the severe retrenchment of the Great Leap Forward. Some urban workers also lost their factory jobs at that time, but they were reassigned to employment in rural firms and projects, not laid off or fired.[64] Under the

59 Lee, *Against the Law*, 125 *ff.*
60 Interview, June 29, 1996; Lee, *Against the Law*, 128–129.
61 Lee, *Against the Law*, 127 *ff.*
62 Ibid., 199.
63 Qin Gao, *Welfare, Work and Poverty: Social Assistance in China* (Oxford: Oxford University Press, 2017); Dorothy J. Solinger, *Poverty and Pacification: The Chinese State Abandons the Old Working Class* (Lanham, MD: Rowman and Littlefield, 2022).
64 See p. 54.

structural reforms, employment security has declined for all categories of workers. Dorothy Solinger has concluded that it is impossible to arrive at a defensible figure for Chinese unemployment, a position with which China's flagship *People's Daily* subsequently concurred;[65] but it surely also runs into the tens of millions. Tens of millions of workers have seen their jobs disappear, though some have been affected more severely than others.

Official unemployment statistics do not count workers who are "laid off" for under three years during which they retain a formal tie to their enterprises entitling them to some paltry services and possible recall to work if openings develop. Even leaving them out, unemployment nearly doubled from 1990 to 2015.[66] This was due heavily to the 1997 decision to privatize, merge or close many state-owned enterprises. Around the turn of the century, the number of laid-off workers increased over tenfold to 21 million (at a time when official unemployment statistics were around seven million).[67] Most were urban-resident workers. But in 2007 and 2008, for the first time large numbers of rural migrants were also laid off. While starting in the early 1990s jobs for rural migrants were plentiful, especially in the construction and export sectors, the 2008 depression saw over 20 million lose their positions.[68] Unlike the urban-resident laid-off of previous years and some of the urban-resident unemployed, they were not entitled to any benefits whatsoever. Most went home to their villages, though they soon returned when the labor market perked up.

Unemployment is also very unevenly distributed, with peaks in the rustbelts of Manchuria and in poorer inland provinces with cities dominated by now shuttered "third front" factories.[69] In Liaoning Province, part of the Manchurian heavy industrial heartland that boomed under the Japanese occupation and then the Maoist era, employment in manufacturing dropped from 4,618,000 in 1990

65 Dorothy Solinger, "Why We Cannot Count the 'Unemployed'," *China Quarterly* 167 (September 2001): 671–688; "城镇失业率"数字打架:专家:会误导决策建议废除," *人民日报*, April 7, 2009, http://politics.people.com.cn/GB/1026/9084260.html.

66 Calculated from *China Statistical Yearbook 2016*, Table 4-17. The data are aggregated by province, and exclude Chongqing and Tibet, for which there were no 1990 data.

67 Li Peilin, "中国经济社会发展的问题和趋势" ("Issues and Trends in China's Economic and Social Development"), in Xin Ru, Lu Xueyi and Li Peilin, eds., *2004年:中国社会形势分析与预测 (2004: Analysis and Forecast of Chinese Society)*. Beijing: 社会科学文献出版社 (Social Science Documentary Press), 2004; cited in David S. G. Goodman, *Class in Contemporary China* (Cambridge, UK, Polity, 2014), 132.

68 "20 Million Laid-off Migrant Workers May Send China's Unemployment Rate to 10%," *China Stakes*, February 6, 2009, http://www.chinastakes.com/2009/2/20-million-laid-off-migrant-workers-may-send-chinas-unemployment-rate-to-10.html (accessed June 6, 2015).

69 The "third front" was a program of development begun in the early 1960s to create heavy industrial plants in remote parts of inland China, partly for defensive reasons—so that an attack on the more vulnerable Manchuria would not deprive China of all such factory capacity—and partly for redistribution.

to 1,447,000 in 2004.[70] In Benxi, a Liaoning city of 1.5 million in which state and collective heavy industry was the mainstay of the economy, 98 percent of jobs in those firms were lost between 1993 and 2002, and unemployment has run to a staggering 70 percent.[71] Across Manchuria (Heilongjiang, Jilin and Liaoning Provinces), the official unemployment rate in 2006 was 15 percent higher than the national average, with Liaoning the highest in the country. It was also at least 10 percent higher than the national average in inland Hunan, Ningxia, Sichuan and Tibet. The actual figures are bound to be more unequally distributed than this. Unemployed workers in such places huddle in decrepit old factory apartment blocks, often without heat, electricity or even adequate food.

China's urban laid-off and unemployed workers have faced three broad alternatives: private sector employment, self-employment or long-term unemployment. Former state and collective industry workers generally lack the skills, inclinations and demographics to land work in the private factories, where youth, education and assiduity are prized, and bosses have been reluctant to hire workers with lingering Maoist-era sensibilities. Self-employment can include everything from starting a business to driving a cab to peddling. The opportunities for entrepreneurship depend, of course, on the state of the local economy, the availability of start-up capital, good information, and business acumen, all of which come together only in a small minority of cases. For most unemployed workers—85 percent in one 1999 survey—there has been little way out, and they are forced into very early retirements on meager and rapidly shrinking "benefits" and humiliating dependence on their children.[72]

Workers who have dodged the bullet live with the constant fear of further cutbacks, especially if they work in factories in economic difficulty. They actually report that this anxiety has provided an incentive to work assiduously.[73] In such firms workers also often expressed the hope that a foreign investor will come along, even though they were also well aware that in private firms, with their generally more intensive labor processes and draconian management, there is a higher risk than in state and collective ones of being fired on the basis of "cause" even in the absence of workforce retrenchment. Some are even willing to countenance corruption if the management is doing it to help lure an investor.[74] One worker compared the loyalty to and sense of identification with their firms that prevailed in the Maoist period to a different kind of tie today.

70 Lee, *Against the Law*, 74.

71 William Hurst, *The Chinese Worker After Socialism* (Cambridge: Cambridge University Press, 2009), 32.

72 Hurst, *The Chinese Worker*, chap. 4.

73 Interview, June 18, 2002; Stephen E. Philion, *Workers' Democracy in China's Transition from State Socialism* (New York: Routledge, 2009), 104.

74 Philion, *Workers' Democracy*, 103.

> People have feelings for their firm today because they cherish the opportunity to work. The workers have a sense of crisis (危机感). They are concerned that if the factory has a crisis, it will affect them.[75]

So desperate are workers in troubled firms that in some cases they have paid more than a year's wages to employers in bribes and "fees" to keep their jobs.[76]

...

Overall, then, Chinese workers' absolute levels of compensation and material life under structural reform offer a mixed picture. While urban workers who have held on to employment have seen significant increases in real wages compared with Maoist days, many others have lost their jobs altogether and been unable to find reemployment. And even the employed have lost the benefits and economic and job security to which they had become accustomed, even as they all remain housed one way or another. Significant inequalities have developed regionally and among various strata of the working class. Workers often have trouble getting paid at all or receiving the pensions and insurance contributions to which they are entitled. They are subject to a great deal of forced, uncompensated overtime, and all manner of deductions and fines, and complex piece rate schemes that make it hard to know how much they are going to be paid or why.[77] Some actually have to pay in order to land a job. Some are not paid at all. Rural migrants have suffered mightily, often in sweatshops, to achieve extremely modest incomes that are an improvement only in comparison with the prospect of little or no income at all in their home villages.

As the structural reforms matured in the new century, the economic situation of China's working class began to homogenize. Whereas in the Maoist period and the first decades of structural reform urban-resident workers maintained multiple advantages over rural migrants in wages, benefits, working conditions and employment security, increasingly the former have descended to the position of the latter. While urban-resident and rural migrant workers remain divided by the household registration system and the institutional, political and legal frameworks that have grown up around it since the 1950s, in material terms the differences between them are shrinking. Kevin Lin has argued that "the distinction between migrant workers in the export sector and many workers in the state sector [is] less dichotomous than it appears."[78] Many scholars and

75 Interview, July 9, 1996.

76 Personal communication from Prof. William Hurst.

77 See p. 128.

78 Kevin Lin, "Recomposing Chinese Migrant and State-Sector Workers," in Anita Chan, ed., *Chinese Workers in Comparative Perspective* (Ithaca: ILR Press/Cornell University Press, 2015), 69.

advocates for the plight of rural migrants have argued for the abolition of the household registration (户口) system, seeing it as the institutional and political basis for their subordination within the working class. But a very different and much quieter economic change has actually pushed in the opposite direction. China's structural reform is beginning to reshape the working class itself by flattening the distinction between urban-resident and rural migrant workers. Instead of the latter potentially rising to the level of the former, the very opposite is starting to occur.

In terms of China's macro-economy, there is a broad consensus among Western and many Chinese economists that state enterprise "reform"—involving at least partial privatization, management changes to emulate the private sector, and deregulation—is the essential next phase if the country is to continue its industrial growth. What often gets lost in such discussions is that such structural change carries a big price for urban-resident Chinese workers who, for the first several decades of the structural reform, remained better off in state-owned enterprises than private ones as well as in comparison with rural migrant workers. But ongoing "reform" has begun to produce a race to the bottom that portends the homogenization of China's working class, a profound development in working class re-formation that could carry with it potentially very significant political implications.

Social Aspects of the Fall of the Working Class

Structural reform radically upended working class social life quantitatively and qualitatively. The working class ballooned, incorporating huge phalanxes of rural migrants; moreover, they became proletarianized in the formal sense—employed as capitalist wage laborers rather than as state socialist workers who enjoyed significant guarantees and protections. Meanwhile, the urban-resident stratum that had been the mainstay of the working class in the Maoist period shrunk to a shadow of its former self. The working class also became even more deeply cleaved than before into widely different strata: not just rural migrant and urban, but employed and unemployed, male and female, older and younger, skilled and unskilled, native and adventive. Old communities grounded in the congruence of workplace and home fractured. Social hierarchies and workplace power relations were turned upside down—or, from the vantage point of the newly capitalistic mode of production, right-side up.

Size

Since 1978 but especially 1992, when urban industrial development took off, China has produced the biggest, most rapid spurt of proletarianization in world history. Precise numbers do not exist, but the scale is well into hundreds of millions. In 1985, there were 381 million workers; three decades later, there were

623 million.[79] They emanated overwhelmingly from rural migration—296 million in 2022[80]—rather than urban population growth.

Such astonishing growth did not occur smoothly. Figures 3.3 and 3.4 track the number of urban-resident "staff and workers"[81] in manufacturing, mining, construction and transport, warehousing, post and telecommunications[82] from 1978 to 2010 and 2013 to 2018. (The categorization of enterprises shifted in 2010 and again in 2013, making a continuous series impossible.[83] Thanks to Chris Bramall for this reference.) Their ranks grew around 50 percent through the early 1990s. As real industrial GDP rose an average of 11 percent per year from 1978 to 1993,[84] most of which was extensive rather than intensive growth grounded in productivity gains, the working class had to expand dramatically.[85] It was only in 1993 that the structural reform of industry and especially labor began in earnest. As firms began to experience increased competitive pressure on their bottom lines, and gained the latitude to shed workers, the urban-resident working class began to shrink gradually. It fell off a cliff in 1998, the year that the deep retrenchment of state industry began, accompanied by massive layoffs. The size of the urban-resident working class kept plummeting through the early years of the new century, when the employed industrial working class began slowly to grow once again. In 2012, it grew 6.8 percent over 2011,[86] but then began to decline from 2013 onward (Figure 3.3), due in large part to ongoing retrenchment or privatization of state and collective firms that employed urban-resident workers, which is evident in Figure 3.4.

79 *China Statistical Yearbook 1986*, 192; Andre Thibaud, "Indispensable but Sidelined: The Chinese Working Class" Beijing: Daxue Consulting, October 20, https://daxueconsulting.com/chinese-working-class/.

80 "Migrant Workers and their children," *China Labour Bulletin* September 6, 2023, https://clb.org.hk/en/content/migrant-workers-and-their-children.

81 As such, it may overstate the ranks of the blue-collar working class a bit, since "staff" includes managers and technicians. Note that it also excludes the huge phalanx of rural migrant labor, of which more below.

82 Chinese statistics data do not report a category for industrial workers. These sectors provide an approximation.

83 中国统计局人口和就业统计司 (China Statistical Bureau Population and Employment Department) and 人力资源和社会保障部规划财务司 (Ministry of Human Capital and Social Insurance Department of Planning and Finance), 中国劳动统计年鉴2014 (*China Labor Statistics Yearbook 2014*).

84 Calculated from *China Statistical Yearbook 2007*, Table 3.4.

85 Moreover, labor force reductions were neither yet envisioned nor politically possible. As this was a time of relatively dilatory policy tinkering with the structure of industry, firms' budget constraints remained soft. Moreover, the leadership both in the government and the firms still had vivid memories of the working class's political juggernaut during the Maoist period, particularly the Cultural Revolution, which ruled out layoffs.

86 It is impossible to calculate 2011 in relation to 2010 due to the discontinuity in the data mentioned just above.

FIGURE 3.3 "Staff and workers" in manufacturing, mining, construction and transport/storage/post, 1978–2010.

Source: *China Labour Statistical Yearbook 2001* (*中国劳动统计年鉴2001*) (Beijing: China Statistics Press, 2001), Tables 1-16, 1-17, 1-18; *China Statistical Yearbook 2002*, Table 5-7; *China Statistical Yearbook 2003*, Table 5-7; *China Statistical Yearbook 2004*, Table 5–9; *China Statistical Yearbook 2005*, Table 5-9; *China Statistical Yearbook 2006*, Table 5-7; *China Statistical Yearbook 2007*, Table 5-8; *China Statistical Yearbook 2008*, Table 4-6; *China Statistical Yearbooks 2009–2011*, Tables 4-4.

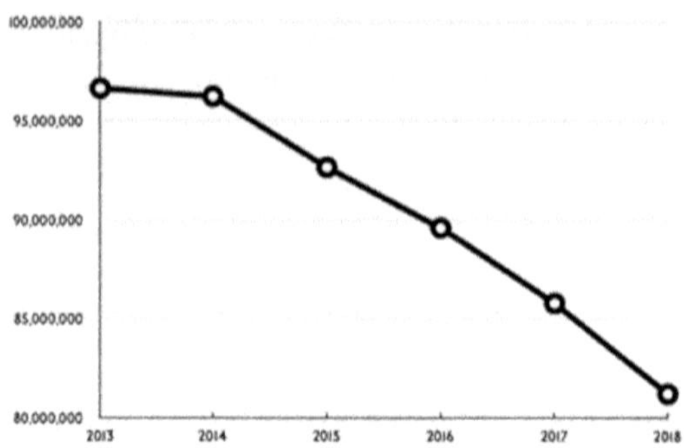

FIGURE 3.4 "Staff and workers" in manufacturing, mining, construction and transport/storage/post, 2013–2018.

Source: *China Statistical Yearbooks 2014-2019*, Tables 4-4.

The urban-resident working class also experienced pronounced changes in the kinds of enterprises in which they worked (Figures 3.5 and 3.6).[87] The transition to capitalistic relations of production got underway in earnest in the latter 1990s, accompanied by massive layoffs in state and collective firms that in

87 Once again, a discontinuity in the categorizations of the Chinese data rules out a continuous series.

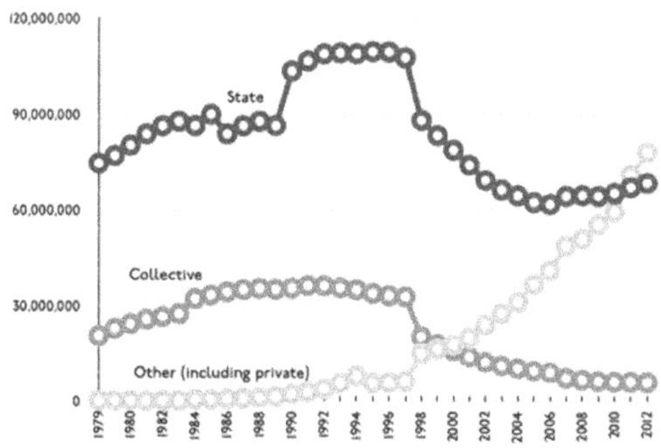

FIGURE 3.5 "Staff and workers" in manufacturing, mining, construction and transport/storage/post by ownership sector, 1978–2012.

Source: *China Labour Statistical Yearbook 2001* (*中国劳动统计年鉴 2001*) (Beijing: China Statistics Press, 2001), Tables 1-16, 1-17, 1-18; *China Statistical Yearbook 2002*, Table 5-7; *China Statistical Yearbook 2003*, Table 5-7; *China Statistical Yearbook 2004*, Table 5-9; *China Statistical Yearbook 2005*, Table 5-9; *China Statistical Yearbook 2006*, Table 5-7; *China Statistical Yearbook 2007*, Table 5-8; *China Statistical Yearbooks 2008 and 2009*, Tables 4-6; *China Statistical Yearbooks 2010 and 2011*, Tables 4-5; *China Statistical Yearbook 2012*, Table 4-4.

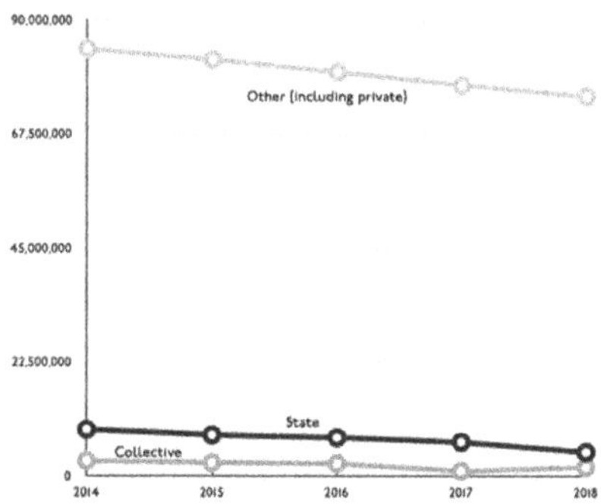

FIGURE 3.6 "Staff and workers" in manufacturing, mining, construction and transport/storage/post by ownership sector, 2014–2018.

Source: *China Statistical Yearbooks 2015–2019*, Tables 4-4.

the newer enterprise forms—"joint," "LLCs," "shareholding LLCs," "private," "foreign funded" and "others"—started ramping up. In 1997, when massive layoffs in public enterprises took place, the shift from state and collective firms to newer ownership forms—"joint," "LLCs," "shareholding LLCs," "private," "foreign funded" and "others"—was dramatic. The number of workers in the latter category grew by one-third, while the former shrank by a similar amount. Thereafter, state and collective enterprise employment continued to decline while that in the newer ownership forms grew apace. All the growth in the number of employed workers that began again in 2002 for the first time since the shrinkage began a decade earlier (Figure 3.3) took place in the new ownership forms. In 2012, the number of workers in the new ownership forms surpassed those in state and collective firms. In short, since 1978 China's working class went through a sharp cycle of employment increase and decrease, while it also began to move out of the world of state and collective industry within which it had achieved such significant gains in the Maoist period.

But the biggest story about the size of the working class is the addition of a huge phalanx of rural migrants. In 2007 there were 137 million rural migrants working in China's cities, excluding non-working family members. This amounts to a 60 percent increase since just 2001. Around 60 percent—80 million—were employed in industry,[88] a figure that dwarfed the 56,742,000 urban industrial workforce. In 2020, there were 286 million rural migrants in China's working class, compared to 81 million urban-resident workers. Rural migrant workers also experienced a roller-coaster ride of radical expansion and contraction: over 20 million rural migrants lost their positions, though they soon returned to industrial employment. But the rural migrant stratum experienced steady expansion from 253 million in 2011 to 296 million in 2022.[89] As a century earlier, the vast majority of Chinese workers were first generation proletarians who had been born into farm families. Almost all of them worked outside what remains of the state and collective sector.

Taking all these categories together, China now boasts an industrial working class of around 400 million, not including dependents, which makes it around half of the country's total employed, 30 percent of the total population, and more than the total population of every other country in the world except India. This was proletarianization on a vast scale and in a double sense: hundreds of millions of farmers became wage laborers, and so did tens of millions of state workers who had previously worked on state socialist rather than capitalist terms.

88 In 2003, 30.3 percent of migrants were employed in manufacturing, 22.9 percent in construction, 3.4 percent in transport, and 1.8 percent in mining. Poverty Reduction and Economic Management Department, East Asia and Pacific Region, World Bank, *From Poor Areas to Poor People: China's Evolving Poverty Reduction Agenda — An Assessment of Poverty and Inequality in China* (Beijing: The World Bank, 2009), 96, 100.

89 "Migrant Workers and Their Children."

Social Composition

From the outset of the rapid industrialization starting in 1992, the new Chinese proletariat underwent significant feminization. By 2022, women comprised 43.5 percent of the working class, and only 36.6 percent of its rural migrant stratum.[90] The mechanism was, of course, that the huge influx was far more female than the preexisting workers (Table 3.1). And it occurred despite the fact that a disproportionate number of workers laid off in the late 1990s were women: 45 percent, even though women made up only 36.5 percent of the workforce.[91] In 1997, 56 percent of state industry workers were men, a figure that rose to 58 percent by 2002, after the massive layoffs of 1998 and thereafter, when women were more likely to be fired. In the less prestigious and well-paid sector of collective industry, the reverse was true: in 1997 the gender balance in collective industry was almost equal, but by 2002 women comprised 60 percent of the labor force. For other ownership forms, the 1997 ratio of 55 percent males to 45 percent females dropped to 51 percent to 49 percent by 2002.[92] This was probably a result of the influx of young women into export sector employment, since in 2002 57 percent of all women workers and staff were under 35, compared with 48 percent in 1997; moreover, in 2002, 56 percent of the workforce under 35 were women, compared with only 48 percent in 1997.[93] One young woman in

TABLE 3.1 Age cohort by gender, 2002

Age cohort	*Male*	*Female*
35 or under	43.4%	56.5%
36–50	51.2%	48.8%
51 or over	81.3%	18.7%

Source: *中国职工状况调查,数据卷1997*, 1272; *第五次中国职工状况调查,数据卷*, 853; 全国总工会政策研究室 (All-China Federation of Trade Unions Policy Research Office) ,*中国职工状况调查,数据卷1997* (*1997 Survey of the Condition of Chinese Workers and Staff*), 1272; 中华全国总工会政策研究室(All-China Federation of Trade Unions Research Office), *第五次中国职工状况调查,数据卷* (*Survey of the Condition of Chinese Workers and Staff in 2002*) (北京:中国工人出版社,2006), 853.

90 Ibid.

91 Mo Rong, "就业新世纪面临的挑战与抉择" ("Employment: The Challenge and Choice that the New Century is Facing") in Li Peilin, Huang Ping, Lu Jianhua (eds), *2001年:中国社会形势分析与预测* (2001: Analysis and Forecast of China's Social Situation) (北京:社会社会科学文选出版社), 218–19; cited in Dorothy Solinger, "Chinese Urban Jobs and the WTO," *China Journal* 49 (January, 2003), 70.

92 *中国职工状况调查,数据卷1997*, 1269; 中华全国总工会政策研究室(All-China Federation of Trade Unions Research Office), *第五次中国职工状况调查,数据卷* (*Fifth Survey of the Condition of Chinese Workers and Staff, Statistical Volume*) (北京:中国工人出版社 [Beijing: China Workers Press], 2006), 850.

93 *中国职工状况调查,数据卷1997*, 1270, 1273; *第五次中国职工状况调查,数据卷*, 850, 853.

a Japanese-owned electrical products plant, confirming the usual stereotypes, put the reasons thus: "My plant is 80 percent female. They hire this way because they think women are more obedient. In addition, women are more dextrous."[94] Thereafter, however, women's employment in manufacturing declined from 43 percent in 2003 to 39 percent in 2012, 2015 and 2017, possibly because women were gravitating increasingly to the service sector, where discrimination is rife, including in gig work.[95] (Still, women make up a far greater portion of industrial employment in China than Brazil, Mexico, the UK or the U.S.) They have tended to be concentrated in less skilled industrial occupations, less technologically sophisticated sectors, and less modern plants.[96] They are also employed at far higher rates among rural migrants than urban-resident workers.[97]

Despite the stereotype of callow youth working assembly lines in Chinese sweatshops, the country's working class began aging noticeably by the turn of the century (Table 3.2). By 2022, the average age of rural migrant workers was forty-two compared with thirty-four in 2008. Thirty percent of rural migrant workers were over 50, while "the proportion of workers aged 16 to 30 meanwhile has fallen from 42% in 2010 to 19.8%."[98] But workers in the state and collective sectors were older than those in the various private sector categories.[99] In general, employers in these new ownership forms—and especially, of course, in the export sector—have preferred to hire younger workers, whom

94 Interview, May 24, 1999. The point about dexterity may not be mere stereotype. In one electrical components plant, during hiring trials "women repeatedly beat the men in both speed and efficiency of assembly…" (Calvin Chen, *Some Assembly Required: Work, Community and Politics in China's Rural Enterprises* [Cambridge, Mass.: Harvard University Asia Center, 2008], 104).

95 Suki Dasgupta, Makiko Matsumoto, and Cuntao Xia, "Women in the Labour Market in China," *ILO Asia-Pacific Working Paper Series* (Bangkok: International Labour Organization, 2015), 14–15; National Bureau of Statistics Department of Population and Employment Statistics and Ministry of Human Resources and Social Security, *China Labour Statistical Yearbook 2016* (Beijing: China Statistics Press, 2017), Tables 1-13 and 1-15; National Bureau of Statistics Department of Population and Employment Statistics and Ministry of Human Resources and Social Security, *China Labour Statistical Yearbook 2018* (Beijing: China Statistics Press, 2018), Table 5; "Women workers in China's gig economy face discrimination, lower pay, unsafe conditions," *China Labour Bulletin* [May 23, 2023]: https://clb.org.hk/en/content/women-workers-china%E2%80%99s-gig-economy-face-discrimination-lower-pay-unsafe-conditions.)

96 全国总工会 1999: 1269; 中华全国总工会: 850; National Bureau of Statistics Department of Population and Employment Statistics and Ministry of Human Resources and Social Security, *China Labour Statistical Yearbook 2016* (Beijing: China Statistics Press, 2017), Tables 1-13 and 1-15.

97 "Between the Lines: Listening to Female Factory Workers in China," n.p., Business for Social Responsibility, March 2013, 3.

98 "Migrant workers and their children."

99 While I could not locate data for rustbelt areas, these figures make it a good bet that a large number of unemployed workers in the northeast and the inland "third front" cities were of a similar age profile.

TABLE 3.2 Working class age cohorts, by firm ownership type, 1997 and 2002

	1997			*2002*		
Ownership	*Under 35*	*35–50*	*Over 50*	*Under 35*	*35–50*	*Over 50*
State-owned	46%	46%	14%	24%	62%	19%
Collective	44%	50%	10%	20%	66%	18%
Other	55%	41%	7%	35%	55%	14%

Source: *中国职工状况调查,数据卷1997*, 1272; *第五次中国职工状况调查,数据卷*, 853. 全国总工会政策研究室(All-China Federation of Trade Unions Policy Research Office) ,*中国职工状况调查,数据卷1997* (*1997 Survey of the Condition of Chinese Workers and Staff*), 1272; 中华全国总工会政策研究室(All-China Federation of Trade Unions Research Office), *第五次中国职工状况调查,数据卷* (*Survey of the Condition of Chinese Workers and Staff in 2002*) (北京:中国工人出版社,2006), 853.

they regard as more malleable and energetic, and less affected by the working class politics of the Maoist period. The average age of migrant workers in 2003 was only twenty-nine, compared with forty-one for the working class overall in 2002.[100] And finally, between two-thirds and four-fifths of workers laid off in the 1990s—who came from state-owned enterprises with older workforces—were over 35 years of age.[101] That was both particularly insulting to them, in light of their long service, as well as injurious since it made it all the more difficult for them to find reemployment.

> Around half of the laid-off workers in Tianjin are people in their 40s or so. They never finished school due to the Cultural Revolution, so they are basically illiterate. So they are the first to be fired. For the same reason, they have a hard time finding other work. So all they can do is go out on the streets and sell stuff on the sidewalks. For this they might earn ¥10 per day or so. They cannot depend on their kids for their livelihood, since their kids are still in school. So they have a really hard time.
>
> But many do not have to pay rent—they have housing allocated free from their old units. Moreover, if their apartment has some extra space they will rent it out to earn a little more. So their expenses are low and they find ways to scrape by.[102]

100 World Bank, *From Poor Areas to Poor People*, 101; *第五次中国职工状况调查,数据卷*, 924.

101 "10城市企业下岗职工和离退休人员基本庄稼矿的抽样调查" ("A Sample Investigation of the Situation of 10 Cities' Laid-off Enterprise Employees and Retirees"),*中国劳动* (China Labor), 12 (2000), 51–3; Zhao Yao, "下岗女职工:出再就业服务中心'情况的调查' ["Laid-off women staff and workers: an investigation of the situation of leaving the 'reemployment service center'"],中国工人 (Chinese Worker), 3 (2001), 12–13; and Mo Rong, "就业新世纪"; cited in Dorothy Solinger, "Chinese Urban Jobs and the WTO,": 70.

102 Interview, May 24, 1999.

TABLE 3.3 Working class age cohorts, by gender, 2019

	Total	*Male*	*Female*
Under 24	8.2	8.5	7.2
25–29	12.5	12.7	12.1
30–34	15.8	15.6	16.5
35–39	13.3	12.5	15
40–44	16.1	15	18.6
45–49	15.7	14.8	17.7
[35–49]	[45.1]	[42.3]	[51.3]
50–54	11.7	12.8	8.8
Over 55	6.9	8	4.1

Source: 中国劳动统计年鉴2019, Table 1-47.

The coping strategies he mentioned work better in Tianjin than in rustbelt areas in the northeast or the older cities dominated by now shuttered "third front" factories, where "opportunities" for peddling and subleasing are much scarcer if they exist at all. By 2019 (Table 3.3), the working class had grown younger again, as the older generation of Maoist-era workers had retired. Women comprised slightly larger proportions of the middle-aged cohorts, mainly because they retired younger.

China's working class was relatively well educated by the turn of the century (Table 3.4). As early as 1984, one Tianjin electrical pump factory required all new hirees to have finished high school.[103] In both 1997 and 2002, the modal category for educational attainment was high school or vocational high school. In the "other" ownership category, the increase from 1997 to 2002 in the percentage of primary educatees and the drop in high school graduates reflects in part the enormous influx during those years of rural migrants (even though, it must be said, those migrants were generally better educated than the villagers they left behind).[104] There was, however, a corresponding outflow of relatively poorly educated workers from the labor force, since the majority of workers laid off in the late 1990s had junior-high school educations at best.[105] By 2019, 72 percent of migrant workers had junior or senior high school educations—a significant increase.[106]

...

In short, China's working class was strongly though somewhat decreasingly feminized, growing older in general but also relatively younger in its fastest growing section of rural migrants, and ever better educated.

103 Interview, June 29, 1996.

104 World Bank, *From Poor Areas to Poor People*, 101.

105 "10城市企业," Zhao Yao, "下岗女职工"; Mo Rong, "就业新世纪."

106 CEIC Data (n.d.) 'China Migrant Worker: Average Age', https://www.ceicdata.com/en/china/migrant-worker/migrant-worker-average-age.

TABLE 3.4 Education by firm ownership, 1997 and 2002

	Illiterate	*Primary*	*Junior high school*	*High school/ vocational high school*	*Technical college*	*University*
			1997			
Total	0.4%	2.4%	26.1%	42.8%	20.1%	8.2%
State	0.5%	2.1%	22.1%	41.8%	22.6%	11.0%
Collective	0.7%	4.5%	37.2%	43.8%	10.6%	3.2%
Other	0.4%	1.0%	20.4%	54.8%	13.9%	9.5%
			2002			
Total	0.30%	2.10%	22.4%	41.90	22.9%	10.5%
State	0.23%	2.36%	26.5%	45.8%	18.9%	6.3%
Collective	0.57%	5.49%	41.5%	43.0%	8.1%	1.4%
Other	0.18%	4.44%	24.7%	47.3%	17.7%	5.7%

Source: *中国职工状况调查,数据卷1997*, 1293–4; *第五次中国职工状况调查,数据卷*, 881–2.

Residence

The relatively strong overlap of workers' workplace and residence in the Maoist period has been weakened considerably. In some flagship state-owned enterprises the factory-based welfare state lived on well into the era of structural reform. For example, in 1995, Yunnan Steel was still providing its workers with not just housing but the likes of discounted phone service, free bus transportation and free supper for the night shift.[107] But in many cases workers still live in the same factory-built housing blocks that they occupied decades ago even though their firms have closed or been restructured, with the attendant layoffs. In these cases the workers may live together but no longer work together. Where the residents have been able to find new work, their old sense of workplace community is, of course, largely gone. In rustbelt areas where they have generally not been able to find new work, the community has also weakened, though the old pattern of concentrated residence surely proved important in reigniting solidarity during the pitched battles over severance packages in 2002.[108] Many workers who are still employed in state and larger collective firms that once provided housing have now moved on to new or at least different dwellings that are no longer occupied only or even mainly by other workers in their enterprise.

Firms outside the state and collective sector have generally not provided their workers with housing in the first place, so their workers do not live together as

107 Interview, December 5, 1995.
108 See p. 166*ff.*

neighbors. The exception is the dormitory quarters provided to young rural migrants by export sector firms. Of course, these places are not what we normally think of as residential communities—historically rooted places where continuous social relationships can develop—but, rather, temporary digs for the teenagers and twenty-somethings who stay a few years only. Nonetheless, they are places where intense (if transient) social relationships are formed. Workers inhabiting them share gossip, news and, often, their deepest feelings.[109] They also act spontaneously to strengthen bonds of community. "Workers frequently changed beds to form kin and ethnic clusters because they found it easier to cope [when connected] with each other."[110] Yet such bonds are also easily and summarily dissolved by the continuous shifts in employment.[111] Moreover, management undermines the breadth of community by providing several levels of housing accommodation, with the best to educated specialists and slightly less good but still better than ordinary rooms to shop floor line leaders.[112] But homogenizing the ordinary workers may actually strengthen their sub-community, which of course is a large majority in any factory anyway. In some cases the overlap of workplace and even such transient residence has helped fuel resistance.[113] But this same residential pattern provides an obstacle to such protest becoming politicized *vis-à-vis* the state, precisely because the state and its politics are so utterly absent from the almost totally encapsulated world of the factory/dormitory.

Social Status

If in economic terms structural reform has produced gains and losses for China's working class, in social terms the picture is much more clearly negative. As one factory official described the state socialist years, "At that time the best thing was to be a worker. It was even better than being a cadre."[114] The not atypical decision made by one bright Maoist era high school graduate to take a factory job rather than a university seat, because workers were so exalted while being an intellectual caused too much trouble (太麻烦),[115] is simply unimaginable today.

109 Pun Ngai, *Made in China: Women Factory Workers in a Global Workplace* (Durham: Duke University Press, 2005).

110 Pun, 105.

111 Lee, *Against the Law*, 196.

112 Pun, 124, 126.

113 Chris King-Chi Chan and Pun Ngai, "The Making of a New Working Class? A Study of Collective Actions of Migrant Workers in South China," *China Quarterly* 198 (June 2009): 287–303.

114 Interview, June 8, 1999.

115 Interview, December 1974.

> We don't have the same status as before. We no longer feel it's our enterprise. In the old days we were seen as the masters of the enterprise (主人翁), but now everything's down to the say-so of a few people. That's the difference. It's like we're just hired hands…[116]

Already in 2002, just a decade into the deepened structural reform of industry, only 0.7 percent of workers hoped their children too would become workers; the most popular aspiration by far was that they become government officials (38.1 percent, more than twice the runner-up [technical work]).[117] 46.3 percent of workers said that over the previous five years their position as "masters of the enterprise" had declined a great deal (19.8 percent) or at least somewhat (26.5 percent).[118] One older worker reported that "Workers today are having more trouble getting married, an indicator of their declining social status."[119] Another, who married a worker decades earlier, said "she would never let her daughter marry a worker. 'Even a peasant entrepreneur is richer than a worker.'"[120] The collapse in workers' social status is greatest among the hard-core unemployed, who live a miserable material existence that has forced many to become supplicants to the state or their children.[121]

> Unemployed workers have low self-esteem. In Tianjin, 33.7 percent think that they have become a burden on their families, 17.4 percent feel powerless (无能为力), and 9.3 percent feel they have been abandoned by society. Even some of those who have gotten other work feel that their social status has dropped. Social prejudice only aggravates this feeling. This is a major reason why many unemployed workers don't have any interest in reemployment.[122]
>
> Actual social status affects how satisfied people are with their living conditions. The unemployed and those recently put out of work are the most dissatisfied. …70 percent of the unemployed are not [satisfied with their social status], according to a survey by the China Social Stability Research Unit in 1999.[123]

116 "'We Simply Lack the Rights': A female state-owned enterprise worker in Zhejiang discusses enterprise reform," *China Labour Bulletin* (Hong Kong), March 8, 2004.

117 See also Chen Meixuan, "Workers' State(s): Changing Self-Images and Social Relations of Chinese Workers 1970–2002," Thesis, School of Foreign Studies, Nanking University, 2002, 15.

118 *第五次中国职工状况调查,数据卷*, 1239–1241, 1260.

119 Interview, June 29, 1996.

120 Chen "Workers' State(s)," 16.

121 See p. 104.

122 朱光磊, *当代中国社会各阶层分析* (天津:天津人民出版社, 1998), 187–188.

123 Wang Shaoguang, Hu Angang and Ding Yuanzhu, "Behind China's Wealth Gap," *South China Morning Post*, October 31, 2002. In the ellipsis, the authors do say that "Most of the employed are satisfied" according to a survey. This is consistent with data from the

Some of the unemployed even try to compensate by condescending to rural migrants, though in this they are joined by the higher-status employed urban-resident workers, not to mention middle- and upper-class urbanites. Rural migrants are referred to, both in common parlance and in government media and policy discourses, as "peasant labor" (民工), the connotation of which is that they are not workers by occupation or identity but rather, literally, just "people who work."[124] They are said to have come to the cities in an "unbridled [literally, blind] flow" (盲流). Under China's household registration system, they are not entitled to live in the city permanently. At best they qualify for temporary permits, and at worst they are subject to roundups and deportations (for which they have often been charged a transportation fee).

> We are second-class citizens, and not even that sometimes, just beasts[125] in the eyes of the police. When they came to raid our houses in the middle of the night, they rode roughshod over us, forcing us to squat on the ground, with our hands raised and folded behind our heads. They treated us like criminals. Even if we could show them our temporary residence permits, they would tear them up, and ask, "Where are your papers?"[126] Migrant workers have no rights at all, because we are not locals.[127]

In daily life they are ignored and condescended to by shopkeepers, hounded with special severity by police and security guards, and subjected to epithets such as "coarse" and "dirty."[128] If they complain to government officials, they are likely to be received with impatience and ridicule that would not be dished out to urban workers.[129] They are also denied compensation for layoffs or unemployment, and entitlements to urban housing allocations, education for their children, and access to public medical services.

Urban workers are often the most hostile to them, fearing vaguely the labor market competition they are thought to provide, even though many urban workers aver that they would not want the jobs that migrants can get, and despite the

---

quinquennial 2002 labor union survey, which reported that 28.6 percent of workers felt their social status had risen over the previous five years, while 22.5 percent had reported a decline and nearly half felt no change (*第五次中国职工状况调查,数据卷*, Table 99). But none of that speaks to the more epochal change from the heyday of the Maoist period.

124 民工 can be short for 农民工 (peasant worker). But in leaving off the first character, the literal translation is "people who work," which is distinct from "worker" (工人). See also p. 153 *ff.*

125 Note the similarity to workers' plaint a century earlier of being treated "like cattle and horses," p. 25.

126 The resonance to the chilling police-state trope "Your papers, please" is unmistakable, though it's very unlikely this informant was aware of it.

127 Lee, *Against the Law*, 198.

128 Pun, 159–161.

129 Personal communication with a source who must remain anonymous.

fact that in many cases they could not get such jobs from employers who prefer to hire migrants, who will work for less and whom they believe are easier to dominate.

> The gap between the city and the countryside causes some urbanites to feel superior. They feel that their status is higher than peasants', that they should have the more comfortable jobs, and leave the more miserable, filthy and tiresome work for the farmers.[130]

One unemployed worker's account demonstrates the depth and texture of the cleavage between even the lowest status urbanites and rural migrants.

> Unemployed workers feel bad today as their income is so low and they are looked down upon by others. When they get a chance, they look down upon others. They unconsciously choose peasants to attack, because they are the only class lower than workers. Mr. Li [an unemployed worker], pointing to a new 'Giant' (a famous brand for bikes) said scornfully, "If a peasant worker rode it on to the street, he'd be stopped and checked by the police to see whether he had stolen the bike or not. But every time I ride it, no policeman will stop me even when I rode it slowly on purpose around Xingjiekou (a business and shopping center). The police won't blindly stop a cyclist. It depends on who rides what kind of bike." Mr. Li's remark shows his and the police's prejudice against peasants. They assume that peasants are often bike thieves. By mocking peasants, Mr. Li tried to demonstrate that he, a city dweller, had a higher status than peasants. Mr. Li strived to bolster his sagging self-respect at peasants' expense. Ms. Su [another unemployed worker] said in a disappointed tone, "Even a peasant entrepreneur is richer than a worker," indicating that she thinks peasants are always poorer and lower than city dwellers, and that even though they make much money, they are still peasants, and so still lower than workers. Her prejudice against peasants is deeply rooted. We can also recall [the unemployed] Ms. Du's remark that her cleaning work "should be done by peasants." Ms. Du thinks that peasants should do the cleaning work which she sees as degrading. Workers believe they are superior to peasants — even though they are both looked down upon by others. One way many people make themselves feel good about themselves is to look down upon others. Workers' rejection of peasants suggests that workers feel insecure and impotent. Their feelings of powerlessness are channeled toward those who they are able to attack—the peasants—the one class weaker than workers.[131]

130 朱光磊, *当代中国社会各阶层分析*, 183 *ff.*
131 Chen, "Workers' State(s)," 19–20.

In short, China's working class has suffered a massive drop in its social status since Maoist days. Even employed workers who are reasonably satisfied with their lives do not want their children to become workers, which was a proud ambition of the past. The urban unemployed have sunk to almost predatory depths. Rural migrants no doubt feel superior to the villagers they left behind, but in the city they experience a life laced with extreme disrespect and hostility from the urbanites around them, including, perhaps most pointedly, other workers. The consequences for working class fellow-feeling, much less solidarity, are obvious.

Intra-firm Stratification

As enterprises have expanded, their workforces have often grown more heterogeneous, and social relations among their workers concomitantly more complex and often strained. Two Wenzhou private firms studied by Calvin Chen, which began as rural workshops and grew into major urban factories, provide an example. They began essentially as extended family operations, in which the founders worked their kinship networks to hire relatives close and distant, as well as fellow villagers, for the new companies. Over the initial years, they developed patriarchal labor relations in the best senses of the term as well as the more negative ones. Management treated the workers with respect, such that workers were able to respond positively to demands for overtime and much extra effort. "[T]he personal charisma and commitment of firm founders and the informal norms of trust and reciprocity enhanced accountability and a sense of common purpose, which, [*sic*] in turn stabilized shop floor dynamics."[132]

But as the firms succeeded beyond the founders' wildest dreams, they first had to upgrade their product and production lines. That forced them to hire technical experts, which in turn required them to go beyond the local networks on which they had thus far relied. These people fractured the communitarian social basis of the firm. Not only were they outsiders to the firm, but also outsiders to the area, which brought into play the pointed regional animosities that have plagued China for millennia. They did not speak the local dialect, which transformed the very basis of day-to-day communication in the plant as the locals had to switch from their beloved Wenzhouese to standard Mandarin. Moreover, the newcomers had to be paid a great deal more than the locals and offered all manner of other emoluments (including mistresses). All that, along with the new status hierarchy that it brought in tow, demoralized the original local staff and undermined their commitment to the firm.

Several years further on, the firm's continued growth had exhausted the locally available pool of line workers, forcing it to bring in a second wave of

132 Chen, *Some Assembly Required*, 26.

outsiders. Many came from much poorer rural areas, which rendered them more grateful for the employment, more accustomed to back-breaking labor, and therefore more exploitable than the local workers, whom the management had treated, as fellow locals and kin, with kid gloves at least in relative terms. Management now found the new wave of workers more pliable and began to complain that the original workers had grown spoiled and lazy. Naturally, this produced further resentment from the locals around issues of work, factory life and social relations more generally. "Outsiders have different habits than we do...Most outsiders are dirtier." The newcomers replied: "[L]ocals don't care about the quality of their work or whether they stay employed."[133]

In his study of a Korean-owned apparel plant in Qingdao, Jaesok Kim discovered other important, consequential cleavages around nation, ethnicity, authority and gender.

> To establish their superiority over the Chinese labor that was not immediately acknowledged, the managers worked diligently to make the space and organization of the factory reflect an inviolable hierarchical difference between Koreans and Chinese. For example, they assigned the core part of the factory space to themselves, while putting the Han-Chinese workers in factory dormitories located just outside the factory space... [T]he discrimination against the Chinese workers created new differences between Koreans and Chinese and maintained the sense of cultural superiority among the Korean managers... [who had] various methods ... to maintain...[their] superiority over the local Chinese labor... [M]anagement's arbitrary understanding of the cultural differences between Koreans and Chinese... contributed to the production of those methods.[134]

They also cultivated differences between Han and Korean-Chinese workers.

> The Nawon management heightened the ethnic tension between its Korean-Chinese and Han-Chinese employees and increased their ethnic consciousness by implementing discriminatory policies that heavily favored Korean-Chinese.[135]

And the employees themselves also did so on their own.

133 Chen, *Some Assembly Required*, 116–123. See also Pun, *Made in China*, 126–131.

134 Jaesok Kim, *Chinese Labor in a Korean Factory* (Stanford, CA: Stanford University Press, 2013), 11.

135 Kim, *China Labor*, 13.

> The Korean-Chinese employees justified their privileged status in the corporation by their belief in an alleged Korean-Chinese ethnic or cultural superiority [over Han Chinese].[136]

Finally, the predominantly female shopfloor employees condescended strongly to the "underclass" of the young, male haulers.

> The guys in our factory? I've never imagined that one of them could be my spouse. They receive low wages, which are even lower than mine! They completely lack skills so they only can do menial jobs. They have no future.[137]

The women even excluded the men from a strike they staged, which of course undermined their own interests and power.

In short, as Chinese industry grows larger, more sophisticated, and more oriented to regional, national and international networks of production and distribution, myriad cleavages have developed among workers and between them and managers, along personalistic, localistic, regional, national, ethnic, gender and authority lines. These are bound to create new obstacles to working class unity, much less solidarity.

Shop Floor Power Relations and Labor Process

The gains that China's working class achieved during the Maoist period in power relations on the shop floor and in employment terms are broadly gone. In state-owned enterprises, the situation ranges widely from despotic to relatively relaxed. Yet even the latter amounts to a setback for workers.

State Enterprises

Into the 1990s, relations between management and labor in many state-owned enterprises maintained affinities with the more egalitarian and participatory situations of the Maoist period. A worker in a state-owned accordion plant in Tianjin reported:

> There is no big social gap between workshop heads and workers. The workers don't fear them. Moreover, each workshop has several teams. The team heads are pretty much engaged in production full time—say, around 97 percent of the time. There is not much of a gap between them and the workers.

136 Kim, *China Labor*, 13.

137 Jaesok Kim, "From "Country Bumpkins" to "Tough Workers": The Pursuit of Masculinity Among Male Factory Workers in China," *Anthropological Quarterly* 88, no. 1 (Winter 2015), 146.

The team heads get the same wages as the workers, though they also get a slightly higher bonus. Workers supervise their own work.[138]

Such a pattern is more likely in work environments that, like this one, require highly trained personnel, of course. But even in plants demanding more moderate levels of skill, such as a welding equipment factory:

Workers don't need permission to go to the bathroom. This sort of thing happens more in some [foreign] joint venture plants…

Most people come to work on time. There's no problem if you show up late once in a while—you just settle it with the team head. Once in a while there are crackdowns, and they fine people.[139]

We complain to our factory manager all the time. Naturally, we don't go to their office to do it, but we just do it while joking with them in the plant. For example, some workers will be chatting in the factory, and if the boss comes over, we would just say that things should be done this way and not that way. We can speak very frankly. We raise suggestions to them. For example, our factory has two labs, both of which have lots of administrators and experimentation personnel; but they have nothing to do. No new products come out of there. The people who are supposed to be doing research there just sit around and play cards. We feel that the bosses should make them go do some other work, or at least close one lab and put them all together so the other building can be vacated and used for a factory or rented out. You know our factory has a great location, and the rent could pay some of our workers' salaries.[140]

Such free and easy relationships do not, of course, amount to worker democracy or even influence.

But the boss said he won't do it. He likes to have two laboratories around... We workers shouldn't have to pay for this. But the manager runs the factory like a patriarch. Our leaders are numbskulls (脑子比较僵化); they don't think flexibly.[141]

An older woman laid off from an oil filter factory in Tianjin reported:

We did criticize the leadership for its incompetence. We did this at the workers' representative assemblies. Discussions there are very free and open; you

138 Interview, June 30, 1996.
139 Interview, July 2, 1996.
140 Interview, May 25, 1999.
141 Interview, May 25, 1999.

> can speak frankly. We often raised opinions about issues such as the system and distribution of incentive pay. Moreover, there was a workshop head who was using his little bit of power to get some personal advantages from other factories with whom we dealt. We exposed this and criticized him, and he was fired. Yes, the factory leadership listened to workers' opinions at the workers representative assembly and took them seriously. After all, we elected them. But of course the power to make decisions is theirs. In general it was not fully democratic—the leadership still made the decisions—but it was not undemocratic either. It was semi-democratic.[142]

Yet while in general there were no vestiges of the participatory, much less confrontative, shop floor processes of Maoist days, in many state-owned enterprises inertia was still operating in workers' favor in the 1990s:

> In my former state factory, they are still "eating out of one big pot" (大锅饭). The main reason has to do with the workers' and the leaders' attitude. They have been doing this for a long time, so they're used to it. If they change it, they fear things could go bad. If you asked workers to work for piece rates, they just wouldn't do it.[143]

Moreover, workers were often able to exercise considerable control over the labor process even under the now ubiquitous piece rates. In the welding equipment factory,

> Workers on piece rates can earn ¥600–700 per month. The basic wage is ¥600. The other ¥100 can be earned by going over the quota. It's not too hard to get to the extra ¥100...When the weather is hot, workers just make the basic quota and stop.
>
> There's an informal maximum set by workers in opposition to rate busters.
>
> When there are rush jobs, and the workshop director wants to increase production, he raises the basic quota. To compensate for that, he also raises the bonus piece rate. No, he would never just lower the basic piece rate. In doing this, the workshop director takes the workers' reaction into account. He only sets a quota that can be reached.
>
> [Q:] Why?
>
> Mainly he considers the needs and conditions of production. He knows what the feasible maximum is.

142 Interview, June 10, 1999.
143 Interview, July 9, 1996.

[Q:] But wouldn't there be uncertainty about the maximum, especially with your factory's new equipment?

No. He can just check with other plants about the capacity of the new equipment.

The fact that we are all neighbors and co-workers is not a major reason he doesn't jack up the rates higher. It does have something to do with the fact that this is a socialist country, so you can't squeeze the workers too much.

These quota and rate increases for rush jobs are not intended as trial runs for a general change in the rates.

The first-line production workers have kitties.[144] The team heads know about this, and they don't mind. They are pretty close to the workers. The workshop head may know about them too, but he may not, since he's not on the production floor. But in either case he doesn't use the existence of the kitties to try to raise the quota. Of course the workers don't want to put too much into their kitties, as a hedge against this happening. The workers will occasionally help each other out by loaning each other pieces from their kitties.[145]

In the oil filter plant:

Workers understood that they should not overfulfill the quota too much, or else the quota would be raised. There was a small majority who overfulfilled quite a bit. Yes, we looked down on them and *vice versa*. Most workers just meet the quota and then stop.

Workers also kept kitties for their own use in case they got sick or ran into other problems, or to help out fellow workers.[146]

All this helped contribute to feelings that "the factory is like our home" (以厂为家), which continued to prevail in some state-owned enterprises at least through the late 1990s.[147]

Yet piece rates can also produce conflict among workers.

Although our salary is calculated by piece rates, if you examine it, there's definitely no one getting more than ¥1,400. There's a limit on how much you

144 These are small caches of products that workers keep rather than turn in to the factory, as a hedge against machinery breakdown, input shortages, illness or other problems that they may experience. Workers often loan fellow-workers products from their kitties as well. For a discussion of their significance, see Michael Burawoy, *Manufacturing Consent: Changes in the Labor Process under Monopoly Capitalism* (Chicago: University of Chicago Press, 1979).

145 Interview, July 2, 1996.

146 Interview, June 10, 1999.

147 Interviews, July 2, 1996; July 3, 1996.

> can earn, but at the same time there's no limit on how low your salary can get. So a lot of workers only get less than ¥800 a month — 30 per cent get only ¥500 to ¥600… [A]mong the workers themselves, they often fight to get just one to two more machines in order to make a little more money (operating one machine brings in ¥4 more). Because of this competition there is often conflict between workers.[148]

Nonetheless, even in firms with such relatively favorable environments, worker–management relations have generally become more alienated and commodified compared with Maoist days.[149]

> Interpersonal relations were better in the 1950s, among workers and between workers and leaders. People treated the property of the factory as if it were their own. If someone tried to damage it, they would protect it. They also protected the reputation of the factory. If someone insulted the factory, they would come to its defense, and get angry. This was based mainly in political feelings.
>
> In those days, people were really happy when a police officer came around. Now they assume it means they did something wrong.
>
> People worked for both material and moral [精神] incentives then. But moral incentives were really a big deal then; much bigger than material ones. Today people just want the money.[150]
>
> Today, things are different. The nature of competition between workers has changed. People used to compete for promotions or bonuses, which provided incentives to work hard. Now, workers compete on the labor market for jobs. This doesn't contribute to labor activism [劳动积极性]. So I think there was more labor activism in the past despite the iron rice bowl.[151]
>
> In the past people really listened to the factory leadership. We were together in shared responsibility for meeting the quota sent down from the higher levels. We all took seriously our responsibility for meeting the quota; indeed, we wanted to meet it. At that time, people really listened to Mao and to the leadership. Now it's different. If the leadership wants workers to do more, it has to pay them more.[152]

148 Wong, *Voices From Below*, 105.

149 Eva P. W. Hung and Stephen W. K. Chiu, "Voices of *Xiagang*: Naming, Blaming and Framing," in Thomas B. Gold *et. al.*, eds., *Laid-off Workers in a Workers' State* (New York: Palgrave Macmillan, 2009), 108.

150 Interview, July 9, 1996.

151 Interview, June 8, 1999.

152 Interview, June 10, 1999.

Yet under the pressures of the newly competitive environment within which state-owned enterprises increasingly had to operate,[153] far more authoritarian and draconian labor-management relationships have also emerged. As early as 1993 and 1994, state-owned textile mills in Henan Province, far from the private-sector sweatshops in the southeast that get all the headlines, workers were doing forty hours per month of mandatory overtime at only standard pay. Explicitly Taylorist approaches were deployed, including the likes of the "full load method" in which quotas were set at the maximum of human exertion based on careful observation. As if that weren't enough, management then imposed further speedups.

> In order to improve productivity, some changes were made to the machines in January and the workshop has reorganized production since then. As a result, the workers' workload has been drastically increased. Before the change, two women attended one machine, sitting side by side, and their shift production quota was 36 rolls... Since January, only one woman has to look after the same machine, and she is expected to inspect 20 rolls, and twice, all in one shift. You see, her workload has been more than doubled! How do the workers like it? Of course, they hate it. But they have no choice. They have to do what they're told.[154]

Workers who did not measure up were not just docked, but publicly shamed. The following sign observed in a workshop was typical:

> A SERIOUS WARNING — 1,236 POINTS WILL BE DOCKED FROM OPERATOR WANG XIAOFENG'S WAGES THIS MONTH, DUE TO HER SUCCESSIVE BREACHES OF THE OPERATING INSTRUCTIONS... FOR EXAMPLE, SHE ALWAYS FAILED TO STAND AT THE RIGHT POSITION PRESCRIBED IN THE INSTRUCTIONS...[155]

Adding "Toyotism"[156] to Taylorism, management also expected workers to monitor each other's output, reducing its own workload and, of course, dividing the workforce.

153 Mary Gallagher, *Contagious Capitalism* (Princeton, NJ: Princeton University Press, 2001).

154 Minghua Zhao and Theo Nichols, "Management Control of Labour in State-Owned Enterprises: Cases From the Textile Industry," *The China Journal*, 36 (July 1996), 6.

155 Zhao and Nichols, "Management Control," 6.

156 Knuth Dohse, Ulrich Jürgens, and Thomas Malsch, "From 'Fordism' to 'Toyotism'? The Social Organization of the Labor Process in the Japanese Automobile Industry," *Politics & Society* 14, no. 2 (1985): 115–46.

> "Self-control", explains the manager, "means workers compete with and watch over one another for product defects... Before, workers depended on cadres for evaluation; now they depend on one another to compare, compete, and check."[157]

Plant physicians had quotas for the amount of sick-leave they can approve, and were docked for going over it, while ill workers lucky enough to land a day off received only 30 percent of their pay or in some cases nothing but a worthless ¥1 in "living expenses."[158]

In terms of pay, piece rates are almost universal now, except in production processes unsuited to them (such as assembly lines),[159] though even in those cases management often works to find a way to use piece rates or other forms of incentive pay.[160] But in the name of "flexibility," many workers have been subjected to constantly shifting quotas and formulae, to the point where they lose all expectation of understanding what they will earn and why. A worker in one of the Henan plants in the early 1990s reported:

> You never know how much money you will be given for the month. Your wage is calculated daily according to the specific task you conduct that day. The task changes constantly because of the constant change in products, which are determined by the constant changes in the market. They say that this is supposed to link our performance with our wages, and that it agrees with the socialist principle of fair distribution: to each according to their work. We don't know how the fairness is worked out. It's really confusing. We don't know how much money we can get at the end of the month.[161]

Workers' body movements and behavior were also tightly regulated, and infractions penalized.

1) not to spill food leftovers or tea on the shop floor – or 5 points off;
2) not to put things on lockers – or 5 points off;
3) not to have baths or showers during the shift – or 10 points off;
4) not to go to the workshop barefoot – or 2 points off;
5) not to be late to meetings – or 2 points off;
6) not to be late or absent from political-ideological study – or 5 points off.[162]

157 Zhao and Nichols, "Management Control," 9.
158 Ibid., 10–11.
159 Interview, July 3, 1996.
160 Interview, July 5, 1996.
161 Zhao and Nichols, "Management Control," 15.
162 Ibid., 18.

And Maoist labor emulation, which offered non-material rewards for improved labor performance, has been adapted to promote labor discipline and the production of surplus value. It now involves not just rewards (material or not) but also shaming.[163] And the material rewards are sometimes paid for by deductions from all workers' wages.[164]

The effects on the workers are, of course, devastating and go well beyond the physical. According to a doctor in one of the Henan plants,

> [T]here has been a sharp increase in cases of mental illness among the front-line workers. We have over fifty such patients. That's in a single mill. Most are women, because most of the women work as front-line machine operators. The number is much bigger than you would expect. As doctors, we are really concerned. This is absolutely abnormal. More seriously, it isn't something that is only happening in our factory. All the other cotton mill clinics in the city are finding the same thing.[165]

Private, Joint-Venture and Foreign-Invested Firms

As in state-owned enterprises, power on the shop floor in private, joint-venture and foreign-invested enterprises runs the gamut from the more relaxed to the draconian. Yet in general a more frenetic pace and more authoritarian forms prevail outside the state sector.[166] As noted above, one state factory worker reported that "workers in our plant don't need permission to go to the bathroom. This sort of thing happens more in joint venture plants."[167] A comment of a young stock worker in a Japanese-owned electrical products factory in Tianjin was typical: "The work is more tiring than in the state-owned enterprise where I used to work."[168]

On the more salutary end of the spectrum, many workers in such plants report a relatively easygoing relationship with their management. A worker in a formerly state-owned Tianjin electrical implements plant that had become a Sino-American joint venture in 1994 described a relationship between management and the workers that was relatively unchanged from its former days.

> Workers talk all the time about how they think the plant should be run—on the shop floor, in talking to each other, and in talking to the managers. In our plant they said that when it entered into its joint venture, the workers were

163 Ibid., 9–10.
164 Interview, July 5, 1996.
165 Zhao and Nichols, "Management Control," 21.
166 Interview, June 18, 2002.
167 See p. 123.
168 Interview, May 24, 1997.

> not consulted, which is why things haven't gone well. They're not afraid to tell the managers this sort of thing.[169]

Yet the opposite can also be true in privatized state firms.

> Workers in enterprises like ours which used to be state-owned and later reshaped into private ownership were not treated as well as workers in enterprises that were private from the start. Those enterprises were still in the development stage and they had high demands on their workers. They could only keep their badly needed employees by paying them better while the workers in the reformed enterprises were severely exploited. They had to suppress their anger and remain silent, since most of them worked on the production line and were not competitive in the employment market due to their lack of special skills. The enterprise considered them a burden and would do whatever it took to drive them out. As soon as they reached 40 years of age they would be either transferred to the service department of the enterprise or sent back home on a long "holiday."[170]

Calvin Chen's longitudinal study of two private electrical implements companies in Wenzhou bears out at least part of this account. It traces a trajectory from patriarchal to draconian forms of management power. When the firms were new and struggling to survive, "the managerial signature emphasized a collectively oriented spirit of cooperation as well as the wide-scale sharing of benefits."[171] Management worked on the shop floor alongside workers, fostering "camaraderie and 'human feeling' (人情)." A plant manager put it thus:

> I don't like to use a tough, cold approach. If I have a problem with a worker, I call that person into my office and we talk. I discuss the problem and ask how the worker feels. It's a discussion, not a scolding… If you think the worker is here to serve the factory and the factory has no need to serve the worker, the factory will eventually fail. You can't go around ordering people to do whatever you want them to do.[172]

This produced "a rough sense of egalitarianism and fairness within the enterprise." Quotidian interactions between management and workers were informal, and they socialized outside the factory. But this patriarchal approach did not preclude conflict. "Workers grumbled about unpaid back wages and the long overtime hours they were asked to work." But when they did, they also eventually accepted management's explanations and reassurances.[173]

169 Interview, June 8, 1999.
170 Wong, ed., *Voices From Below*, 100.
171 Chen, *Some Assembly Required*, 74.
172 Ibid., 76.
173 Ibid., 79–80.

Yet as the firms began to expand, paternalistic authority eventually gave way to a much more, and much more oppressive, bureaucratic authoritarian approach. A strict division of labor and Taylorist methods came into use, including an elaborate system of work rules and fines. "Enforcers" inspected the shop floor regularly. Managers' private discussions with errant workers gave way to public shaming and even collective punishment for the entire line (in the form of significant fines) if those responsible for production snafus could not be identified. Workers who in the early days used to go along with management demands for intensive work for the sake of the enterprise (in whose welfare they of course had a material stake) now began to resist through slowdowns and spreading salacious gossip.[174]

This account of his boss by a young stock worker in a Japanese-owned electrical products factory in Tianjin was typical of China's new private factories.

> The biggest problem in the plant is that the Chinese shop floor manager curses the workers when they don't do what he wants. They have no recourse but to take it, since he can fire you if you argue with him.

Strict physical controls are also common.

> I am not allowed to talk to fellow workers while on the job, except about work-related matters. But we do so anyway, secretly in whispers.[175]

Chen describes a Wenzhou private firm that demanded military-style boot camp for new employees.[176] Some factories also endeavor to control workers' personal behavior on and off the shop floor, such as draconian prohibitions against "crass speech and vulgar behavior," smoking and sex.[177]

And as in the more abusive state-owned enterprises such as the Henan plants discussed above, management often works to increase piece rate quotas, producing a complex game of push and pull which it wins although workers can sometimes, as in this case, find ways to slow the process and set an upper limit at least in the short run.

> We have a simple quota system: you have to make a set quota. If you overfulfill it, you don't get any bonus, but if you don't make the quota you have to stay until you make it. The quota can be reached, but it's getting harder. The manager has raised it little by little over two years from 30 units/hour

174 Ibid., 101–116.
175 Interview, May 24, 1997.
176 Chen, *Some Assembly Required*, 77–78.
177 Ibid.

> to 43. It has been cat and mouse: the manager would raise the quota, and the workers would refuse to meet it, just working to the old quota. They just kept working at the old quota rate. This was not a formally organized strategy, but just something all the workers understood and did. Because it's an assembly line, each person on the line can affect all the workers down the line. But this way it was hard for the management to tell which worker was slowing things down, because everyone did slow down a little. He wanted to raise it further, but the workers resisted. Still, over my two-and-a-half years he has managed to raise the quota quite a lot. At this point, the work is pretty intense.[178]

It is in the private sector—and especially the export-oriented plants of the southeast—that China's worst sweatshop conditions have been found. Migrant workers have been incinerated in factories lacking the most rudimentary safety equipment.

> In 1994 ninety-three were killed and 160 injured in a Zhuhai textile factory when a fire led to the collapse of the building. In 1993 eighty-seven women died in the Zhili toy factory fire in Shenzhen, China. At Dongguan, a raincoat factory burned in 1991 and killed seventy-two people. Also in 1993, a textile plant fire killed sixty-one women in Fuzhou province.[179]

Such deaths also result from predatory management control of workers.

> Eighty-one people died on Friday when fire swept through a doll factory with locked doors and windows near the southeastern China city of Shenzhen, trapping hundreds of workers in the smoke-filled building, officials said.
>
> Smoke rather than flames was the major killer and most of the victims died of suffocation in the factory, officials said. Thirty-one people were injured.
>
> "During the fire, most of the doors and windows were locked to keep people inside the factory during working hours," said the spokesman for the municipal government of Shenzhen.[180]

Draconian control takes many oppressive if non-lethal forms as well. Factory regulations often prohibit all forms of socializing on the job,[181] forbid work-

178 Interview, May 24, 1997.
179 William Greider, "Global Agenda," *The Nation*, January 13, 2000.
180 "Fire Ravages a Doll Factory In Southern China, Killing 81," *New York Times*, November 20, 1993. This incident is redolent of the infamous Triangle Shirtwaist fire in lower Manhattan in 1911, whose legacies included a major boost to the labor movement, the passage of progressive legislation to protect workers' safety, and the development of the New York Fire Department.
181 Interview, May 24, 1999.

ers from leaving their dorms after work,[182] require them to get permits to leave the plant, and much more. Workers who seek redress for grievances or injuries have been kept imprisoned by their employers.[183] Harsh punishments are levied for infractions, such as fines of three days' pay for lateness[184] and immediate dismissals for making a phone call during work.[185] While workers

182 Interview, September, 2002.

183 Interview 7C/113–, October 29, 2002; 7B/8–113, September 2002.

184 Interview, September, 2002.

185 This set of rules is common:

Production regulations

1. Workers should do all preparations such as wearing work cap, electronic prevention belt, gloves, and so forth five minutes before the on-work time. To prevent any dirt on the products, no one is allowed to comb their hair or do anything that may cause dust or dirt. Each violation is fined 2 yuan.

2. All workers should obey the production arrangements of the higher authorities. If anyone has a different opinion, complete the job first before seeking out the authorities.

3. Workers are not allowed to leave work positions or change work position (*sic*) during work time unless approved by the supervisors. If leaving the work position for personal reasons such as going to [the] toilet the worker must apply for an out-of-position permit. Each violation is fined 2 yuan.

4. No one will be allowed to leave the factory unless there is a company exit permit signed by the affiliated department manager and the personnel department and examined by the security guard before leaving the factory. Leaving the factory without permission will be seriously punished and each violation is fined 50 yuan.

5. Punching a timecard for others or asking another person to punch a timecard for you is prohibited. The first time of violation will be given [a] serious warning and fined 20 yuan; the second time will be fined 100 yuan and the worker will be dismissed at once.

6. All workers must arrive at work on time. Arriving over five minutes late will be counted as late for one hour, while wages will be deducted at two hours rate (*sic*).

Daily behavior regulations

1. No talking, eating, playing, chasing, or fighting is allowed on the shop floor.

2. No dumping waste and no spitting. Each violation is fined 5 yuan.

3. Receiving or making personal phone calls is not allowed. If discovered, no matter how long the call, the worker will be immediately dismissed and all wages deducted.

4. For stealing factory property the worker will be dismissed at once and fined 50 to 500 yuan. If the case is serious, the offender will be sent to the Public Security Bureau.

5. The normal period of wear for an overall is one year. If one requires a new overall, there should be a reasonable explanation; otherwise, 50 yuan will be deducted from the wage.

6. The normal period of wear for a pair of work shoes is eight months. If there is unreasonable damage, 12 yuan will be deducted from the wage.

Job leave and resignation regulations

1. No job leave unless there is permission from the line leader, foreman, and department manager. A leave permit should be signed by all of them and then sent to the personnel department for approval. The leave permit should then be signed by the applicant to make it effective. Otherwise, all leave will be considered as absence.

2. For those who are ill or on personal leave who cannot attend overtime work, prior permission should be gained and the proper procedures completed. Otherwise, all such leave will be considered as absence. Absence for one night of overtime work will be deducted half a day's wage, absence for one day will be deducted three days of wages.

have derived a modicum of relief from the fact that these rules were not always tightly enforced, they have often been subjected to a much spookier panopticon using surveillance cameras, which cause more anxiety precisely because workers have no way of knowing how the devices are being used.[186] Significant levels of forced overtime[187] and corporal punishment are not uncommon.[188] Neither are violations of regulations designed to protect workers from pollution and injury.[189] To the government's credit, such matters are reported with some regularity in China's own press,[190] and the government has passed impressive legislation against them (such as the 1995 Labor Law). But it has proven unwilling or unable to enforce its own laws with anything close to the level required to bring the problem under control.

In enterprises with large numbers of young migrant women, patriarchy permeates and intensifies factory power relations. In such plants, management and especially skilled technical and staff are heavily male, while line workers are predominantly female. In one electronics factory, even the most capable female workers chosen as deputy line leaders were no match for the rest of the (male) management. One male boss admitted:

> It is difficult to find the right people for leaders among the line girls. Girls are so talkative when they crowd together. But at work, they are so timid and afraid to criticize others.[191]

And the fact that the gender-based division of labor produces significant functional and pay differentials[192] of course only reinforces the patriarchal nature of power relationships in the factory.

---

3. Absence for two days will be deducted six days of wages. Continuous absence for three days will be considered as voluntary leave and all salary voluntarily given up.

4. Basic workers who intend to resign should give notice fifteen days before leaving; staff should give one month's notice. Otherwise, wages will be deducted for fifteen days.

5. For those new workers and staff who resign before completing two months of work, seven days of wages will be deducted for training costs.

Pun, *Made in China*, 101–102.

186 Ibid., 106–107. Chen also reports the lack of draconian enforcement as well as the use of surveillance (Chen, *Some Assembly Required*, 77, 110).

187 See p. 97.

188 Interviews, 7C/T113–, September 2002; October 29, 2002; January 12, 2003.

189 Interviews, 2002–2003; Anita Chan, *China's Workers Under Assault* (Armonk, NY: M.E. Sharpe, 2001).

190 For just two examples, see "Nine arrested for fatal factory fire in south China," *People's Daily*, September 28, 2008; "At least 65 die in textile factory fire," *China Daily*, February 25, 2006.

191 Pun, *Made in China*, 149.

192 Ibid.

Summary

Overall, then, factory power relations and shop floor politics in Chinese industry are growing more authoritarian and alienated. For the first two decades of structural reform, many state and collective enterprises continued to be home to a somewhat more reciprocal or balanced relationship between labor and management. But into the new century they have gradually adopted the more bureaucratic, alienated and draconian approach pioneered by private, joint-venture, and foreign-owned firms. The latter have incubated some of the most dreadful factory conditions in the world. The influx of young women into industrial labor has augmented the process, adding a distinctly patriarchal element. In general, then, China's working class is experiencing increasingly oppressive workplace power relations.

...

Structural reform, starting cautiously in 1978 and ramping up in the early 1990s, radically reconstituted the social world of China's working class. In overall size, the proletariat went on a roller coaster, expanding faster than any working class in history through 1993, then shrinking even faster until 2002 to levels below the end of the Maoist era, and beginning a more moderate expansion and subsequent decline since then. All this entailed dramatic changes in who the workers were and are and where they have worked. Tens of millions of urban-resident workers were laid off, an unknowably large proportion consigned to lives without any further work at all. They were replaced by an even larger influx of rural migrants—mostly young people, a large minority of whom were female. They were getting their first experience of industrial work, which they preferred to rural life despite often being subjected to the most dreadful employment in economic, social and political terms. In a stunning development, by the early years of the new century these migrants comprised a large majority of China's working class. Though they were better educated than the villagers they left, they were less well educated than many of the older urban workers they replaced or the younger urbanites who managed to join the working class when they did.

The tight overlap of workplace and home provided by the "work unit" has been broken apart by the structural reforms, though it has been replaced in a monstrous form by dormitory housing for young, unmarried workers in large plants. In many cases, the old state-owned enterprises closed, leaving people as neighbors but no longer co-workers, and often as hard-core unemployed. In many other cases where factories remain open, their housing stock has been privatized, demolished or both, scattering co-workers to neighborhoods far and wide. The close social bonds produced by the "work unit" and the Maoist-era urban working class's high level of social homogeneity have been further broken apart by unemployment, an increasingly stratified status hierarchy, an ever more elaborate and technologically diverse division of labor, the increasingly regional, national and international reach of labor markets, and the deepening cleavage between urban workers (employed and unemployed) and rural migrants.

Finally, both urban workers and to an even greater degree rural migrants have found themselves in a world of increasingly authoritarian management power, where draconian rules and punishments are meted out and there is little recourse when frequent abuses take place. With the continuing decline of state-owned enterprises that were once home to a rather different pattern of workplace authority and power, and the continuing pressures of the market economy for ever higher profit, this trend is more likely to strengthen than to abate.

How have Chinese workers come to understand these profound changes, and transformed their understanding of themselves?

Cultural Aspects of the Fall of the Working Class

Structural reform produced a second sea-change in the ways Chinese workers understand themselves, the forces acting on them and the possibilities before them. Gone is the oppositional, workerist sensibility of the radical state socialist decades. It has been replaced by several distinct, complex ways of thinking, each of which is loosely associated with specific sets of material and social conditions that tend to prevail in particular regions of the country. In the rust-belts of the northeast and inland areas with "third front" factories, where unemployment has gone sky high and opportunities for reemployment have been minimal, the largely unemployed working class has developed a desperate, moralistic, nostalgic focus on bare subsistence. Where unemployment is lower and the labor market more lively, as in northern and central China, workers tend to evince a commitment to muddling through, blaming the victims, including themselves, if they fail. Under still better employment conditions, such as the central and eastern coast, both employed and unemployed workers have by and large accepted the hegemony of the market and the state that have undermined the working class's elevated position. Rural migrant workers' thinking, which in Maoist days featured assertive outrage at their inferior economic and social status *vis-à-vis* their urban co-workers, has been transformed into a fatalistic, and by turns depressed and self-sacrificing sensibility that is now focused on abusive factory managers rather than, as in the Maoist period, the state and the structural gap between rural and urban institutions it had established. Overall, then, the working class's consciousness has become much more variegated, divided, complex, introverted and apolitical.

Rustbelt Atavism

Where the great heavy industries that were the pride of China's import-substitution industrialization in the 1950s and 1960s have been shuttered with little or nothing to replace them, unemployed and even some still employed workers' sensibility begins with a wistful look backward to those better days, which in each respect they compare favorably to the situation after structural reform. Workers remember themselves as honest, conscientious, assiduous and earnest (老老实实).[193]

> In my day, workers worked to serve the country. At that time, people's labor activism was higher than now—really. Yes, there were lazy people then, but very few. The pace of work was harder, and people exhausted themselves more at work. This was not due to pressure from leadership—it was due to the workers' attitudes toward work and the atmosphere in the factory. Nowadays people's thinking is more chaotic. They are not clear who they work for: the country, the factory, their children, the factory leadership, or themselves. If workers only consider themselves, there's no way for the enterprise to do well.[194]
>
> Workers did work hard in those days despite the iron rice bowl. That's because there was some genuine competition: among wage grades and for bonuses, both of which were limited. In addition, people really were enthusiastic about building up the plant and the country. There was lots of propaganda about this, and on the whole it fit people's life experiences. People looked down on slackers. Moreover, there was genuine participation in factory affairs: in awarding bonuses and in criticizing bad behavior among cadres. At that time, the best thing was to be a worker. It was even better than being a cadre. Today, things are different. The nature of competition among workers has changed. People used to compete for promotions or bonuses, which provided incentives to work hard. Now, workers compete on the labor market for jobs. This doesn't make people more assiduous. So I think there was more enthusiasm for work in the past despite the iron rice bowl.[195]

Workers recall wistfully that relative equality prevailed, both among workers as well as between them on the one hand and factory and party officials on the other. Incomes were low, and life was simple, but workers enjoyed security of employment and social provision. "Society was stable and the masses had a sense of purpose."[196]

193 Hung and Chiu, "Voices of *Xiagang*," 96.
194 Interview, June 29, 1996.
195 Interview, June 8, 1999.
196 Lee, *Against the Law*, 144.

> Our old factory director was very concerned about workers' welfare. For women workers in particular we had a clinic — they distributed sanitary napkins to women — a nursery, a mess hall, a factory bus, a barber shop, a workers' culture palace [a Mao-era institution for movie screenings and other cultural events]...When the new director came, there was nothing left. Now I understand what *exploitation* means. We are really pitiful. In the old days, if you needed housing, the factory would give you housing. Now, no single apartment has been built. Mine is a three-person household and we still cannot buy our own apartment unit... Gradually, all kinds of power the masses had under Mao have been taken away bit by bit.
>
> In the past, when my kid was sick or my family had financial difficulty, I went to the union chair. He would study the problem and come back to me with allowances. This is gone now. Our Workers' Congress has not had a meeting in years. The union chair works only for the director who appoints him. Workers have no protective gear on the shop floors, no working shoes, antitoxic masks, soap or towels, nothing. They cannot even reimburse you 50 percent of your medical expenses. In the days of Mao, no matter how poor, the factory could not ignore you when you got sick. Now, without money, you just wait for death when you get sick.[197]

Workers were also given the opportunity to become educated and develop skills.[198]

> The current system in our country slights skills. When we first joined the factory [in 1970], we spent many hours taking skill classes. Every Monday, Wednesday, and Friday, every week, in the evening we stayed in the factory after work to learn systematically different types of welding, different raw materials and their mixture, and how to read blueprints. These days, when young workers come in, they know nothing and learn nothing in the factory. Our country is regressing...When the Chairman [Mao] was alive, poor students who really wanted to go to school and did well would get scholarships. It was a way to preserve the strength and quality of our nation. Now, without money, you cannot send your child to school.[199]

Education and skill enabled workers develop *esprit de corps*, to feel part of something larger than themselves, to be willing to sacrifice, to take pride in their work and their contribution to the country, and to be confident and fulfilled as human beings.

197 Lee, *Against the Law*, 142.
198 Ibid., 143.
199 Ibid., 143.

> I felt particularly excited and content because I could learn new technologies. I was very hard-working…At that time, production was for our country, for building socialism. I had a very advanced mentality. [Interviewer: Was it only a slogan?] It's what the slogan said, but it's also my genuine feeling. We were very different from young people today.[200]

> At that time, we did not consider rewards. We just had faith. The more difficult the production task, the more willingly we worked…Once a fire broke out in the factory. I took the lead in fighting it. I was not afraid…Now, no more. I don't care if I make substandard products, because the factory defaults on my wage payments. It's natural that we are producing many rejected goods because no one feels responsible for their work. What a contrast with the past, when we volunteered to study how to improve production.[201]

> Even in the early 1960s, when we had to endure hunger, we did not complain… We had to do voluntary labor. Perhaps because we were young and strong, we never complained. It was something we "should" do. I saw my father working in the factory continuously during the Great Leap Forward and coming home to rest only once every two weeks. He did not get extra pay… Workers became lazy and calculating only after the Cultural Revolution. When bonuses were introduced, workers became reluctant to work if the bonus was small. People also had more conflicts with one another on how to distribute bonuses.[202]

There is also a strong and distinctly (if not consciously) Marxist sense among older present and former state industry workers that the industrial achievements of the Maoist period were very much products of their own labor. This produces feelings of pride, but also both rightful credit for creating their factories and identification with the state, which formally owns them. What Ching Kwan Lee terms "[t]his extraordinarily deep and unique 'class feeling'" helps fuel outrage when state firms are put into bankruptcy; the assets being liquidated are, many workers feel, *theirs*, and their losses are nothing less than exploitation in the sense of appropriation of the product of their labor. And when they protest they feel they are protecting not just their own economic class interests but also those of the state.[203]

To workers' minds, the shop floor transformations and expropriations wrought by structural reform have not just happened unintentionally or resulted from inexorable structural forces. On the contrary, they represent a betrayal. At the famous Daqing protests of 2002,[204] laid-off workers complained bitterly.

200 Ibid.,146.
201 Ibid.,143.
202 Ibid., 145.
203 Ibid., 91.
204 See p. 166 *ff.*

> [When we were persuaded to apply for our layoff buyout,] we were completely cheated. No wonder everyone is so angry now.[205]
>
> Workers in the Daqing Oilfield have made a great contribution to the country, earning it tens of billions [of *yuan*] every year. But they simply sold out the senior workers. I mean, we were cheated.[206]

The theme of officials being bad parents—a particularly profound and damning accusation in China's still "Confucian" culture—is common.

> Everyone needs someone to back them up. We bring up children hoping they will look after us when we are old. If we didn't need to be backed up, we wouldn't have to bother having children… It's a socialist country, so there should be somebody to take care of us.[207]
>
> We simply became lambs to be slaughtered. We are like the children deprived of mothers.[208]

Moreover, the betrayal involved trickery. This last worker continued:

> The government is brainwashing us every day. Who believes their propaganda?!
>
> The workers are brainwashed, blindfolded and fooled. Officials use their authority selfishly to obtain benefits for themselves.[209]
>
> They cheated us to agree to layoffs, and then made policies to fool us.[210]
>
> If we knew they were going to change the policy, we would not have agreed in the first place.[211]

Yet some also blame themselves for being gullible or naïve, feeling they should have known.

> The sly and cunning would have left the enterprise long ago, or they would have profited, like the managers, by taking advantage of the enterprise. It was the workers, the honest and simple-minded, who thought of nothing but their loyal service to the enterprise, who were met with the fate of [being laid off].[212]

205 Interview, March 2002.
206 Interview, March 2002.
207 Interview, March 2002.
208 Wong, *Voices from Below*, 102.
209 Interview, March 2002.
210 Interview, March 2002.
211 Interview, March 2002.
212 Hung and Chiu, "Voices of Xiagang," 105.

Their palpable anger is mixed with heavy doses of depression.

> I felt very depressed after being laid off two years ago. I just stay at home, feeling depressed. I had worked more than twenty years, after all. After I was laid off, I felt completely aimless.[213]

> [In the past] my heart felt balanced and relaxed. [Now] I cannot feel the bottom of my heart. In the past, I never felt this empty inside… "Eating from one big pot"[214] may not be good for our country's development, and it impoverished and exhausted workers, but psychologically we felt better.[215]

> Look at the suffering and pain we tens of thousands of workers have to endure! Some threw themselves on the railroad and got killed, some hung themselves, some went insane.[216]

> Now everyone says, "This is so meaningless."[217]

> Leaving the enterprise was equal to committing suicide.[218]

> We can just simply kill ourselves when we think we can't live any longer.[219]

> I heard about one family with an income of only around 200 RMB a month. The parents couldn't even buy steamed bread for their children, so the whole family committed suicide together.[220]

The word "pitiful" keeps coming up in workers' self-descriptions.

> We are a pitiful lot in the city.[221]
>
> How can a technical employee of the best-equipped factory in China become so pitiful?[222]

Like the downtrodden in so many places, many also feel shame.

> I have a neighbor, a laid-off worker, whose wife divorced him. He cannot work because of his illness, so he can only live on the dole. Seriously, who

213 Interview, June 18, 2002.
214 A slogan—吃大锅饭—denoting state socialist egalitarianism and social provision.
215 Lee, *Against the Law*, 141–2.
216 Daqing protest leaflet, quoted in Wong, *Voices from Below*, 119.
217 Lee, *Against the Law*, 143.
218 Wong, *Voices from Below*, 100.
219 Interview, March 2002.
220 Wong, *Voices from Below*, 79.
221 Lee, *Against the Law*, 199.
222 Ibid., 150. See also p. 138.

> wants to go on the dole? It's such a shameful thing! It is not a free gift. In order to get it, you have to go clean public places, or go to serve in government-sponsored activities, and you are frequently called in to be educated about how to reshape your life.[223]

All this adds up to feelings of powerlessness (弱势群体), a term that has entered common parlance. Once again, this starts with the past. In Maoist days management may have been autocratic, but it was not systemically mired in ruinous corruption; moreover its highhandedness could be dealt with through Party-led efforts to develop new, more participatory factory politics. Workers had *power*, but no longer.

> The most important thing is that today's workers have no power, the power that Mao gave workers, the power to criticize the director and write big-character posters.[224]
>
> Everyone here says this: our lives would be so much better if there were still struggle meetings and political campaigns…Back then [in Mao's time], we masses had a weapon against corrupt cadres. Many people miss mass campaigns. People always say these cadres would have been criticized and executed many times over now for the amount of their graft.[225]
>
> "The working class takes leadership in everything" was a popular slogan under Mao and now workers bitterly and self-mockingly describe their situation by turning the claim into "Everything leads the working class."[226]

This toxic combination of depression and feelings of powerlessness leaves most rustbelt workers not just pessimistic, but hopeless.

> Now we're all just donkeys, harnessed, and day and day [*sic*] pushing to grind the mill. You want to get out of the harness, but it's completely impossible.[227]

Urban Working Class Hegemony

Outside China's rustbelts, and even in them to some extent, many workers, including the unemployed and those in economic straits, broadly accept the basic values of the state and the structural reforms it has fostered.

> Enterprises' development should not all proceed the same way. I support reform. It is necessary. Competition is right.

223 Wong, *Voices from Below*, 89.
224 Lee, *Against the Law*, 144.
225 Ibid., 119.
226 Ibid.,114.
227 Wong, *Voices from Below*, 103.

This sentiment was surprising coming from a 47-year-old worker whose building materials factory was economically endangered, who was not readily re-employable, and who also had serious complaints:

> Competition is right. But what should we do about the workers in bankrupt enterprises? I think the government should have a policy to guarantee the workers' basic livelihood. There are lots of things about which I am dissatisfied. I go to work every day, and make contributions to the factory, but my wages are so low. My wife goes out to work, and together the two of us try to support our family. But we barely have enough to eat, and can't save anything. Our life is pretty tight. The factory leaders ought to have some sympathy for the workers, but they're not like that.[228]

One sea-change for workers brought about by structural reform occurred when, starting in the middle to late 1980s, their wages and livelihoods became dependent on the economic health of their particular enterprise rather than on the state more broadly. As enterprises became more fully independent economically, for the first time workers in prosperous firms experienced higher wages, better employment security, and more ample benefits than those in economically struggling firms. For workers, the economic health of their enterprise was often a matter of the luck of the draw. If they happened to find themselves in a sector that was faring badly, or in a plant with particularly incompetent management, they would lose out, often seriously, compared with their more fortunate fellows. *Prima facie*, this new economic structure provided an objective material basis for a sense of injustice among workers on the losing end. Yet none of the workers I interviewed in Tianjin in the late 1990s had developed such sentiments. Whenever I raised the issue, most developed a puzzled, faraway look indicating that they had not thought about their circumstances quite that way before. It was difficult to get them to understand the changed situation to which I was inviting their reaction, even though they lived it on a daily basis.[229] The values of the market were hegemonic. When I succeeded in engaging a few with the possibility that they might have been subject to a kind of lottery in which some benefited from being assigned years ago to factories that now happened to be doing well while others suffered from unlucky assignments, the following responses were typical.

228 Interview, May 28, 1999.

229 "They do this without being aware of it..." Karl Marx, *Capital* Vol 1 (New York: Vintage, 1977), 166–167.

> Yes, I guess it's unfair that some people lose out simply because their enterprises are doing badly. I felt this. But I didn't express it. Partly this is because I saw that enterprises all over Tianjin were suffering. Mine wasn't the worst.[230]
>
> The change [from all workers being treated the same to some doing better and some doing worse because of the condition of their factories] happened in 1995. Yes, now that I think of it, this was a big change.[231]

As they thought about it and even admitted the unfairness, most nonetheless accepted it, grounding their acquiescence in the logic of the market.

> It's fair that factories that can sell their products should do better than those that cannot.
>
> [Q:] Is this really fair?
>
> No, I suppose it's not fair that the workers should have to suffer because of these differences.[232]

Somehow, the market principle was fair even though its consequences were not.

Once they began to think about the new enterprise-based inequalities among them, whom or what did workers hold responsible? Many drew a blank.

> In the 1970s all workers were paid around the same. Now the differences are pretty large. I do feel this is unfair. Some people earn too much money, and some earn too little. They are all workers, so why should the differences be so great? So ordinary people don't understand why the differences should be so great. I can't say whose responsibility this is. There are lots of ways of understanding this...
>
> I don't know why workers who do a good job have to be laid off...
>
> Maybe it's that the country is too large and overpopulated—I can't figure it out. There definitely are lots of unreasonable things going on. Ordinary people can't say clearly what's happening.[233]

> Yes, of course it's unfair that I worked for a factory that was doing poorly while others did not. I have a classmate who today has ¥100,000,000.
>
> [Q:] Who has responsibility for this?
>
> I don't blame the government. I just blame the situation (现象). But what can you do? Things are still better today than they were before the reforms started. Even those worse off than me would say so.[234]

230 Interview, June 10, 1999.
231 Interview, June 7, 1999.
232 Interview 2, May 25, 1999.
233 Interview, May 28, 2009.
234 Interview, May 29, 1999.

They interpreted the question of responsibility in terms of possible ameliorative efforts, not cause. This exchange is typical:

> No, it's not fair that the workers should have to suffer because of these differences.
> [Q:] Who is responsible for this suffering?
> The union is useless in this regard.
> [Q:] Is the government responsible?
> Yes, the government is responsible for assuring a livelihood for workers.

Tellingly, even here he let the state off the hook.

> But what can the government do? There are so many workers who are doing poorly that there is nothing the government can do about it.[235]

Underlying these responses is a strong sense of fatalism among many.

> Many workers just feel that they have a bad fate (命运), that they went through the wrong door (走错门)—*i.e.*, if they had joined another industry when they first started work, things would be alright.[236]

And the logical outcome of such thinking is passivity.

> There are so many workers who are doing poorly that there is nothing the government can do about it. There is no point in protesting.[237]
> We older workers would not make trouble. If we have opinions, we raise them to the higher levels, and after they investigate the government will take some measures to address the problem.[238]
> We were owed six months' accumulated wage arrears—not six months straight, but six months' altogether. Workers were unhappy about this, and some protested to the management—not to the government. But everyone knew that the factory didn't have money, so what's the point? I was too embarrassed to raise opinions about this.
> Yes, of course it's unfair. But if you don't accept it, you still have to accept it (你不接受夜得接受). There's no way around it (没办法).[239]

For this worker, the employment lottery was more like the weather than a policy of his government.

235 Interview 2, May 25, 1999.
236 Interview, May 25, 1999.
237 Interview 2, May 25, 1999.
238 Interview, May 28, 1999.
239 Interview, June 7, 1999.

For many other workers, though, the causes of their problems were clearer: poor management rather than government policy.

> The main responsibility for the factory's problems is the factory. The government's policy is to let everyone get rich. Whoever is capable will have food to eat. The government doesn't want to see factories do poorly, and doesn't want workers to lack for food. But some factory leaders' methods are mistaken. If you're a worker, what can you do? China's workers don't fear exhaustion, but only want to have work to do, to have hope. They are just afraid that their factory will not do well.
>
> In the past our leadership helped other districts build small factories. We gave them our technology free of charge. Now these factories' costs are lower than ours, because they have fewer people and because their business methods are very flexible. Whoever sells their products gets a commission; but our leaders never do this… So now our products don't have buyers.[240]
>
> Some workers in my plant did express their dissatisfaction about the factory's economic problems. Mainly it was people whose livelihoods were hurt most by the layoffs, and whose personalities were such that they would speak out. They sought out the plant leadership to complain. No one sought out the government. I didn't feel that the government has responsibility for solving this, since there are enterprises all over the city in this situation.[241] Moreover, the reason for the problem wasn't the government, but the enterprise leadership, which wasn't too smart.[242]
>
> Even those who are doing poorly after being laid off do not hold the government responsible for their welfare. They hold their enterprises responsible, and they think that the government's responsibility is limited only to making sure that enterprises live up to policies. You can't hold the government responsible; there are so many laid-off workers, and the government can't support them all. Workers generally know this.[243]

The scale of the damage that structural reform did to the working class did not stimulate workers to think of equally large-scale political causes in government policy, but rather to let the government off the hook. A small number did blame local government officials.

> Yes, of course, it's unfair that my wages are lower and I have to endure wage arrears just because I happen to work in a plant that is not doing well.

240 Interview 2, May 25, 1999.

241 Of course, the ubiquity of the problem could very well suggest precisely the opposite conclusion—which suggests the operation of market and/or state hegemony.

242 Interview, June 10, 1999.

243 Interview, June 7, 1999.

> [Q:] Does the state have responsibility?
>
> The state's policies are good. It's the implementation that is no good. Sometimes middle-level officials mess things up...
>
> Some people just turn bad after becoming officials.[244]

> I still think Deng [Xiaoping] is good. It's just that many of the people below him are not so good—*i.e.*, they are just out for themselves.
>
> [Q:] But isn't such behavior an inevitable result of the market, which Deng brought in?
>
> Yes, it's a contradiction.[245]

Yet of course holding local officials responsible is a different matter from blaming the government, and in most cases is, on the contrary, a way of insulating it and depoliticizing the question—*i.e.*, evidence of state hegemony.

These workers' penchant for hegemonic thinking in terms of the inevitability and implacability of the market rather than any underlying political causes is reflected too in their behavioral responses.

> Yes, of course it's unfair that some workers lose out just because their factories are doing badly. But most workers think that the way to deal with the inequality is to try to make more money for themselves... At first, most workers were afraid of being laid off. But then after it happened most found out that it wasn't so bad; that they could make do in various ways. Many are better off now... Most workers in my old plant found some way to make a living. You have to eat, after all. Some go into petty business, some find jobs on the labor market.[246]
>
> All the laid-off workers in my plant found other work making about what they made before or more.[247]

Others said that workers' dependence on their ailing firms increased labor incentives.

> If the plant does badly, people know they won't have work to do. So everyone works hard. When there's a lot of work in the plant, people go all out.[248]

Workers thought such economic reactions far more advisable than political ones.

244 Interview, May 28, 1999.
245 Interview 2, May 25, 1999.
246 Interview, June 7, 1999.
247 Interview, June 8, 1999.
248 Interview, May 28, 1999.

> I have heard that some workers create disturbances. But there's no use in doing so. The workers in our factory have not done so. Every worker is trying to think of a way to make money, to change their position. If you create a disturbance, you can't make much money.[249]

Those who do think politically are pessimistic.

> Now it's just a matter of the [factory] director having complete control. The present leadership is more like a mafia group…The workers have no security or power and the future is bleak.[250]

Quantitative Analysis

Quantitative research corroborates these findings, which are based, after all, on overwhelming but nonetheless anecdotal evidence.[251] Reconstructive, Q- and factor-analytic methodologies underpinned a questionnaire I designed probing underlying patterns of thought at the turn of the century among a snowball sample of Tianjin workers. They were presented with phrases drawn from their own quotidian discursive universe (the "reconstructive" method) and asked to agree or disagree on a seven-point scale. Their responses were analyzed in a way that sought out *the pattern of relationships among their responses* (the "Q" method and factor analysis) rather than simply looking at their attitudes on individual items (the common survey approach, known as the "R" method). Three main patterns, which could be thought of as distinct world views, emerged. Each is coherent but also complex and nuanced, involving incompletely resolved contradictions.

Market Socialism

Emerging most strongly from the factor analysis was a world-view that could be called "market socialism." It appreciates the value of the market and the political relations behind it both in the enterprise and the wider state, while still retaining a commitment to some core socialist values. Workers should remain "masters of the enterprise," but it's no longer clear if they actually are. Workers are responsive to the needs of their firms even though those are now understood to be significantly market-oriented. While managers should give workers more leeway on the shop floor, management is also right to exert authority to keep

249 Interview 2, May 25, 1999.
250 Philion, *Workers' Democracy*, 108.
251 This section summarizes the findings in Marc Blecher, "What—and How—Have Tianjin Workers Been Thinking?" *Journal of Chinese Political Studies* XIII, no. 3 (October 2008): 249–267.

indolent workers on their toes. Workers retain some capacity to resist egregious management demands such as unpaid overtime, though they also fear faulting the management. Workers believe, by contrast, that managers do not fear them, and in fact sometimes treat them as not fully human. They do not respect workers' knowledge and talent, and they are much more distant from workers than they should be.

The piece rate wage system is fair and consistent with socialism, and management does not generally abuse it. Markets are basically fair. They do bring unemployment, which is serious but unavoidable. Unemployment has weakened affected workers' attachment to their work units. They provide fewer benefits than before, though those still provided are distributed fairly. Yet workers should not rely too much on their work units for economic security. But for those still in work, the factory is still like a home (以厂为家) and an important locus of social life, even if it is the enterprise's bottom line that is now most important.

The market produces reasonably fair outcomes. It is only mildly unfair that workers' livelihoods now depend on the economic health of the enterprise in which they happen by sheer good or bad fortune to have found themselves when marketization was brought in in the late 1980s. Class does not determine people's life chances particularly strictly. Yet inequality is something of a problem, and it is undermining class solidarity. The working class's position in society is declining, and workers are exploited.

At the level of the state, policy and ideology, there is no alternative to state enterprise reform. Yet that need not mean the triumph of capitalism: socialism should be, and in fact is being, reformed, not abolished, which limits exploitation. Piece rate wage systems are consistent with the socialist principle of pay according to work. Yet unions do need to be stronger, and workers need more representation in the Party.

What, finally, of workers' politics? Normatively, it may be desirable and even possible, though disappointing in its actual practice. People, not just leaders, are responsible for what happens both to them and to society. Bureaucratism, which is still a problem, can be fought. Protests such as slowdowns are not particularly dangerous. Yet politics today is not too useful. Workers only complain, but lack consciousness to organize to address their complaints. The state has only the mildest fear of workers.

Realism/Workerism

This worldview combines "workerist" sensibilities with hardheaded pragmatism. Workers who think this way are realistic about the requisites and effects of China's structural economic reforms, but also think that workers have managed or can manage to stake out a place for themselves and moderate structural reform's effects somewhat. There are some limits on managerial authority. Like market socialist thinking, workers should be "masters of the enterprise"; unlike it, though, they actually still are to a significant degree. Social attitudes and relations bolster workers' capacity and autonomy. Unlike market socialism, management does fear the workers and does not treat them as mere labor power to be ordered about. The leaders do respect workers' talent and knowledge. In return, workers are more willing to sacrifice by doing unpaid overtime. They do not hope for more daily contact with factory leaders, though; to put it the other way around, they are more content with quotidian autonomy from their bosses. They do fear faulting the management, but notably less than under market socialism.

Markets are viewed as less fair than by the market socialist worldview. By contrast, though, the labor market in particular is reasonably fair—a place where workers can receive their due. Realism/workerism is much milder in attributing unemployment to reform. Workers should seek their own benefit by following the market. Therefore, unemployment is not a big worry even though state benefits are insufficient to allay concerns about it. Compared with market socialism, here workers need retain even less loyalty to their state or collective firms now that employment security and benefits are gone. Wage differentials are not too great, and do not undermine working class unity. Perhaps partly for this reason, wage differentials based on the economic health of the firm are not particularly unfair.

Piece rates are fair. Quotas may be set high, but workers can find ways to reduce the pace of work. Nevertheless, some level of labor discipline does help prod lazy workers and, therefore, improves the factory. Workers' spirit of commitment to shop floor cooperation was greater in the 1960s than it is today, but the gap is not as great as the market socialist view would have it. Workers today do take pride in their work, though again not so much as in the market socialist way of thinking.

There are serious questions here about the work unit. One's firm is a focus of sociability and, somewhat less, identification, even in the face of extended unemployment. But it need not provide housing for people to get married, and in general it is not an effective provider of security. Moreover, such benefits as are provided are not distributed fairly. As in market socialism, what matters most about the enterprise is its bottom line.

The working class's position in society is not declining. Inequality is not a major problem, as it is for market socialism. Nor is it corrosive of class solidarity. Like market socialism, workers are exploited, but class is not a strict determinant of life's outcomes.

Turning to the state, policy and ideology, like market socialism, state industry must reform, and socialism should be reformed rather than abolished. Yet, consistent with its workerist sensibility, socialism has been undermined, and exploitation has gone quite far. Unions should be stronger and more workers should join the Party. In line with its realism, though, a worker should not lead the country, and bureaucracy is not such a problem. Workers cannot be expected to be more altruistic; it is all right for them to pursue their self-interest.

In terms of workers' politics, people should control their own destiny and are partially responsible for social outcomes. Yet popular forces are on balance less effective than good leaders. Nonetheless, there is some space for worker politics in China today, even as the prospects of that happening are low.

Mild Contentment

This way of thinking is basically satisfied with and, therefore, acquiescent to the status quo. Here views about authority relations within the firm are the blandest. There is the weakest commitment to the view that workers should be "masters of the enterprise." Management is not oblivious to workers' capabilities, so workers do not have it especially hard. Managers still don't sufficiently respect workers' talents, but this view is less pronounced than under market socialism. Likewise, management doesn't fear the workers, and does tend to treat them as labor rather than people, but less so than in the view of market socialism (though, to be sure, more than realism/workerism). Workers fear faulting managers. They do like autonomy from shop floor management, but managerial discipline is also needed to keep lazy workers in line.

Markets are marginally fair. Unemployment is not a serious concern, and losing one's job is not a big worry. Moreover, the inequalities in pay resulting from different enterprises' economic performance are viewed somewhat positively.

On the shop floor, piece rates are fair, even though there is some doubt about their consistency with socialism. Workers are somewhat responsive to the needs of the firm, *e.g.,* by doing a good job coping with shortages. Work is a source of pride. Workers' commitment to work and the level of shop floor cooperation were not much better in the 1960s. The factory is like a home and something of a source of sociability even in the face of extended unemployment. But there is ambivalence about the value of benefits such as housing and economic security, and the fairness with which they are distributed.

Class is not so determinative of individual outcomes despite a definite sense of exploitation. The working class is in decline, though that does not necessarily conflict with the general theme of contentment in light of the relatively low salience of class.

There is only weak conviction that state enterprises must reform. Likewise, there is a strong sense that the country is still socialist, that exploitation is limited, and that socialism should be reformed rather than abolished. In this same vein, there is the weakest support for strengthening unions, and no sense at all that it would help workers for more of their younger ranks to join the Party.

Looking finally at workers' politics, ordinary people share responsibility with leaders for social outcomes, and people should control their own destiny.

Yet politics is only minimally useful and, unlike the other views, mildly risky. As in market socialism and realism/workerism, however, worker politics so far is not effective.

...

In short, the main components of urban working class thinking outside the rustbelt are: broad acceptance of the market, including the labor market, even by those who have suffered layoffs; disinclination to blame the government for workers' problems; fatalism; political passivity; and a demonstrable sense that the solution for workers in need is, in the time-honored words of The Silhouettes, to "get a job."[252] The positive valuation of the potential of the labor market echoes William Hurst's finding that a dominant frame for these workers is to "keep your head down and muddle through," as well as Dorothy Solinger's argument that for Wuhan workers protest is inhibited by their incessant employment, or search for employment, in the informal labor market.[253] Indeed, Ching Kwan Lee found that even rustbelt workers, who live in the most unfavorable labor market in China, actively seek to cope with their dire straits through irregular work as much or more than protest.[254] Quantitative analysis of the structure of working class thinking in Tianjin is broadly consistent with this hegemonic view of the market and the state, even as it reveals some differences over the relations and balance of power between workers and management, levels of satisfaction with marketization, the functioning of work units, the social status of the working class, and the role and prospects of proletarian politics.

Rural Migrants: Attraction/Repulsion

The workers from farm families who now comprise most of China's working class are, in a very real sense, a class apart from the urbanites who also work in the country's industry. As we have seen, their economic situation is structurally different. For a long time, they received significantly lower wages (until the urban-resident workers began to converge with theirs)[255] and, all too often, no wages at all. They enjoy no benefits or services, either from their employers or the governments of the cities to which they have come. Their employment lacks any security. Socially too, they are the lowest stratum of the urban status hierarchy, suffering discrimination and abuse from the urbanites among whom

252 "Get a Job (song)," *Wikipedia*, last modified March 30, 2024, https://en.wikipedia.org/wiki/Get_a_Job_(song).

253 Hurst, *The Chinese Worker*, 119; Dorothy Solinger, "Labour Market Reform and the Plight of the Laid-Off Proletariat," *China Quarterly* 170 (2002): 304–326.

254 Lee, *Against the Law*, 130–139.

255 p. 106 *ff.*

they live. The same goes for social relations in the workplace, where they often endure more draconian management authority. They often live in miserable migrant ghettoes such as shanty towns or factory dormitories. Little wonder, then, that they also develop a distinctive world view.

It begins with a definite sense of being profoundly different from urban workers. Ordinary language makes this clear to both groups. Urban workers, including even the rustbelt unemployed, are known as *gongren* (工人), composed of the characters for "work" and "person." But to engage in migrant labor is termed *dagong* (打工). *Da* is "a generalized verb of doing with specific meaning determined by its object,"[256] so *dagong* means, literally, one who does work. Where *gongren* connotes an identity or occupation, *dagong* is simply an activity. The work (*gong* [工]) could be done by anyone, including those who are not workers (*gongren*). When the verb *dagong* is nominalized, things get worse. The noun that is appended is not *ren* (person), but *mei* (妹), which means "younger sister," or *zai* (仔), which means son. Rural migrants, then, are not workers, but, despite being adults, "boys" or "girls" who work. Implicit as well is the fact that they hail from the countryside. (As discussed above,[257] another term for migrant workers is *nongmingong* (农民工), which means farmer or peasant worker.) And implicit in their rural origins, but not identical to it, is the fact that they are also "outsiders" (*wailaigong* [外来工]), a pejorative even within the rural or urban areas. Inscribed in language itself, then, is a quadruple subordination of migrant workers: they are peasants, outsiders, youngsters and specifically defined by gender in a way that "workers" (*gongren*) are not.[258]

Migrants experience deeply the burden of their rural origins; it is an albatross they feel, rightly, they can never throw off. "As a peasant, I just feel naturally inferior. I cannot explain why."[259] They refer to themselves as "low level" (底层的).[260] Bosses regularly berate female migrants as "rural girls" (乡下妹) with "coarse hands and feet" (粗手粗脚).[261] This leads to feelings of confusion and disorientation.

256 John deFrancis, ed., *Wenlin Software for Learning Chinese* (Eureka, CA: Wenlin Institute, 2009).

257 See p. 153.

258 Where females are the object, definition by gender is, in societies still suffering from patriarchy, obviously a form of subordination. But even for males, and in the context of differentiation by age and home place, the specification by gender of some but not all also suggests a need for different treatment that is appropriate to an inferior. That is, in this case of a lower order like rural migrants, gender matters in a way that it does not for urban workers, much less for the middle class.

259 Lee, *Against the Law*, 217.

260 Eric Florence, *Struggling around "Dagong": Discourses About and by Migrant Workers in the Pearl River Delta* (Ph. D. dissertation, Université de Liège, 2008, 274).

261 Pun, *Made in China*, 116–117.

> We are neither peasants nor workers. I don't know how to farm the land anymore after so many years away from home… We are not real workers either. With so little education and skills, and the job market so fluid, we can be dismissed anytime. How can you build a long-term career, when there is no security and we have no skills?[262]
>
> Ever since I started working in 1987, I have always worked in Shenzhen. If I judge my own ability, I feel I am better than I was in the past. But then, I also feel that after fifteen years, I still have not earned much money, that I am not as good and competent as other people who can start their own businesses here… Every time [I returned to my village], I was reluctant to go home. But once I got home, I was reluctant to come back to Shenzhen. When I am home, I say to myself: in the past, this place was so backward and poor; but even after so many years of *dagong*, I still have very little extra. So I don't want to leave. But once I am in the city, I am anxious to earn more money to improve the life of my family, and therefore I don't want to return home so soon. Most of the time, I don't even know what I think or want, village or city?[263]
>
> I missed my home while I was out to *dagong*. When I returned home, I thought of going out again.[264]
>
> Regardless of what work I do, I get the feeling of being looked down upon.[265]
>
> There's nowhere I could find myself happy. No matter where I go, I'm not calm and balanced.[266]

As Pun Ngai and Lu Huilin put it:

> The gates of the urban and industrial world remained closed to the second generation of migrant workers. The *nongmin gong* has had nowhere to go and nowhere to stay, as expressed in [a] workers' poem: "You say your life is destined to a state of wandering" and you chose this route to becoming nobody because you are neither a *nongmin* (peasant) nor a *gongren* (worker). You are always a *nongmin gong*, somebody caught in between a rural citizen and a worker—a social identity that is always quasi. Acquiring this quasi identity, the individual, however, feels responsible for himself or herself and

262 Lee, *Against the Law*, 224–225.
263 Lee, *Against the Law*, 225.
264 Pun Ngai and Lu Huilin, "Unfinished Proletarianization: Self, Anger, and Class Action Among the Second Generation of Peasant-Workers in Present-Day China," unpublished paper. The choice of the verb "going out" implies the persistence of the rural as a definite point of reference.
265 Interview 8/T1–60, October 2002.
266 Pun and Lu, "Unfinished Proletarianization."

> is compelled to try to overcome the difficulties of becoming: "Never gonna regret, even though you have to suffer from tremendous difficulty." This is the motto of the new generation of *dagong* workers, who are trying to overcome their experience of incompleteness.

Still worse, migrants can develop feelings of worthlessness and even self-hatred.

> I felt that the value of my labor was really insignificant....We workers didn't consider ourselves to be worth much...I really didn't have any status.[267]
>
> People with money look down on poor people. I am a peasant, but I myself despise peasants because we are so poor.[268]

Evident here is the ideological hegemony in an almost pure form: acceptance, however reluctant and depressing, of the world view of the superordinate.

Pun and Lu's point about rural migrants feeling responsible for themselves has its dialectical opposite: they are alone, alienated, with no one to rely on but themselves. They express this alienation in all the forms enumerated by Marx.[269] Materially, they are alienated from their labor and the product they produce. Migrants refer to *dagong* employment as "selling one's body" (卖身), which of course is also used for sex work. Continuing this trope, they are also alienated from the process of production.

> In the factory, your entire body is under his [the employer's] control. You lose control over yourself. You have to do whatever he wants you to do. It's like you're sold to him.[270]
>
> He [the boss] treats workers like machines. As long as we can earn him money, he does not care about workers' health and bodies...[271]
>
> We worked like machines that kept running continually, to end up stupid.[272]

Moreover, they are alienated socially. As Pun and Smith point out,

> Workers in dormitories are alienated from their hometown and their parents, working within factories dominated by unfamiliar others, languages, food, production methods and products. Yet these objects and subjects confront

267 Interview, September 2002.

268 Lee, *Against the Law*, 217.

269 Karl Marx, *The Economic and Philosophic Manuscripts of 1844*, Edited by Dirk Struik (New York, International Publishers, 1964).

270 Lee, *Against the Law*, 197.

271 Ibid., 197.

272 Florence, *Struggling around "Dagong,"* 278.

> the new worker virtually 24 hours per day, seven days a week and often throughout the year.[273]

And in existential terms, migrants are alienated from what Marx called their species-being.

> It's like in the old society, I give you my money and you become my slave, a lesser human being. In the countryside, even if you are poor, people look down on you but still as a human being.[274]

They invoke the very same terms that workers before 1949 used, describing themselves as being treated like "cattle and horses."[275]

> We are second-class citizens, and not even that sometimes, just beasts…[276]
> How can we go on with such inhuman treatment?[277]
> We are not considered human beings.[278]

Mordant jokes have grown up around the "common feeling in the workplace that the employees 'worked like dogs'."

> Is it your only regret that you weren't born a foreign dog?
> Next incarnation, remember to be born elsewhere (than China), even as a dog.[279]

One worker's poem weaves together these themes.

> Dance, dance, dance, someone says
> What I dance is a dance of survival.
> Dance, dance, dance, what we dance is pain and anger
> That supplant our humanity and dignity.
> Together with skinny shoulders
> We creep upon the alien land haplessly.[280]

273 Pun Ngai and Chris Smith, "Putting Transnational Labour Process in its Place: The Dormitory Labour Regime in Post-Socialist China," *Work, Employment and Society* 21, no. 1 (2007): 32–33.
274 Lee, *Against the Law*, 197.
275 See p. 25.
276 Lee, *Against the Law*, 198.
277 Isabelle Thireau and Hua Linshan, "The Moral Universe of Aggrieved Chinese Workers: Workers' Appeals to Arbitration Committees and Letters and Visits Offices," *China Journal* 50 (July 2003): 98.
278 Thireau and Hua, "Moral Universe", 99.
279 Pun, *Made in China*, 183.
280 Pun and Lu, "Unfinished Proletarianization."

Most migrants understand themselves as exercising extremely limited yet heroic agency under conditions of extreme constraint. Their decision to migrate in the first place is generally driven both by an implacable necessity to escape rural poverty in the only way possible, but also by the wish to make a success of themselves by earning money and acquiring skills, not to mention the lure of the city's bright lights.

> I come from the North-West of Jiangxi, the Xishui district (...) Up to now, there is not a single company: it is still completely empty. Even at the township level, not a single factory. Not a single one. Well there are a few very small factories (...) The problem is that there are [*sic*] no place to sell the goods. There has not been any systematic development. In these conditions, for most people to go out to *dagong* is the only way out. They can not stay at home.[281]

> Because my family was so poor, I had to allow my brother and sister to study as well as to care for my grandfather's medicine aimed at his high blood pressure. My parents were really worried for money. Therefore, in order to alleviate my parents' burden, I decided to tell my parents that I would go to Shenzhen for work. Even though they did not want me to wander away while I was so young, covered with debts as they were, they could not help but to let me go.[282]

Yet migrants also manage to express such flight as a choice, albeit a highly constrained one.

> Completing three years of secondary school is not too bad for children in the countryside… After I had done my first three years of junior middle school, I had to quit. My parents had done their duty, but I found this unfair. I was angry at my parents for having taken away my right to an education. Each time I saw them tilling the fields all day however, I felt very sad. So that they did not have to worry any more, I decided not to study any more and to step into the road of *dagong* with my eldest sister.[283]

Moreover, they often have positive reasons for taking up and staying with *dagong*.

281 Florence, *Struggling around "Dagong,"* 258.
282 Ibid., 253.
283 Ibid., [author's re-translation from the Chinese original].

> My sister and I wanted to come out to the city to learn new skills and experience the city way of life… I thought coming to Shenzhen would give me a feel [*sic*] of the real world and society.[284]

> I started working at the factory when I was fifteen… I had very little education or skill and my family wasn't financially well off. There was no point for me to stay home…Farming wouldn't lead me to a bright future. I would just end up spending my entire life in the pit and not learn anything new.
>
> [Q:] After experiencing sweatshop conditions] did you feel like going back home?
>
> Not really. What would I do back home? At least here I had the opportunity to learn new things and better myself.[285]

> [Q:] Why did you choose to come here?
>
> That's hard to say. I guess I just wanted to see the world outside my village.[286]

Both these young women paid for their ambitions with their arms, which were amputated after industrial "accidents." One of these young women had ample warnings about the dangers which she professed made her "quite afraid and nervous about the job"—an uncle had died from chemical inhalation and another relative lost an arm. But she came nonetheless, which speaks terrible volumes about the strength of the forces driving young migrants into sweatshops.

> After all, I was a newcomer from the village with no educational background and a low level of experience. I really did not have any status. So I was left with no other choice but to take up the job.[287]

In another case:

> In my factory there had been three serious injuries in two years. One worker was burned over his whole body, another lost his fingers, and the third is me [who lost an arm].
>
> [Q:] Were you afraid when you saw them injured?
>
> Yes I was.

284 Interview 7C/113–, September 2002.
285 Interview 7B/8–113, September 2002.
286 Interview 7C/T165, September 2002.
287 Interview 7B/8–113, September 2002.

> [Q:] Did you consider resigning and going back home?
> Yes I did think about that. But then I thought there is no choice if I didn't work here and didn't have another job.[288]

The decision, however, is not always made by these young workers. A parent who put his little daughter into child labor in his factory said:

> Well, apart from wanting her to work and earn some money, we as parents also want her to learn some skill from the exposure to factory work.[289]

Another worker explained that he couldn't go home.

> My parents said to stay here, because whatever skills we are able to learn will be ours forever and we can earn a living without depending on anyone else.[290]

What emerges from migrants' experience of material compulsion, draconian oppression, super-exploitation,[291] social exclusion, multi-faceted alienation, physical abuse and bodily dismemberment is a sensibility that somehow combines fatalism and agency, hopelessness and hope. Pun found that "[s]ome workers consoled themselves with the thought that 'fate takes turns, so fate will turn one day.'"[292] As a worker who lost a hand in a factory "accident" put it:

> [Q:] So was it a good move to come here to Shenzhen?
> I guess if the accident didn't occur it wouldn't be that bad. But I can't even blame it on the accident. I cannot regret my decision. The accident was inevitable.[293]

Another injured worker who sued his factory, though personally more inclined to respond actively against his experience, also testified to most of his fellow migrant workers' fatalism and hegemonic acceptance of the wage relationship.

> Suing definitely does help. At least the worker is made aware of their rights. After my suit I know that I won't work for more than twelve hours a day. It's

288 Interview 7C/T165, September 2002.
289 Interview 8/110, September 2002.
290 Interview 8/1–60, October 2002.
291 This term refers objectively to an employment relationship in which the employer extracts so much surplus value as to undermine the process of surplus value extraction itself by destroying the worker who is, after all, the fount of value creation in the first place.
292 Pun, *Made in China*, 183.
293 Interview, September 2002.

> important for all workers to know that they are not required to work to earn money at the cost of one's own health and safety, to make use of labor rights and realize that they are not worthless. They should not allow big business-people to exploit them. Yet most workers do not react favorably to my message, because they feel that if you're paid to work then there is no choice.[294]

Yet migrants don't have to have undergone such dramatic experiences to feel some hope amid the hopelessness. This letter is typical.

> To be a migrant worker is really like living a non-human life (...) You get tired to a point that you do not know what day it is and which year next year will be. The factory I worked in was like that… But it is precisely in this environment that my world outlook has undergone a fundamental change… I received a letter from a friend [who] said that although she was not really smart, by putting in some extra efforts, she would manage to be successful. She just needed to struggle consciously and she would eventually be able to create her place in the sky. Work hard and you'll be rewarded… The *dagong* life is a tempering process and the one who goes forward with courage will manage to go against the tide. The weak will only stagnate. A person can not endlessly be angry at others, and keep saying that his lot is unfair… *Dagong* is a treasure.[295]

Such "agency" is, of course, mainly a treasure—literally—for employers and the state, for it helps sustain a steady flow of exploitable labor while depoliticizing their misery. Most migrants take a dim view of the government. Even a worker who had the temerity to sue over a lost arm, and who won a judgment but was having trouble collecting, said:

> There is no concept of fair or unfair in this state…The court and the local authorities favor the factory owners. Although they know the law, they just don't follow it. The court did not exert its full authority to compel the defendant to pay the damages I was awarded. They do not wish to see the company lose…The government does not carry out its duty… We get pressured by the legal authorities… We are not permanent residents so they look down on us and are not willing to help… They basically act as a mediator between the factory and us workers but they favor them. If they just stood in the middle and remained neutral the problem [of me collecting my judgment] would have been solved ages ago…

294 Interview 7B/8–113, September 2002.

295 Florence, *Struggling around "Dagong,"* 290–291 [author's re-translation from the Chinese original].

> The government is very secretive. We do not trust the government. We have lost all hope [in politics] because they do not help us…
>
> A union won't help. The government is like this; it won't change…
>
> It's all hopeless. The Chinese government is useless.[296]

In short, rural migrants' world view is profoundly contradictory. They are pushed, but also drawn, into a world in which they are regarded and treated as alien, inferior and not fully human. They suffer terribly, but somehow manage to keep some small hope alive. They are fatalistic, but also believe that they can triumph over fate. They are willing, or at least able, to take extraordinary risks for the most meager rewards. They take the dimmest view of their government and politics. Yet as we shall see, such political pessimism of the intellect does not prevent a growing number of migrants from exercising some surprising optimism of the will.

…

The working class's complex economic and transformations produced a new, differentiated and contradictory panoply of ways workers think about their world (or, better, worlds). These divide the working class, and often pit them against each other. In Daqing, for example, an unemployed worker who went into hair-dressing called protesters demanding their pensions "crybabies."[297] What they all share, though, is that none hark back to the radicalism of the Maoist era working class. As such, they are all consistent, each in different ways, with the hegemony of the market and the state, and they reinforce the power of both. Both their variegation and their shared acquiescence have profoundly shaped working class politics, which, though quite active, have remained both fissiparous and deradicalized.

Political Aspects of the Fall of the Working Class

China's working class has responded to the profound, complex ways structural reform has remade it economically, socially and culturally by mounting more labor activism than anywhere else in the world.[298] But the character of its politics has changed radically from Maoist days. Gone is the radicalism of its focus on democratic management in the firm and class and state power beyond it. Instead, working class struggles have become defensive, focused on

296 Interview 7c/T165, September 2002.

297 See p. 170.

298 Beverly J. Silver and Lu Zhang, "China as an Emerging Epicenter of World Labor Unrest," in Ho-fung Hung (ed.), *China and the Transformation of Global Capitalism*, Baltimore: Johns Hopkins University Press, 2009, 174; Eli Friedman, "China in Revolt," *Jacobin*, August 1, 2012.

"bread-and-butter" questions such as wage arrears and social insurance contributions. Why did the high expectations and radical visions of a new world that workers evinced, and for which they struggled so ardently, not prepare the ground for vigorous working class critique of structural reform? Why did the resentment of state socialist authoritarianism by managers and bureaucrats not produce a political critique of the return of genuine factory despotism? Why did the criticism of factory and Party/state officials for starting down a "capitalist road" not produce anything similar now that they have completed the journey, turning into full-blooded and often pretty vicious actual capitalists? Why have workers who were able to extend their struggles to municipal and regional canvases—to stage not just strikes and protests but "waves" of them—reverted almost completely to small-scale, firm-level protests, especially in an age when technology has made coordination all the easier? Why has the working class's fiery struggle for a "world to win" been relegated instead to mere atavistic nostalgia for a "radiant past"?[299]

Good political explanations abound. The Party/state has monopolized and constricted political space, and repressed collective action; in the conceptual language of collective action theory, it has created a particularly inhospitable political opportunity structure for working class politics.[300] It has shown great skill in managing labor protest, combining the stick of arresting radical ringleaders with the carrot of leaving most strikers and protesters unpunished and, sometimes, pressuring management to compromise. In terms of sequencing, structural economic reform was brought in gradually and without first hazarding political liberalization. Contingency played a role: after a decade of dilatory economic and political opening in the 1980s during which opposition or at least hesitance to thoroughgoing structural economic reform remained strong, the imposition of political crackdown in mid-1989 for different reasons inadvertently cleared away lingering political obstacles to price and labor marketization.

Without calling most of this into question, the present approach takes a wider perspective. What can help explain the puzzling contrast between labor politics in the Maoist and structural reform eras is the many interrelated changes in working class formation. Under structural reform, the working class has been remade in ways that correspond broadly to the tepidity of its politics. And since

299 Michael Burawoy and János Lukács, *The Radiant Past: Ideology and Reality in Hungary's Road to Capitalism* (Chicago: University of Chicago Press, 1992).

300 Yet this approach can be questioned. For there have been significant political opportunities—most prominently, the 1989 nationwide protests that shook the régime to its core. Moreover, Dorothy Solinger argues that one aspect of the Party/state's political monopoly—its continued sponsorship of a pro-state, pro-capital labor federation in which workers have no faith at all—actually helps explain why there is more labor protest in China than in France or Mexico, where unions help canalize labor discontent. Dorothy Solinger, *States' Gains, Labor's Losses: China, France, and Mexico Choose Global Liaisons, 1980–2000* (Ithaca: Cornell University Press, 2009).

the political aspects of class formation can help shape the economic, social and cultural ones (rather than just being their product),[301] it is also important that workers' politics in China no longer contribute significantly to reshaping working class economic life, social experience or ways of thinking.

The 1980s: The Silence of the Lions

Structural reform of China's state socialist system of labor allocation and employment began in 1986, with the government's first efforts to institute labor contracts to replace the existing system of lifetime employment. Savvy or skeptical workers—with whom the Maoist period showed that the country was amply endowed—might have been expected to spot this as the "capitalist-roaders'" camel's nose under the tent, and, therefore, to object strenuously. But of course, that is much easier said in hindsight. At the time, the new contracts seemed innocuous and formalistic, and workers would be justified in thinking that they were still firmly in the driver's seat in their relations with managers. The latter were so stung by the Cultural Revolution that even well into the 1980s they dared not implement bonus schemes being pressed by reformers for fear of stirring up a hornet's nest of proletarian opposition. It is little surprise, then, that the 1986 "reform" did not produce a political reaction from the working class.

Neither did the working class take much advantage of the political opportunity presented by the massive protests of 1989. A handful of minuscule workers' outfits that had formed at the outset in April, and been raising working class issues such as wages, inflation and livelihood, eventually joined, were absorbed into, or were subsumed by the Beijing Workers' Autonomous Federation (BWAF). By mid-May, though, the BWAF only had several dozen active members. Moreover, in a development redolent of so much of the history of working class politics in China, the workers who had formed the original groups were now displaced by students and intellectuals. In the last three weeks of the movement, the BWAF dropped its original working class demands and joined the bandwagon of broad social support for the student movement for "democracy." In the last big demonstrations that took place at the end of May, the BWAF turned out only 200 people. As the *denouement* approached, individual workers bravely positioned themselves at key intersections leading to Tiananmen Square, but the BWAF was not involved in that or in any other way.[302]

301 E. P. Thompson, *The Making of the English Working Class* (New York: Vintage, 1966); Ira Katznelson, "Working-Class Formation."

302 Raymond W. K. Lau, "The Role of the Working Class in the 1989 Mass Movement in Beijing," *Journal of Communist Studies and Transition Politics* 12, no. 3 (September 1996): 343–373. Lau's exhaustive article takes issue with earlier studies that mark out a somewhat greater role for working class politics in 1989; see Andrew G. Walder, "Workers, Managers and the

Starting in the latter 1980s and continuing through the early 1990s, a far more portentous and dangerous change ensued. The soft budget constraints of state socialism began to give way as enterprises were gradually expected not just to earn profits, a share of which they could retain, but also to cover their own losses. Workers now became dependent on the economic well-being of their specific firm in a way that none of them ever had experienced. Those fortunate enough to work for prospering factories could receive wage increases and other benefits, while the unlucky ones employed in struggling enterprises faced pay freezes or cuts, wage arrears and layoffs. The differences in the fates of workers with similar skills and work experience were now functions of the employment lottery: where, under the old labor allocation system, they had happened to be assigned when they first left school. The government made no effort whatsoever to compensate for or cushion these random and very serious inequities created by its own "reforms." It is even more surprising that workers quietly acquiesced in this profound structural change, since this affected their material lives palpably and evidently, in ways that the 1986 labor contracts did not.

The tentativeness and even bafflement workers expressed when confronted with this puzzle, documented above,[303] are, however, comprehensible. In the industrial heartlands, there was little basis until the latter 1990s for evaluating the economic health of China's core factories in the first place. Workers can also be forgiven for thinking that the government would always assure their livelihood in any new market environment, or that they had the residual influence and power to force it to do so. Finally, the factory-towns in which some were situated were not places in which a multiplicity of enterprises were evincing heterogeneous economic results. Most fundamentally, it was eminently reasonable for the proletariat of China's primary industries to believe, as Wall Street bankers would years later, that they and their steel mills, oil refineries and power plants were simply indispensable. Workers in China's secondary and tertiary sectors would have been far less justified in thinking this way. But, as we have seen, many of the cities in eastern and central China where they lived were already beginning to grow with sufficient rapidity, especially by the middle 1990s, which could take the edge off anxieties about the fate of a state-sector job.

Thus, at the very moment when structural reforms were setting China off on a new and controversial path toward marketization and capitalist transition, its politically powerful industrial working class did not object. Only a few years later, when the path was firmly set and they had become dependent on it, did

State: The Reform Era and the Political Crisis of 1989," *China Quarterly* 127 (September 1991): 467–492; Andrew Walder and Gong Xiaoxia, "Workers in the Tiananmen Protests: The Politics of the Beijing Workers' Autonomous Federation," *The Australian Journal of Chinese Affairs* no. 29 (January 1993): 1–29.

303 See p. 143 *ff.*

they start to react. But in this new path-dependent situation, it was too late to reverse the "reforms," and the best workers could do was to demand a bit more material resources to help them cope.

Rumbles in the Rustbelt

Some of the core of the Maoist-era working class did become politicized in China's former heavy industrial heartland of Manchuria, but only once it had been reduced to a shuttered shadow of its former self. The 1997 state enterprise reform blessed a process that had been proceeding for several years, stipulating that state enterprises were now to be converted into share-holding firms and sold off as public, quasi-public or even private enterprises that would, as such, be responsible for their own profits and losses. Those that could not be disposed of in these ways would be put into bankruptcy and sold off wholesale or piecemeal. Pension and wage arrears, which had already been growing serious, now skyrocketed, and with them protests. In Heilongjiang Province, the number of large demonstrations (involving over 500 people) nearly tripled between 1998 and 1999, with more than half demanding unpaid wages.[304] Between January 2000 and September 2002, there were almost 10,000—almost thirty per day. And this extraordinary figure actually represented a decline from 1999.[305]

When the petition drives with which they usually began failed to produce results, protests often moved on to sit-ins at government offices, factory occupations, traffic blockages, seizures of management officials, and sometimes even riots.

> [I]n early 2000, workers here [in Yangjiazhangzi, Liaoning Province] were angered not just by rampant layoffs but also by months of unpaid wages, pensions and stipends that left many desperate. Adding to their rage was evidence that mine officials were profiting as they sold off equipment from the worn-out molybdenum mines that anchored the town's existence.
>
> Tempers boiled over when a group of petitioners was beaten by the police. Some 20,000 workers and their relatives raged down the main street, damaging police cars, smashing windows and barricading the road with fire…
>
> [T]he riots ended in three days as droves of police officers and soldiers took up positions, and 20 "troublemakers" were arrested.[306]
>
> Northeast China, once the robust heartland of Chinese state-owned heavy industry, has been the epicenter of demonstrations staged by SOE

304 Lee, *Against the Law*, 76.

305 Murray Scot Tanner, "China Rethinks Unrest," *The Washington Quarterly*, 27, no. 3 (Summer 2004): 137–156.

306 Erik Eckholm, "A Mining Town's Sullen Peace Masks the Bitter Legacy of China's Labor Strategy," *New York Times*, April 14, 2002.

> workers…In mid-2001, as many as 10,000 coal miners from the Jilin province town of Jishu, inflamed by wage arrears and corruption in the local mining bureau, blocked northeast China's most central rail line for more than three days. Slightly more than a year later, another coal mining town in Jilin, Taonan City, was wracked by worker demonstrations. Livid about withheld pay, faulty mining equipment, and hazardous work conditions, 2,000 miners marched on the offices of the city party committee and shouted incendiary slogans that the CCP could interpret as treason: "Overthrow the dark government and put the evil-minded mining bureau on trial!" In December 2002, 2,000 chemical plant workers owed several years' back pay formed a human chain across the Avenue of the Red Flag in the Liaoning district of Shuangtaizi. In the same month, 2,000 unemployed paper-mill workers in Jiamusi, Heilongjiang barricaded the city's two primary national transport conduits, the rail line to Beijing and the road to the airport. Stirred to action by the usual dose of local state venality — in this case officials helping themselves to the mill-workers' living allowance fund — the Jiamusi demonstrators refused to back down even when military police arrived on the scene. Most alarmingly for the CCP, in January 2003 textile workers robbed of their retrenchment entitlements took to the streets in Dandong, a city in Liaoning that had already witnessed protests by defrauded investors and demobilized soldiers in the same month.[307]

Even bigger alarm bells for the state had rung the previous March in Daqing and Liaoyang, where massive protests began to spread among enterprises and cities.

Daqing

Daqing was an especially ironic and dangerous site for such an outburst, inasmuch as it had been not just the country's main oilfield, but also the Maoist-era national model for industrial development, whose "iron men" were presented in ongoing propaganda campaigns as exemplars of proletarian heroism to be emulated by one and all. Daqing represents a classic case of the effect of capitalistic restructuring on the state socialist working class. In November 1999, the China National Petroleum Corporation spun off its best assets, including Daqing, into a new company called PetroChina. Under pressure from international markets—it became listed on the New York and Hong Kong stock exchanges in April 2000—it laid off tens of thousands of workers, including eventually half

307 John Gulick, "Insurgent Chinese workers and peasants: The 'weak link' in capitalist globalization and U.S. imperialism," in Eddie Yuen, Daniel Burton-Rose, and George Katsiaficas, eds., *Confronting Capitalism: Dispatches from a Global Movement* (Brooklyn, NY: Soft Skull Press, 2004), 292–308.

of those in Daqing. With profits in the range of $30 billion, it offered severance packages of under $500 per year of service in lieu of all health, heating and pension benefits. The company made the "offer" on a take-it-or-leave-it basis, accompanied by threats that this was the workers' last chance and that the firm, with its aging wells, was in danger of bankruptcy that could result in their being left with nothing at all. PetroChina trumpeted this message on local television so that workers' families would pressure the recalcitrant among them to go along.

Some sporadic protests had broken out in the spring of 2001, but the promises of benefits as well as the above-mentioned cleavages among workers helped keep them from escalating. Only when the local government reneged on those benefits did significant mobilization get underway. On March 1, 2002, 3,000 retrenched workers marched on Iron Man Square and the Daqing Petroleum Administration Bureau (DPAB) building, producing broken windows but no injuries. It only took three days for the demonstrations to grow almost twenty-fold to 50,000. Ominously for the government, the streets were now filled not just with workers, but basic-level cadres, engineers, technicians, technical assistants, and teachers and professors as well. Until now, workers' plight, and even less their protests, had not attracted any cross-class attention in Daqing or, for that matter, the rest of the country. On the fourth and fifth of March, workers blocked the railway, causing transport delays. This plus an attack on the DPAB canteen impelled the police to arrest three workers, one of whom, charged with hanging a banner, was beaten in detention. Another, a woman in her fifties who went on a hunger strike, urged workers to stop destroying property lest they play into the hands of the Falungong, a sizable religious cult on which the government had cracked down in 1999, and whom the government was accusing of being the black hands behind the protests. Yet despite her pleas for calm, the police also arrested her and roughed her up. The workers laid siege to the DPAB headquarters. Negotiations collapsed when the workers' representatives were arrested. The workers organized a provisional independent union, led by better educated workers with some knowledge of the law. Meanwhile, miners in Fuxing (Liaoning), oil workers in the also renowned Shengli Oilfield (Shandong) as well as in the Liaohe (Liaoning) and Xinjiang Oilfields organized solidarity demonstrations.[308] By the middle of the month, labor protest in China was, for the first time, beginning to metastasize across the country. Moreover, as in May 1989, just before the climax of the "Tiananmen" movement,[309] workers and their social allies were beginning to organize themselves.

These were two developments that the government had never countenanced; the latter violated the most basic principle of the Leninist state's political monopoly. Pushed beyond the brink, it now cracked down. On March 19, hundreds of

308 See p. 170.
309 It actually played out in cities across China.

armed police converged on the protesters. The next day the central government declared its determination to use force to stop the protests. Orders were given to arrest leaders of unauthorized trade unions, and casualties were reported.

The following week saw a tense standoff, in which thousands of workers faced a thousand armed police and paramilitary, some in full riot gear. The protests were broadly peaceful and sometimes even festive, including poetry readings. Workers petitioned and looked into filing lawsuits. They planned a mass ceremony in which Party members would resign. They also blocked roads and railways. The demonstrations were marred only by some vandalism (including overturned cars) and the beating of a motorist who had driven a car into a crowd of 30,000 protesters. The government responded with its characteristic combination of carrots and sticks. On the one hand, it offered economic concessions and promises to investigate corruption claims, and even organized public *majiang* (*mah-jong*) games and a folksong competition. Enterprises convened meetings of workers' representative congresses. On the other, it threatened to go no further with such offers and to respond in the future with police sanctions; it ramped up arrests and fines; it made vague threats against protesters' children; it went house to house to persuade workers to stay home and threaten those who did not with retribution against themselves and their families. A stalemate continued over the next several months.

Liaoyang

At the very same time, another spectacular working class protest took place in the Liaoyang Ferro-Alloy Factory in neighboring Liaoning Province. According to Ching Kwan Lee, it was

> the most radical episode in labor activism in more than two decades of reform, rais[ing] the specter of a class-based uprising. It involved interfactory coordination and political demands for the removal of city officials. These two features of the Liaoyang incident set it apart from every previous worker protest, and it received enormous attention from the international media and the Chinese régime.

Quoting one activist,

> "The whole struggle went through a conversion, a 'qualitative leap'"... from petitions to protests, from single-factory to multi-factory joint action, and from economic to political demands.[310]

310 Lee, *Against the Law*, 101–102.

The factory had begun to lose money in 1995, and stopped paying its workers' pension contributions, medical reimbursements and insurance premiums, housing subsidies, minimum welfare support payments, and in some cases even wages. Production was periodically suspended starting the following year. It took until 1998 for a small group of workers to organize an open letter of protest addressed to the highest levels of the Party/state.[311] In 2000, 600 workers blocked a main highway, resulting in beatings and arrests by the paramilitary police. A year of negotiations on the issues and the arrests followed, with no result. Another year on, in May 2001, the removal of equipment and raw materials provoked another demonstration by a few thousand workers. The city government promised to investigate and report within a week, which never happened. In October, the factory convened a meeting of the workers' representative congress to discuss formal bankruptcy. The day before the planned meeting, 1,000 workers blocked the main highway again, resulting in the stick of arrests and the carrot of negotiations. The latter stalled. Within weeks, the enterprise declared bankruptcy.

The following March, amid ramped-up security and arrests of workers' leaders, Liaoyang Ferro-Alloy convened a second meeting to discuss the bankruptcy. Provincial Governor Gong Shangwu inflamed the situation by telling "a Liaoyang TV reporter that in his city 'there were no unemployed' and that the city had handled the economic transition swimmingly."[312] 17,000 workers, mainly the laid-off, immediately took to the streets. Amid their denunciations of government indifference to official corruption and the workers' plight, they had the temerity to demand the resignation of Governor Gong, which gained even more gravity because at that moment he was representing his province at the National People's Congress in Beijing. A high-level delegation led by the city's Deputy Party Secretary undertook immediate negotiations with the incandescent workers. Though it guaranteed the workers' urgent request that there would be no arrests, four days later Yao Fuxin, one of their key leaders, was bundled into a car and driven away. The next day, even in the face of a very heavy armed police presence, over 30,000 workers from twenty other Liaoyang factories—a novel and portentous development—took to the streets. Over the next two days, the demonstrations diminished in the face of cold weather and continued armed force. Still, 2,000 older workers, many retired and female, persisted in demonstrating at a government building, thinking their age and sex would help protect them. Their main demand was Yao's release. When one broke through the police cordon, got inside, and was detained, one hundred

311 The text can be found in Human Rights Watch, "Paying the Price: Worker Unrest in Northeast China," *Human Rights Watch* 14, no. 6 (August 2002), Appendix 1.

312 John Pomfret, "With Carrots and Sticks, China Quiets Protesters," *Washington Post*, March 22, 2002.

workers stormed past the defenders and managed to spirit him out. Hours later, the police attacked a group of thirty older workers protecting him, arresting four. Over the subsequent weeks, protests continued and the crackdown intensified. In one case, a man complaining to the police about the beating of his elderly mother was himself beaten and detained.

Metastasis and Collapse

The Daqing and Liaoyang protests, the latter of which itself had begun to spread from the Ferro-Alloy plant to the rest of the city, stimulated proletarian protests across China. In Fushun, 140 km away, over 100,000 miners and factory workers had been laid off in the late 1990s, producing serious protests such as railway blockages. They also stimulated renewed ones by thousands of workers in March 2002. The government responded with the carrot of minuscule payoffs and the stick of arrests for those who would still not disperse. At the same time, similar protests broke out far afield in the Maoist model Shengli Oilfield in Shandong Province, as well as others in Gansu, Hebei, Lanzhou, Shandong and Sichuan Provinces and even as far across the country as the Xinjiang Uyghur Autonomous Region.[313]

In the end, the government pushed the terrifying genie of metastatic working class protest back into the bottle by combining ruthlessness and skill. The Daqing workers proved no match for the multifaceted repertoire and skillfully modulated response of the Party/state. It combined armed force with salami tactics, dividing the working class by mobilizing still employed workers to visit the homes of unemployed protesters they knew to tell them that the government would withhold their own bonuses unless the demonstrations stopped.

Yet much more than the government divided the Daqing workers. As one unemployed worker who had become a hairdresser put it in 2002, in the midst of the movement:

> Daqing workers are a bunch of crybabies. Our factory shut more than two years ago. We got no compensation. We started the salon with our own funds. I don't support the demonstrations. They got money, which we didn't. They are all over 50.
>
> Protest is no use. It can't resolve things. I grew up in Daqing. There are people with money here, and some without money. Each year we earn ¥8,000. There are also lots of migrants here. They are much worse off than

313 See, for example, Philip P. Pan, "Oil Protest Shows Spread of Unrest in China," *Washington Post*, April 24, 2002.

> the protesters. They don't protest because they can find their own work; they rely on themselves.[314]

A barber expressed the same sentiment.

> The protesters just depend on the state, not themselves. They have the old way of thinking. Things are actually getting better all the time.[315]

By the middle of 2002 the Daqing movement had burned itself out, and the exhausted workers reverted to their homes and, for some, jobs.[316]

In Liaoyang Ferro-Alloy too, the government eventually prevailed partly by its skilled response. It combined repression with concessions: the workers' leaders were eventually sentenced to long prison terms, but so were the enterprise's former director and several other officials on corruption and smuggling charges. It combined its repressive stick with carrots such as revised and better-monitored bankruptcy proceedings and modest payoffs of benefits to entitled workers. It played divide-and-conquer by coopting some workers' leaders with plum jobs even as it intimidated dozens of others. Moreover, as in Daqing, the Liaoyang workers too could not sustain their political mobilization due partly to their lack of solidarity. Retirees denied pensions actually resisted allying with workers denied wages. Both groups thought they were competing for monies from the same pot. Moreover, retirees thought they had the moral high ground in terms of deservedness compared with active workers, whom they sometimes urged to go find another job. To make the prospects for working class solidarity dimmer still, even retirees from the same enterprise had trouble allying, since under state socialist China's complex retirement system they faced different pension entitlements depending on seniority and skill. Of course such divisions made alliances across enterprises even more unlikely.[317]

Taking advantage of latent cleavages within the working class, the Party/state's deployment of time-honored tactics of carrot and stick, cooptation, and divide-and-conquer formed a repertoire of response that worked like a charm to enable the state ultimately to survive the incipient metastatic working class protest. In Fushun, for example, it doled out minuscule payoffs to workers blocking the railway and main highway, while arresting those who would still not disperse. Yet such tactics could succeed thanks to the nature of working class formation on which they rested. Fissures between the employed and unemployed, between migrants and urban-registered workers, and between those inclined to

314 Interview, courtesy of Jocelyn Ford, March 2002.
315 Ibid.
316 Interviews, Beijing, 2002.
317 Lee, *Against the Law*, Chapter 3.

identify with the "radiant past" and the political victories and economic guarantees the working class had won in the Maoist era on the one hand and, on the other, the opportunities presented by the brave new world of capitalist transition, also undermined the working class's capacity to create a broad political movement that could threaten the Party/state's legitimacy and power, both then and subsequently.[318]

Contention in the New Century

The structural reform of Chinese industry has produced complex economic, social and cultural transformations and challenges for China's working class. Little surprise, then, that labor protest has grown rapidly, along a continuum from peaceable, civil and legal forms to more politically contentious[319] (*i.e.*, confrontative, extra-legal, illegal and, at the far end, criminal) ones—more specifically, from informal factory-level discussions, to formal mediation, arbitration and lawsuits, to strikes, slowdowns, demonstrations, occupations, riots and violent attacks.

The number of labor disputes that entered the arbitration and legal systems rose steadily from the mid-1990s, spiking sharply in 2008; in 2012, they numbered 650,000.[320] There are few precise figures for contentious labor disputes. According to Elfstrom and Kuruvilla,

> [Chinese] Sociologist Yu Jianrong estimated that roughly 30,000 strikes and protests by workers occurred in 2009 alone — a number that roughly matches the figure obtained when the percentages of Wedeman and Chen's "mass incidents" that relate to labor disputes (36.7% and 32.3%, respectively) are projected onto the total number of incidents that the government acknowledged occurred in 2005 (87,000 incidents).[321]

Contentious disputes in 2009 were way up on 2008—by 30 percent according to *Caijing*, a respected Chinese business magazine. It attributed the spike to the

318 Not until the 2010 wave of automotive sector strikes did Chinese workers come close to converting cellular, firm-by-firm protest into a broad mobilization. It was stimulated by a very different stratum of the working class that was operating within very different economic, social and cultural parameters. Yet it too promptly abated, though for very different reasons. See p. 182 *ff.*

319 Of course, civil and legal disputes are also contentious. Here, though, the term is meant to reference the kinds of political conflict connoted by the political science term "contentious politics."

320 Eli Friedman, *Insurgency Trap: Labor Politics in Postsocialist China*. Ithaca: ILR Press, 2014, 4.

321 Manfred Elfstrom and Sarosh Kuruvilla, "The Changing Nature of Labour Unrest in China," *ILR Review* 67, no. 2 (2014): 455.

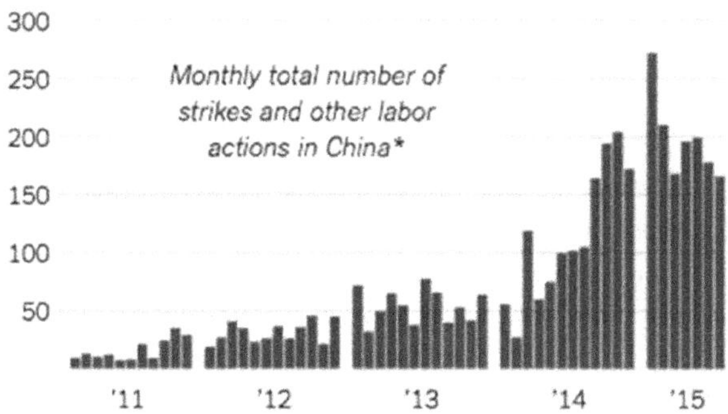

FIGURE 3.7 Contentious labor disputes, 2011–2015.
Source: Keith Bradsher, "China Turned to Risky Devaluation as Export Machine Stalled," *New York Times*, August 17, 2015.

2008 economic crisis and the promulgation of the Labor Contract Law that same year.[322] Keith Bradsher assembled a database for subsequent years (Figure 3.7), grounded in compendia of actual reports compiled by *China Labour Bulletin* and *The New York Times*; it is, then, a sample, of indeterminate validity, of what made it into public reporting in the press or online. *China Labour Bulletin* estimates that the actual number of disputes is ten to twenty times greater than the number reported,[323] bringing the order of magnitude to somewhere between 25,000 and 50,000 per year in 2015. Moreover, assuming some rough consistency in the representativeness of the reports he was able to capture—which is a big assumption—labor contention was on the rise from 2011 to 2015, with a big spike in the second half of 2014. In 2019, the estimated number had dropped back to 2014 levels, which still breaks down to between 38 and 75 per day nationwide.[324]

Even in the absence of solid data, though, there can be no doubt that labor conflict is significant and that it has been rising in the new century.

> For the duration of the Hu-Wen administration (2002–12), the volume, and seemingly the intensity, of labor conflict increased dramatically. Officially adjudicated disputes rose continuously until 2007 and spiked sharply in 2008 because of the economic crisis and the passage of new labor laws. While the number of disputes declined somewhat following the resumption of rapid

322 " Rising Rate of Labor Disputes in China," *Caijing*, July 13, 2009.
323 Peter Symonds, "Signs of Rising Levels of Workers' Struggles in China," *World Socialist Website*, February 18, 2019, https://www.wsws.org/en/articles/2019/02/18/chin-f18.html.
324 *China Labour Bulletin* reported 1,385 incidents in 2019. See https://maps.clb.org.hk/?i18n_language=en_US&map=1&startDate=2019-01&endDate=2019-12&eventId=&keyword=&addressId=&parentAddressId=&address=&industry=&parentIndustry=&industryName=.

> growth in 2009, they increased again in 2012 and remain incredibly high in absolute terms. Autonomously organized strikes, road blockades, riots, and worker suicides continue to upend social order. In at least two high-profile cases, workers who murdered their bosses were widely hailed as heroes on the Internet. Just one week after the Guxiang riot,[325] an even more spectacular worker insurrection took place in the Guangzhou suburb of Zengcheng. Workers blocked a national highway and set fire to a police station — and the unrest continued for days until the government deployed the military to quell the uprising. By 2012 the government was spending renminbi (RMB) 701.8 billion (U.S. $111.4 billion) on internal security, significantly outpacing its national defense budget of RMB 670.3 billion. Clearly, all was not peaceful in the People's Republic.[326]

In 2014, the biggest strike since the onset of the structural reforms took place, when 40,000 Yue Yuen Shoe workers stayed out ten days.[327] Beverly Silver and Lu Zhang argue that China is now "an emerging epicenter of world labor unrest," and Eli Friedman uses the very same word even more definitively in calling it "undeniably the epicenter of global labor unrest."[328]

Stimulants

Material issues have predominated across sectors and regions. The most common complaints have concerned wages and benefits. Here the issue for workers

325 "On the night of June 6, 2011, migrant workers rioted in the southern Chinese town of Guxiang. The protesters were furious over an incident in which a fellow worker had been violently attacked while seeking back wages. On June 1, Xiong Hanjiang, a nineteen-year-old migrant from Sichuan province, went to demand 2,000 yuan in back pay from the ceramics factory where he was employed. Rather than give him his wages, some of the bosses' relatives attacked Xiong with knives, cutting tendons in his hands and feet. Between June 3 and June 6, workers demanding justice for the victim protested in front of the municipal and township government offices, as well as at police headquarters. Protesters vandalized the government buildings, and a number of police were hospitalized with injuries. On the night of the sixth, the workers originally surrounded the Guxiang government offices to continue to press their demands for harsh punishment for the attackers and fair compensation for Xiong. Things quickly escalated as physical confrontations took place with police, leaving dozens injured. Witnesses claimed that more than one hundred cars were smashed, though the official number was just nineteen. Widespread violence between migrants and locals ensued, with one migrant saying, 'If you couldn't speak Chaoshan dialect [the local language], they would beat you.' Riot police were called in to put down the unrest, and the town was placed under martial law for several days." Friedman, *Insurgency Trap*, 1.

326 Friedman, *Insurgency Trap*, 3–4.

327 See below, *passim,* and Marc Blecher, "The Yue Yuen Strike of 2014," in Franceschini and Sorace, *Proletarian China:* 664-673.

328 Silver and Zhang, "China as an Emerging Epicenter of World Labor Unrest," 174; Friedman, "China in Revolt."

is generally not so much their level,[329] dreadfully low though it is, as arrears, whose size and duration are often egregious.[330] Workers obviously need their wages to live on, although mere survival is somewhat less of a problem for those who live and eat in factory dormitories and refectories. What drives rural migrant workers to protest, though, has at least as much to do with migrants' needs to meet their families' expectations of remissions (especially during annual visits home for the Spring Festival, when they cannot turn up empty handed), with their inability to quit (in which case they are very unlikely ever to see the monies due them), and with their loss of social welfare benefits when employers fail to pay their share of the premiums. The biggest strike since the onset of structural reform, involving an estimated 40,000 workers of the Yue Yuen shoe factory—the world's largest—in Dongguan, Guangdong Province in the spring of 2014 was brought on by the revelation that the company had not been making pension contributions for many years. Other common material stimuli of strikes and demonstrations include hours, working conditions, benefits, employment security, relocations and ownership restructuring (with the attendant opportunities for corruption, more draconian management and layoffs).[331] In the 2010 automotive strikes, material concerns—specifically, wage levels—predominated more than in other sectors.[332] Material stimuli are also growing in significance over time, as economic development generally (especially in urban areas), increased information about relative levels of material life (both within China and internationally) and generational change all drive a significant uptick in workers' material expectations. Gig workers are now getting into the act.[333] Elfstrom and Kuruvilla quote Samuel Gompers, of all people: "Chinese workers now appear to 'want more.'"[334]

Humanistic issues such as bullying, disrespect and violence, and moral ones such as corruption, including management absconding with firm assets, also drive labor protest. In apparel factories, management itself provides a

329 Again, with the exception of the 2010 auto sector strikes.

330 See p. 95 and *passim*.

331 Daniel Y. Zipp and Marc Blecher, "Migrants and Mobilization: Sectoral Patterns in China, 2010–2013," *Global Labour Journal* VI, 1 no. (January 2015): 116–126, https://escarpment-press.org/globallabour/article/view/2293. Early 2023 saw a big uptick in strikes "mostly related to factory closures and relocations, which lead to conflicts over outstanding wages and benefits, the terms of the relocation, and severance pay, among other issues." "Factories shut down or relocate, leaving workers out of work and with months of unpaid wages and benefits," *China Labour Bulletin*, March 16, 2023, https://clb.org.hk/zh-hans/node/15779.

332 Zipp and Blecher, "Migrants and Mobilization": 119.

333 Zhao Yuanyuan, "Meituan couriers go on strike in Shanwei," *The China Project* (April 27, 2023, https://thechinaproject.com/2023/04/27/meituan-couriers-go-on-strike-in-shanwei/#:~:text=In%20a%20rare%20display%20of,other%20improvements%20in%20the%20workplace; "Food delivery riders strike for increased pay per delivery," *China Labour Bulletin*, May 18, 2023, https://clb.org.hk/zh-hans/node/15817.

334 Elfstrom and Kuruvilla, "The Changing Nature of Labour Unrest."

FIGURE 3.8 Labor process in apparel and assembly line production.
Sources: Celestica employees work on a production line at the Celestica Technology Co. Ltd, Dongguan, July 29, 2009. (AP Photo/Vincent Yu); Workers make down jackets at a workshop of a garment manufacturer in Hehe town, Yangxin county, Binzhou city, East China's Shandong province, on November 4, 2024. (Photo by Costfoto/NurPhoto via Getty Images)

particularly prominent flashpoint because of the nature of production and the shop floor itself: inputs are valuable, the production is labor intensive and skill dependent, quality and quantity measurement are challenging, and enforcement of labor discipline depends heavily on direct, personal monitoring.[335] By contrast, in the automotive and electronics sectors, management is built more into the routinized and automated labor process of constant-flow assembly line production (Figure 3.8). Moreover, in apparel (though not there alone, of course) monitoring by male supervisors over female workers sets up a ready flashpoint of gender-based, face-to-face friction that readily produces humanistic and moral outrage.

Political concerns focusing on the nature of institutions, governance or legitimacy rarely stimulate labor protest. In a sample of reported protests by migrant workers between 2010 and 2013,[336] only two out of eighty-nine mentioned political demands: in one, workers complained that their union existed "in name only," and there was an anti-tax riot in Huzhou (Zhejiang).[337] Regulatory matters, which are political in the more limited, simpler sense that they are undertaken by governments, have stimulated protest in particular sectors such as

335 Anand Deshpande, "Shop Floor Control in Apparel Production," *Apparel Resources*, May 30, 2016, https://apparelresources.com/business-news/manufacturing/shop-floor-control-in-apparel-production/.

336 Zipp and Blecher, "Migrants and Mobilization": 119.

337 Radio Free Asia (2013) "广州工人罢工取得成果 如愿加薪" ("Guangzhou Workers' Strike Has Achieved Results"), June 20 2013; www.rfa.org/mandarin/Xinwen/bag-06202013143811.html; Fung, Y-y., Xin, Y. and Mudie, L. (2011) 'Officials Blamed for Tax Riots', *Radio Free Asia*, October 28, 2011, www.rfa.org/english/news/china/tax-10282011102227.html.

the taxi trade.[338] Of course, Chinese workers have on rare occasions expressed political critiques during their strikes and protests,[339] but those issues are rarely the core stimulus of their contentious action in the first place.

Repertoires

Labor disputes often begin peaceably, with workers simply complaining to their bosses. They almost never begin with their labor union branch (if they have one, which many private sector firms do not), because workers know all too well that factory-level union branches do not exist to represent workers *vis-à-vis* management. If they don't receive satisfaction from their supervisor, workers can pursue further action individually by seeking arbitration or legal relief. Very few workers—under 1 percent—have done so, and the majority of them have been urban-resident rather than migrant workers. The number of cases accepted for arbitration has risen steadily: cases rose from 50,000 per year in 1996 to over a million in 2020 (Figure 3.9). Nationally, it doubled in 2008, due to crisis-driven layoffs as well as the promulgation of a major new Labor Contract Law; in Guangdong Province, China's main export manufacturing base, it nearly tripled. Workers can also file lawsuits under China's various labor laws. Following the pattern of arbitration, the number of suits doubled from 150,000 in 2007 to 300,000 in 2008 and 2009, falling back only to 200,000 in 2010. Since then, the courts have taken various steps to discourage labor litigation, by refusing to accept collective complaints and channeling individual ones back into the

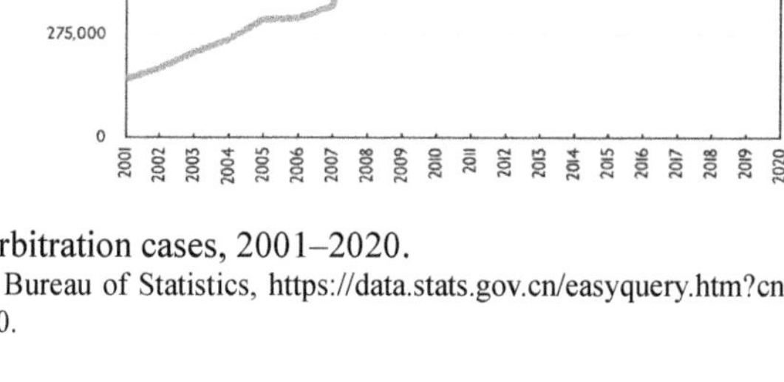

FIGURE 3.9 Arbitration cases, 2001–2020.
Source: National Bureau of Statistics, https://data.stats.gov.cn/easyquery.htm?cn=C01&zb=A0S05&sj=2020.

338 Manfred Elfstrom, "China's Contentious Cab Drivers: A Window on Worker Activism and Policy Change," unpublished paper, 2012.
339 See p. 190.

mediation system.[340] Such mobilization of civil and legal disputation by workers promptly overwhelmed the labor bureaux and courts. It began to take months just to schedule a first hearing, and several years to reach a conclusion. So the government began to urge aggrieved workers and their employers to focus more on mediation. From 1997 to 2010, 43 percent of urban-registered workers' civil and legal disputes concerned wages, 18 percent contract termination, and 17 percent overtime. Twenty-three percent of these complainants were dissatisfied with the outcome, and 40 percent very dissatisfied; the major reasons for their unhappiness were the protracted nature of the process (43 percent), its lack of fairness (23 percent), and non-implementation (13 percent). For migrants, wages, including arrears, were the overwhelming complaint (83 percent). They were happier with their outcomes: 71 percent felt satisfied or very satisfied, perhaps because wage disputes are given to more straightforward resolution, or perhaps because migrants' expectations are lower.[341]

No surprise, then, that contentious labor disputes have proliferated. When complaints and meetings with management fail, workers turn to a wide range of repertoires. Almost none of these benefit from significant planning or organization, for which the Chinese political and industrial relations systems do not allow any space. Most have only loose, novice leadership at best, both for this same reason but also because workers have come to realize that protest leaders make ready targets for repression. All this, of course, puts workers at a grave disadvantage compared with the formidable resources and experience of Party/state. The fact that some have turned for advice to activists of the Hong Kong *China Labour Bulletin* or other such outfits—in the midst of a maelstrom, phoning up to a live broadcast to ask what to do next—provides poignant testimony to the problem.

When aggrieved workers act collectively, most often they just down tools in an impromptu strike. Slowdowns are less frequent, probably because they require more ongoing organization and discipline and also since they leave protesting workers face-to-face with management on the shop floor. Rather than picket, they often take their strike to the streets, staging marches and blocking roads and railways, partly just to express themselves but also hoping to attract the attention of the public, media or government as a way to pressure their employer to meet their demands. In early 2008, one group of Zhengzhou workers repeatedly blocked their boss's luxury car (Figure 3.10). If the local government gets involved, it generally tries to contain rather than suppress such demonstrations, sometimes also working behind the scenes for a settlement. It

340 Hui, *Hegemonic Transformation*, 86.

341 Mary Gallagher *et al.*, "China's 2008 Labor Contract Law: Implementation and Implications for China's Workers." *World Bank Policy Research Working Paper* 6542.

FIGURE 3.10 Workers blocking their boss's Audi.
Source: "*当街堵住欠薪老板的奥迪A8为讨要工钱, 昨晚工人们还围着轿车打起地铺, 截至今日凌晨双方尚未达成一致*," ("Boss's Audi A8 blocked by workers demanding unpaid wages. Last night, the workers surrounded the car and bedded down. As of this morning, the two sides have not reached an agreement.") *Sina.com* January 4, 2008. http://news.sina.com.cn/o/2008-01-04/075413194545s.shtml.

deploys its repertoire of carrots and sticks *vis-à-vis* workers,[342] puts the trade union branch to work to pressure the workers to settle, and meets quietly with management to do the same.

But where such complex, risky tactics, which require great acumen, fail, disputes can quickly turn violent. Police or thugs hired by the local government or the management may beat up workers.

> Migrant worker Lei Mingzhong, 27, is unconscious on a trolley at Heyuan People's Hospital, the sheets stained with his blood.
>
> It is Tuesday night, four days after about 40 thugs in the employ of Fuyuan Hydropower company attacked Mr Lei and 200 other striking workers on a building site in the southern province of Guangdong.
>
> His attackers, wielding shovels, axes and steel rods, bashed Mr Lei and other workers last week after they went on strike over more than four months of unpaid wages…
>
> Mr Lei is brain-dead, but being kept alive, fellow workers speculate, because the police are postponing a murder investigation.
>
> "He was dead at the field," Xiang Xiquan, one of the seven workers injured in the clash, says from his hospital bed earlier that night.
>
> "The first shovel blow killed him but after he had fallen they kept beating him," Mr Xiang, who suffered a broken leg, bruising and cuts, said. "They are using artificial means to keep him breathing, but it is just a pretense."[343]

342 See p. 168.
343 Mary-Anne Toy, "Chinese Capitalism Reveals Dark Side," *The Age*, July 7, 2007.

This can produce a riot, as in the Guxiang case.[344] Cars (including police vehicles) are overturned and torched, government and enterprise offices are invaded, and property vandalized. Enraged workers also detain, beat or sometimes even kill their bosses. In 2009, a proposed privatization of Tonghua Steel, in the northeastern province of Jilin, turned ugly.

> [L]ocal opponents feared outsiders might hurt their interests, or even destroy their way of life. One day, those suspicions turned violent. Opposition to the takeover contributed to the beating death of Chen Guojin, 40, a Tonggang manager and father of twins, during a worker protest July 24.[345]

Just weeks earlier, across the country in Guangdong Province,

> Liu Hanhuang, a worker at the Zhan Ming Hardware Producing Factory in Dongguan City of south China's Guangdong Province, quarreled with three Taiwan managers over compensation for a work accident. He then killed two and severely injured one…
>
> Liu stabbed the factory's general manager Lin Yu-teng, vice general manager Shaw Cheng-chi and production manager Lai Chen-jui with a knife. Shaw was killed on the spot and Lin died in a hospital.[346]

While such murders might result from the heat of the moment, workers' threats of violence demonstrate their premeditation and deadly seriousness. In Sichuan,

> Chen Fayuan, director of the Chengdu Municipal Supply & Marketing Cooperative, went behind the Guixi workers' backs and sold the co-op's store for over 220 million yuan. The workers wrote letters asking for help from various state organs, including the "National General Cooperative", but no one was willing to help. So finally the workers decided on direct action. They put a padlock on the store so Chen or the new owners couldn't get in, and apparently they stood guard outside. The photo shows a sign they carried that reads "a blood-letting incident against corruption will soon take place."[347]

344 See p. 173.

345 Luo Changping *et. al.*, "Blood on the Hands at a Bleeding Steel Mill," *Caijing*, August 21, 2009.

346 "Mainland 'Highly Concerned' over Worker's Murder of Taiwan Factory Managers," *Xinhua*, June 17, 2009.

347 "The Limits of 'Defending Rights'," *Boxun*, September 1, 2009, https://en.boxun.com/2009/09/01/the-limits-of-defending-rights/.

In 2001, in three separate incidents in Hubei Province, "[a]ngry laid-off workers and their relatives killed three managers at financially struggling, state-owned enterprises."[348]

Desperate, depressed and aggrieved workers have also inflicted violence on themselves. Between 2010 and 2011, 24 young migrant workers in Foxconn plants attempted suicide, several in waves; all but four succeeded.[349] In 2012, 150 Foxconn workers in Wuhan climbed to the roof of the plant and threatened to jump if the company did not cancel planned job transfers.[350] In January 2004, a Zhengzhou construction worker, owed ¥6,000 in wage arrears, set himself on fire on the site.[351] In 2013, six laid-off police officers from Heilongjiang Province in China's northeast attempted suicide outside Zhongnanhai, the central Party compound in Beijing. In May 2015, thirty taxi drivers, also hailing from northeast China, journeyed to the swanky Wangfujing shopping district in Beijing, where they drank pesticide and collapsed (Figure 3.11).[352] In 2007, a wave of layoffs at the Henan No. 5 Provincial Construction Company [in Zhengzhou] drove one worker out of his mind.

> He came unhinged under the strain of supporting his wife and daughter, grew paranoid and delusional. Convinced that the police would charge him with murder, he tried to drown himself in a barrel of water. Today he's in a mental institution while his wife peddles dumplings of fatty pork and mustard greens under the soot-covered trees. "People here have sympathy," Mrs. Xie says, "but I can't eat sympathy and they don't eat enough dumplings."[353]

On a lighter note, workers have also shown their creativity and even their ironic sense of humor by deploying guerrilla theater.

> On Jan[uary] 31, 5 migrant workers in Beijing, who dressed as anger birds, Garfield, Donald Duck, and the Chinese God of Wealth respectively, sat quietly outside the headquarter[s] of China National Radio. Each held a sign with a Chinese character on it. Together they read, "Pay back my blood-sweat (hard-earned) money."[354] (Figure 3.12)

348 "Angry Chinese Workers Murder State Firm Managers," *Reuters*, February 25, 2002.
349 Chan *et. al*, *Dying for an iPhone*, Appendix 2.
350 Janet Ong and Mark Lee, "Foxconn Workers in China Threatened Suicide," *Bloomberg*, January 12, 2012, http://www.bloomberg.com/news/articles/2012-01-12/foxconn-says-150-workers-at-china-plant-protest-redeployment (accessed May 26, 25).
351 Josephine Ma, "Violence Flares Over Unpaid Migrant Wages," *South China Morning Post*, January 10, 2004.
352 Robert Foyle Hunwick, "Desperate Chinese Are Turning to Mass Suicide to Get Their Government's Attention," *Global Post*, May 19, 2015.
353 Matthew Forney, "Workers' Wasteland: China's Prosperous Surface Masks a Rising Sea of Joblessness That Could Threaten the Country's Stability," *Time Online*, April, 2002.
354 "Migrant Workers in Beijing Dressed in Cartoon Costumes to Protest Unpaid Wages," *Offbeat China*, February 1, 2013.

FIGURE 3.11 Beijing taxi drivers attempt suicide in Wangfujing, Beijing, 2015.
Source: Twitter.

FIGURE 3.12 Cartoon costume protest.
Source: Jan. 31, 2013. CFP.

This set of repertoires—wildcat, unorganized strikes and protests, some leading to violence, garnished with a *soupçon* of black humor—evince the very low level of formal institutionalization of labor relations in China. Strikes are neither legal nor illegal, and are often tolerated. Yet strike leaders know they risk arrest on other grounds, which is why few workers dare step forward to take the helm. Independent "wildcat" unions, which can arise spontaneously during strikes, most certainly are forbidden. These strictures, backed as they are by state repression, of course make it nearly impossible for negotiations leading to a settlement to take place. The local branches of the state trade union rarely involve themselves in strike negotiations, and often take sides with the local authorities, including the police, in trying to suppress strikes. There is certainly neither law nor formal or even informal institutions governing contentious labor protest. In general, then, most strikes end with workers receiving a few carrots from employers or the government, or, more commonly, at best with sticks of defeat and repression for aggrieved workers. That, of course, only keeps on the boil the cycle of discontent and strikes leading to collective protest.

What appeared at the time to be an important departure from this "wild west" pattern of labor relations took place in a wave of automotive sector strikes of 2010. When a small group of workers at Nanhai Honda in southern Guangdong learned that they were not receiving the benefit of an increase in the local minimum wage, a small group began quietly to contemplate a strike and mobilize support among their fellow employees. On day one, only fifty stopped work, but soon all 1,800 were out.

> [W]orkers' representatives engaged in an intense informal bargaining process with the management in the course of which they rejected several offers for wage increases. The negotiations went on through several rounds before an agreement was reached. Government representatives and external advisors, among them a well-known labor law expert from Beijing, needed to be mobilized to help in the negotiations.[355]

Moreover, for the first time since 2002, the strike spread into a significant strike wave.

> [T]he 2010 strikes stretched beyond the boundaries of cities and even provinces. The most significant example of this new pattern was a spontaneous "pattern bargaining" in which workers at different factories adopted similar core demands for wage rises without formal coordination. The willingness of workers to pick up demands of their colleagues in other workplaces facilitated the strike contagion that was evident throughout the automotive industry. In the city of Zhongshan, for instance, local Honda workers demanded exactly the same nominal wage increase their colleagues in Nanhai had already won. In numerous other automotive factories in the southern region, demands echoed those of the Honda workers, suggesting a correlation between the different events. Reports in the national media may also have triggered strikes in other regions thousands of miles away.[356]

Yet, in the end, like the contagious protests of 2002, the 2010 genie of coordinated working class politics was soon back in the bottle. Butollo and ten Brink point out that these strikes were copycats rather than a coherent, even semi-organized movement. Ironically, the success of the novel negotiations at Nanhai Honda obviated their development elsewhere: once other employers saw what had transpired and been agreed there, they caved in with stunning rapidity to

355 Florian Butollo and Tobias ten Brink, "Challenging the Atomization of Discontent: Patterns of Migrant-Worker Protest in China during the Series of Strikes in 2010," *Critical Asian Studies* 44, no. 3 (2012): 430.

356 Butollo and ten Brink, "Challenging the Atomization": 429.

workers' demands. Moreover, Nanhai Honda was very skillful in granting wage increases narrowly while rejecting across-the-board raises and seniority pay, thus maintaining

> the dominant system of low base wages and high incentive pay [which] provided motivation for workers to stay with the company and develop their skills. Honda and Guangzhou Automotive effectively prevented a precedent for car suppliers in China. Jobs would remain low-paid and the [state] union would continue to side with management.[357]

The outcome is consistent with the general preference of employers in other capitalist countries, when squeezed, for wage increases if they will help prevent unionization or, as in this case, an informal equivalent.

Moreover, one important contextual factor that made the Nanhai Honda strike appear at the time to represent a move toward more institutionalized labor relations was the expressed commitment of Chen Weiguang, the Chair of the Guangzhou Federation of Trade Unions (GZFTU), to accomplish precisely this.

> In the labor conflicts at Honda's suppliers…in the city of Guangzhou…our approach was very different and the trade union behaved proactively.… In the event of a strike, even very short ones [*sic*], the trade unions have to be on the side of the workers and may not act as mediators.[358]

Indeed, it was the GZFTU that allowed the strike to continue as long as it did until a settlement was negotiated. The following year, Chen and his Guangzhou union colleagues deepened and somewhat democratized collective contract negotiations at Nanhai—a process that has existed broadly on paper across China for many years but that is usually formalistic and moribund. Some scholars who have studied and even been involved in the labor politics at Nanhai were cautiously optimistic, even as they noted that Nanhai's workers remain quite disappointed about the gains they have made and sullen about the prospects.[359] In the end, though, the GZFTU's success in canalizing labor protest and the general weakness of labor *vis-à-vis* the state in Nanhai and across China combined to undermine the prospect of long-term institutionalization at Nanhai and prevent any further cases.

357 Boy Lüthje, "Auto Worker Strikes in China: What Did They Win?" *Labor Notes*, December 23, 2010.

358 Butollo and ten Brink, "Challenging the Atomization": 432.

359 Friedman, *Insurgency Trap*, chaps. 3 and 5; Chris Rohmberg, "A Turning Point for China Workers?" *In These Times*, April 2, 2015. http://inthesetimes.com/article/17759/a-turning-point-for-chinese-workers (accessed September 17, 2015).

Subsequent developments have dashed further any prospects of institutionalization. In 2015, the Party/state began a nationwide crackdown on labor rights NGOs that had been involved in such apolitical, innocuous work as helping individual workers seek legal redress and/or compensation for on-the-job injuries.[360] Private conversations and public lectures I have presented in China about the effectiveness of American and British labor legislation in enabling governments to regulate and rein in strikes and labor protests have met with uniform skepticism.

In an important new book, Manfred Elfstrom has uncovered systematic variation in the nature of labor politics. "Contained" working class responses—relying on "litigation and petitioning, raising demands concerning basic labour standards, and organising via narrow workplace networks"—are associated with "more capital-intensive industries with more high-skilled jobs." By contrast, "transgressive" politics—"well-disciplined or cross-worksite strikes, demands relating to wage increases in excess of legal minimums or calls for things like union reforms, and organising that involves movement-oriented NGOs and other associations"—are more common in "light industry, construction, and transport."[361]

In short, amid China's structural reform, workers have evinced impressive virtuosity in expressing their anger at their employers and the state, in militating for what they believe they deserve, and in pushing the envelope of labor politics. They did briefly attract the attention of at least one provincial leader who sought to contain labor activism through tentative institutional change, but its significance lies in the fact that it proved, as in Hamlet's famous words, "a custom more honored in the breach than the observance." In general, the repertoires of worker protest continue to operate in a murky, uninstitutionalized, repressive and often frightening environment.

Claims and Frames

Have workers expressed claims as employees and citizens with legal rights, human beings entitled to respectful treatment, proud Chinese (in opposition to a foreign employer), rural migrants, oppressed women, the "people" (人民) or the working class committed to socialism?

360 Congressional-Executive Commission on China, "Prosecution of Labor Advocates Has Chilling Effect on Labor NGOs, Strikes Continue," February 22, 2017, https://www.cecc.gov/publications/commission-analysis/prosecution-of-labor-advocates-has-chilling-effect-on-labor-ngos.

361 Ivan Franceschini,"Workers and Change in China: A Conversation with Manfred Elfstrom," *Made in China*, vol. 5, no. 3 (2020): 145. Of course, the distinction is not neat: much labor protest is "boundary spanning." See also Manfred Elfstrom, *Workers and Change in China* (Cambridge: Cambridge University Press, 2021).

Even when engaged in contentious collective action, workers often appeal to their rights under their contracts and China's labor laws. William Hurst has argued that contentious labor protest in China's central coast and most provincial capitals tends to focus on specific claims for legal enforcement.[362] For example:

> [A] laid-off chemical worker in Shanghai on the verge of retirement said that, although she has sometimes had difficulty making ends meet since losing her job, she would never consider protesting unless her pension is withheld after her formal retirement. When pressed as to why she made this distinction, she responded that she had a "formal contract" with her old firm to supply this pension, and so it is "legally protected" in a way that her other living subsidies are not.[363]

The massive 2014 Yue Yuen strike focused on forcing the company to make the pension payments for which it was legally responsible. One worker said:

> The factory director told us, "If you're looking for us to repay, I can tell you it's not going to happen"... That afternoon, people just started walking off little by little....We're fighting for our rights. Even if I go to prison, I won't regret it.[364]

Strikers marched under a banner (Figure 3.13) that proclaimed: "Return our pensions, return our housing subsidy. Dongguan Baocheng (Yue Yuen)'s disgraceful lawbreaking..."

It's no accident that Yue Yuen is located in southern China's Dongguan. One of the core findings of Ching Kwan Lee's celebrated study of working class protest around the turn of the century was that, in contrast to the rustbelt protests discussed above,

> Chinese migrant workers in the sunbelt, indignant over their treatment as second-class citizens by officials and employers, stage "protests against discrimination." These workers resort first to legal activism such as filing petitions and lawsuits for collective labor arbitration, mediation, and litigation. Only when this institutionalized channel fails (which it often does) do they resort to public disruption. They stake their claims in the law, clamoring against discrimination by officials and employers and violation of labor

362 Hurst, *The Chinese Worker*, chap. 5.

363 Ibid., 113.

364 Dan Levin, "Plying Social Media, Chinese Workers Grow Bolder in Exerting Clout," *New York Times*, May 2, 2014.

FIGURE 3.13 Yue Yuen strikers' march.
Source: http://weibo.com/u/2728385957 (accessed September 8, 2015).

> rights, identifying themselves as weak and marginalized masses needing the protection of the state.[365]

For example, when one factory in southernmost China's Shenzhen announced it would move to nearby Dongguan,

> Line leaders became concerned and they jointly organized the girls in their lines to petition to different government departments, demanding allowances during this no-work period. Line leaders saw that their interests were compromised like those of the workers. And eight hundred workers signed the petition letter to the Labor Bureau. Workers divided themselves into three groups and marched to the Labor Bureau, the district government, and the district court, respectively, deliberately putting public pressure on the authorities to pay attention to their plight. Thus began a tortuous process of negotiation with management, mediation by the Labor Bureau, an appeal lawsuit initiated by the factory, and finally a court settlement.[366]

In another case, workers facing heavy wage arrears organized a march through downtown Shenzhen.

> The march is inspired by what we saw on television and in the newspaper. There was a case of wage arrears that took only one week to resolve. That's because the workers managed to get their story into the newspapers. We organized the march and contacted several newspapers, *Guangzhou Daily, Shenzhen Special Zone Daily, Southern Metropolitan News*, and *Crystal*

365 Lee, *Against the Law*, 9.
366 Ibid., 176.

> *News*, in the hope that the media would report our case. In the end, reporters came but no report made it to print… We are not afraid, because we know we have done nothing illegal. The law should not coerce the public.[367]

In 2011, striking workers at the Hailiang Storage Products Company factory in Shenzhen lifted a banner that proclaimed "we know our rights."[368] In 2012, construction workers employed by the Tongshan County (Hubei) government, upset about wage arrears, submitted a letter asking it to "protect the legitimate rights and interests of migrant workers (确保农民工的合法权益)."[369]

Echoing their working class predecessors before 1949 who railed against being treated "like cattle and horses,"[370] workers in the structural reform era have also burst out in *cris de cœur* against subhuman treatment. Workers at the Brother Industries electronics plant in Shenzhen, striking in 2010 over low pay, miserable working conditions and dreadful food in the factory refectory, shouted, "Heavy workload, no increase in pay, you are treating us like rabbits."[371] That same year, striking workers at the Japanese Plastics Group, also in Shenzhen, complained that "there's no difference between the refectory food and pig slop."[372] In 2012, a striking worker at Youde Automotive Electrical Components said that "in 20 years there will be civil unrest in China if these immoral, inhuman [反德不人] practices continue."[373] In 2010, workers on strike against Pingdingshan Cotton in the Pearl River Delta complained that the management "don't treat us like human beings… They couldn't care less if we lived or died."[374]

367 Lee, *Against the Law*, 190.

368 Agence France Presse, "Hundreds Strike in Latest China Labour Protest," December 7, 2011, http://www.google.com/hostednews/afp/article/ALeqM5jp0UWY1VQB0nS7Jxit4N5ikfmQwQ?docId=CNG.8dc3992299cb598cecde0fffb1db8bcd.551.

369 李军 (Li Jun), "农民工代表向湖北通山县政府跪讨工程款" ("Migrant Worker Representatives Appeal to the Government of Tongshan County, Hubei for Project Funds"), *博讯* (*Boxun*), October 7 2010. boxun.com/news/gb/china/2012/10/201210071949.shtml#.UQqLr1rXlhp.

370 See p. 25.

371 "Strike at Shenzhen Brother Industries Ends After Management Compromise," *China Labour Bulletin*, September 10, 2010, https://www.clb.org.hk/content/strike-shenzhen-brother-industries-ends-after-management-compromise

372 "深圳日资企业工人堵路罢工遭防暴公安殴打" ("Workers of Japanese-Funded Enterprises in Shenzhen Blocked Roads and Were Beaten by Riot Police"), *博讯* (*Boxun*), January 21, 2011, http://www.boxun.com/news/gb/china/2011/01/201101211931.shtml

373 "武汉友德汽车电器公司薪水低微福利全无，老板自食加薪诺言，工人拒绝上工" ("Wuhan Youde Auto Electric Co., Ltd. Has Low Salary and No Benefits. The Boss Promises to Raise Salaries, But the Workers Refuse to Go to Work"), Molihua.org, August 22, 2012, http://www.molihua.org/2012/08/blog-post_3421.html.

374 Bill Schiller, "Labour strife rolls across China," *Toronto Star* June 8, 2010, http://www.thestar.com/news/world/2010/06/08/labour_strife_rolls_across_china.html.

In another continuity with pre-1949 labor protest, workers have sometimes deployed nationalist tropes, blaming foreign employers for their plight. Striking Hailiang Storage workers hoisted banners proclaiming that "Japanese companies shamelessly bully Chinese workers."[375] One worker involved in a 2005 sit-in at his Japanese-owned Uniden Electronics plant recounted that when Chinese police intervened against the protest, "Some workers shouted 'traitor' and accused the police of helping the Japanese."[376] Workers in the strike against Taiwan-owned Yue Yuen Shoes even accused what some in China term their "compatriots" of being "Taiwan devils" (台湾[赤]佬).[377]

> Online forums targeted at migrant workers have become popular with those looking to complain about their Japanese, Korean or Taiwanese employers. "They're not interested in helping us Chinese people at all," said one user… on a forum dedicated to Foxconn, the Taiwanese contract manufacturing company.[378]

Such feelings on the workers' part are understandable in light of many foreign (especially East Asian) managers' condescending and even racist views of Chinese workers.[379]

By contrast, the specific mistreatment, by the government and employers alike, of rural migrant workers compared with urban-resident workers, though felt strongly by the former, has not formed a major flashpoint of labor politics. This is surprising, since the issue was a tinderbox of some of the most pointed labor radicalism during the Cultural Revolution.[380] Yet under structural reform, rural migrants have, by and large, not demanded reform or abolition of the household registration system even as it has deprived them of entitlements to health care, housing and education for their children, and even though for the first two decades or more many state enterprises offered better pay and less draconian employment conditions to their urban-resident workers than those

375 Agence France Presse, "Hundreds strike in latest China labour protest" December 7, 2011, https://www.terradaily.com/reports/Hundreds_strike_in_latest_China_labour_protest_999.html.

376 Edward Cody, "Short-Lived Strike Reflects Strength of Japan-China Ties," *Washington Post*, April 26, 2005.

377 Eli Friedman and Ching Kwan Lee, *"Don't Cry Yue Yuen": A Labor Protest in China*. Cornell Program on Ethics and Public Life (video), http://eplchina.cornell.edu/dont-cry-yue-yuen-labor-protest-today/.

378 James Pomfret, "China's New Migrant Workers Pushing the Line," Reuters, July 5, 2010 (republished by *China Labour Bulletin*, July 6 2010, http://www.clb.org.hk/en/content/reuters-china%C3%A2%E2%82%AC%E2%84%A2s-new-migrant-workers-pushing-line.

379 For a detailed discussion of a Korean-owned textile plant, see Kim, *Chinese Labor in a Korean Factory*.

380 See p. 79.

experienced by rural migrants working in private firms. The solution may have to do with the fact that, unlike in the Maoist period, relatively few factories employ rural migrants alongside urban-registered workers, thereby ameliorating the palpability of the irritant within the firm. After all, most labor protest in the structural reform era has been cellular, organized and focused on the workers' specific enterprise. In short, the drivers of protest are generally restricted to rural migrants or to urban-registered workers rather than cutting across that cleavage.

Gender, too, has not emerged as an explicit flashpoint of labor protest. Women workers have, of course, played central roles in protests and strikes against factories that employ mainly women. And when they have done so, they have occasionally referenced their gender as a source of defiant strength. For example, one 46-year-old woman worker in the 2014 Yue Yuen strike declared:

> I have worked here for 15 years, and I am not going without a proper response… Many of my co-workers are women. They thought we would be easy to pick on, but we are here to prove them wrong.[381]

Still, though, in general (and even in this strike) women workers' demands and discourses rarely focus on issues such as patriarchy, gender discrimination or sexual harassment, even though these problems are all too common. Put differently, women workers' claims are generally broadly similar to men's.

And in another, striking discontinuity from the Maoist era and even the pre-1949 period, conspicuously absent are radical, class-based demands and rhetoric. Protesting workers almost never mention class conflict, exploitation, or even Mao (much less Marx). In one exceptional case from 2001, 400 Zhengzhou workers observing the twenty-fifth anniversary of Mao's death:

> bowed before the statue [of Mao] and laid baskets of flowers with long strips of paper carrying elegial [*sic*] couplets — a traditional Chinese literary form of mourning — around its base. "The Great proletarian leader Chairman Mao lives in our heart forever!" read one message. "We, the working class, miss you!" "Defend Mao Zedong's Thoughts till death. Defend the ruling status of the workers' class [*sic*] till death!" said another.[382]

More telling, though, even two "far left" labor organizers of this very event complained:

381 Friends of Gongchao, "The New Strikes in China," *Libcom.org*. http://libcom.org/blog/newtrikes-china-28072014 (accessed September 9, 2015).

382 "Chinese police detain four workers mourning Mao," *Reuters*, September 10, 2001.

> Workers don't recognize they have the power to protest... As long as they can eat, they'll remain obedient. If they can't eat then they'll sell off their belongings. Workers believe it is right that managers have all the power, and workers have none.
>
> Workers who are employed are afraid if they organize they'll lose their job. Workers who are unemployed cannot organize because they are dispersed.[383]

Since the early 1990s, if not before, workers living outside the northeastern and inland rustbelts do generally seem to have accepted the hegemony of the market and the state,[384] which is a powerful reason for the political success of structural economic reform.

By contrast, older and often unemployed workers, especially those in the rustbelts but also across much of China, have advanced claims for proper compensation for their many years of sacrifice in the Maoist era grounded in a frame of "the people" rather than the "working class."[385] Focusing on what Burawoy and Lukács have called "the radiant past,"[386] they recall with much fondness and pride the days when they felt part of China's collective national project of state socialist industrialization. Of course the most important component of the "people" was the "working class." But here, thanks to the revolution, class has been emptied of class conflict, even though, as we have seen, at key moments workers in the 1950s and 1960s did advance "workerist" claims against the state (which, following the Maoist conceptualization during the Cultural Revolution, included, if not capitalists, then certainly officials "taking the capitalist road"). These older workers have largely forgotten their struggles for workplace democracy, management participation in manual labor, and egalitarian pay and benefits. In the context of their disastrous fall from grace, they remember instead a time when they were the leading class in society and were treated as such politically and economically. Their pride in having been the main driver of China's historical economic and political triumphs leaves them decidedly ambivalent about the Party despite everything it has done to them under structural reform.

> [W]orkers' ambivalent feelings about the reemergence of China complicate their perceptions and experiences of living in poverty. Facing appalling stories of corruption as well as the growing gap between rich and poor, [they] often simply sighed, saying, "This is what China is"... Anger and despair went hand in hand with delight and hope as they recounted the nation's

383 Jiang Xueqin, "Fighting to Organize," *Far Eastern Economic Review*, September 6, 2001.
384 Blecher, "Hegemony and Workers' Politics," 283–303.
385 Cho, *The Specter of "the People*."
386 Michael Burawoy and János Lukács, *The Radiant Past*.

> growing GDP, China's important presence in world politics, the number of gold medals won by Chinese athletes, and so on.[387]

As one laid off worker put it:

> "Northeast China was called 'the eldest son of the republic' [共和国的长子]. Do you know what that means? Northeast China was the first area liberated by the Communist Party during the Civil War. Since then, we *dongbei ren* [northeasterners] have devoted our resources to the state without compensation. What came to us after all these sacrifices? Total neglect! Total betrayal!… Deng Xiaoping said that "development is the solid truth" [发展才是硬道理]. National development is good, isn't it? That's the very contribution that we *dongbei ren* have tirelessly made since 1949!"[388]

In short, the frame of "the people" differs from and actually undermines that of "the working class" by eliding any concept of structural conflict now or in the Maoist past and by providing a basis for workers to take credit for the achievements of the structural reforms rather than to denounce them.

It undermines a frame of class in another sense as well. Consistent with what we have seen, urban workers, including the unemployed, immiserated rustbelt survivors, who think of themselves as part of "the people," also exclude rural migrant workers from that category. In Hadong, which lies deep in the Heilongjiang rustbelt,

> The split within "the people" has become palpable… "Peasants," who had in ideological terms constituted one of the primary classes constituting "the people," along with urban workers, are now excluded when workers invoke "the people."… Urban workers call rural migrants *nongmin* [peasants] to highlight their perceived ignorance. Even peri-urban farmers, who are denigrated as *nongmin* by urban workers, attempt to distinguish themselves from rural migrants by calling them "real" *nongmin* while emphasizing that they themselves are, unlike rural migrants, urban *hukou* [household registration] holders.[389]

Moreover, hegemonically, the migrants have dejectedly accepted the urbanites' exclusion of them from the frame of "the people."

387 Cho, *The Specter of "the People,"* 4.
388 Ibid., 33.
389 Ibid., 43.

> [R]ural migrants continue to describe themselves in a way that magnifies their abandonment and abjection, regardless of the social assistance directed toward them. This differs from the tendency of urban laid-off workers to lay claim to the title of "the people" while grappling with their relationship to the original author of that claim, the Chinese state. The rural migrants… in Hadong were not interested in either the old ideological rhetoric identifying peasants as "the people," and thus the masters of the country, or the state's new ideological description of migrant workers as "an active industrial army spurring the nation's economic development." From "(powerless) common people" (*laobaixing*) to "wolves," poverty-stricken rural migrants in Hadong produced their "downtrodden" identity in ways that differed from the state's attempts to see, name, and count them. These rural migrants identify themselves as powerless outcasts.[390]

The frame of "the people" has shaped rustbelt unemployed workers' claims. As we have seen, the most they expect is compensation for layoffs to which they believe they are entitled for giving their lives to the construction of Chinese socialism. They have not mounted any serious critique of structural reform, even though in the Maoist period these selfsame people united militantly and powerfully within the frame of the "working class" to attack that state socialism even as it treated them much better than structural reform does today. And the rustbelt migrants who also accept not just the hegemony of the frame of "the people" but also their exclusion from it have not even critiqued or claimed even that much, believing themselves lacking so meager an entitlement. In short, in the rustbelt "the people" has replaced and profoundly undermined "the working class" as a political frame.

Timing and Contagion

Strike waves may provide one important indicator of the working class's capacity to transcend immediate local concerns and act in concert, as part of a broader economic, social, cultural, and political collectivity. Chinese workers did so in the 1920s, the 1940s, the 1950s, and the 1960s. What of the structural reform era?

Employers and the Party/state in China have managed to prosper extraordinarily well despite the drumbeat of labor resistance. What they fear most from the country's workers, though, are waves of strikes and protests. For employers, they could presage broad, across-the-board wage rises, threatening profitability and international competitiveness. For the Party/state, they could usher in metastatic political instability. The two major (and very different) strike waves

390 Cho, *The Specter of "the People,"* 122.

that have occurred under the structural reforms—by laid-off workers in the northeast in 2002, and by skilled migrant auto workers in 2010—therefore rang loud alarm bells among both supporters and opponents of labor activism in China.[391] In the end, though, they turned out to be exceptions that proved the rule in Chinese labor relations—that collective action is, in general, basically cellular. It may be, though, that China is beginning to evince the traces of a yet unexplored pattern of clustering that lies between the standard categories of broad protest waves on the one hand and cellularity on the other.

Figure 3.14 compiles data on reported labor protest by migrant workers from 2010 to 2013.[392] In the apparel sector, four of the seven collective actions in late 2011 took place in or around Guangzhou, though none were in the same town, and there is no evidence that the workers were in touch with each other; so the

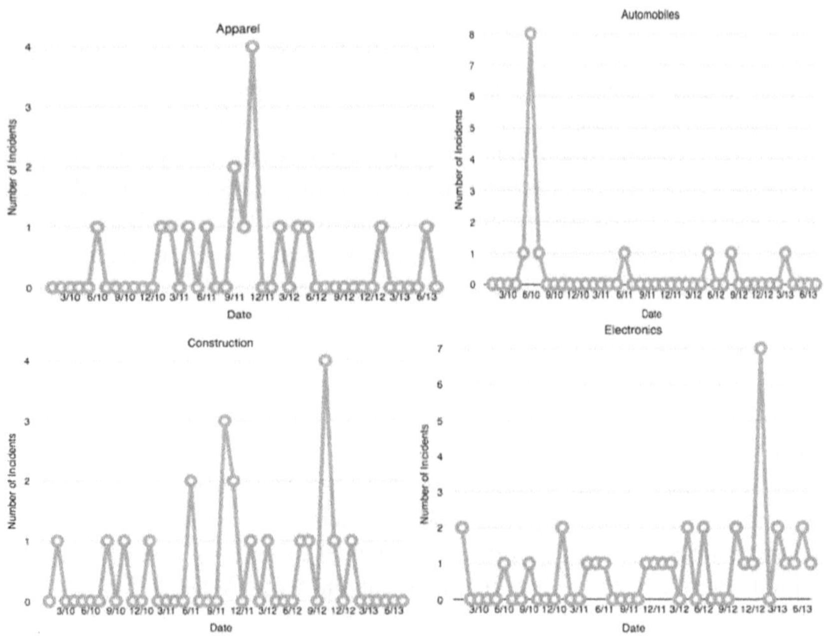

FIGURE 3.14 Dates of migrant workers' collective action by sector, 2010–2013.
Source: Zipp and Blecher, "Migrants and Mobilization."

391 Waves of strikes and protests were also reported immediately after the June 4, 1989 crackdown, in Hangzhou and elsewhere, but little is known about them.
392 Zipp and Blecher, "Migrants and Mobilization."

spike in the data may just reflect random variation. After all, there were only four cases. The spike in the data from May to July 2010 in the automotive sector reflects the clearly documented strike wave in automobile plants, discussed above. While it took place across three provinces, in joint ventures with two different Japanese companies (Honda and Toyota), workers who walked out a few days later had been in communication with the earlier strikers or had news about their strikes.[393] In construction, collective action spiked in 2011 and 2012 across widely scattered locations, both years in October. Workers in one case mentioned the Mid-Autumn Festival in their appeal,[394] which alerts us to the possibility that what we are seeing here is the effect of holiday timing rather than a protest wave. Finally, in electronics, there was a clear strike wave in January 2013 at three plants in Jiangxi, in which workers communicated with and inspired each other.[395] The remaining four were scattered across Beijing, Shanghai and Guangzhou, with no apparent connection except, perhaps, for the timing around the Lunar New Year.

Overall, then, except for the 2010 automobile plant strike wave and one small triad of electronics strikes, there is little evidence that collective action among migrant workers even within the same sector involved significant direct contagion. Moreover, looking across sectors, the spikes occurred at different times, which reinforces the point. Still, capital and the state may wish to resist complacency. Butollo and ten Brink argue that the unusual offensive and contagious strikes in the auto sector could occur because of effective, energetic leadership, which can happen anywhere, but also due to specific structural characteristics of these firms: they employed better educated workers who had graduated from technical schools. The workers also understood that the just-in-time production system in Japanese automobile production gave them real leverage: shutting down one small supplier factory, which is where these strikes occurred, can bring the big assembly plants to a halt in very short order.[396] Insofar as Chinese industry moves over the coming decades toward more sophisticated forms of lean production with more highly trained workers, dangers could lie ahead. For the moment, though, the very factors that made for contagion in the automobile sector militate against it spreading to other sectors where they do not prevail.

Finally, there is a caution here. Strike waves *may* indicate the development of working class political concertation, but they may not, or they may do so only in a partial and contingent way. The automotive strikes of 2010 did not spread to other sectors, and they occurred largely because of the specific characteristics of their sector. Moreover, they involved frames and claims around

393 Butollo and ten Brink, "Challenging the Atomization of Discontent."
394 Li Jun (2010) "农民工代表."
395 Chan, John, "Further Strikes in China as Economy Slows," *World Socialist Website*, January 21, 2013. www.wsws.org/en/articles/2013/01/21/chin-j21.html
396 Butollo and ten Brink, "Challenging the Atomization of Discontent."

bread-and-butter issues rather than structural issues of class relations and political economy. Of course, working class solidarity need not be radical; a highly developed working class can also be one oriented to business unionism, as the United States in the Fordist era shows. The point here, though, is that neither of the strike waves of the structural reform era evinced much in the way of working class coordination, discourse, frames or claims. In 2002 the laid-off northeastern workers sought better settlements for themselves, going so far as failing to support similar demands of their own neighbors. The Honda workers asked for higher pay, not labor protection and subsidies for all workers. Neither, then, is the stuff even of bread-and-butter working class formation. On the contrary, their inwardness reflects the profound fragmentation of China's working class under structural reform.

Efficacy

What difference have proletarian politics made? Have they improved workers' economic or social lives, or changed the way they understand their world and prospects? Have they fostered political momentum?

Material conditions in China's cities have of course improved dramatically, and some gains have trickled down to workers. Average real wages have been rising in the neighborhood of up to 8 percent annually under the structural reforms.[397] The reasons have much more to do with productivity gains and the labor market—bumpily rising demand that outstrips supply—than with labor protest, though. Most labor protest is cellular, and ends with workers in a particular enterprise getting minor concessions at best. In this sense, then, most workers who have experienced economic gains are inclined, as we have heard them say, to chalk them up to economic development rather than collective political action. And that only contributes to the hegemony of their broad support for structural reform.

Moreover, the decades-long drumbeat of labor protest has not produced detectable gains in labor solidarity or collective identification. Workers are more likely to emerge from strikes and protests demoralized and hopeless than energized. As one veteran worker who participated in the huge Yue Yuen strike, but who also said that "I don't see myself as an activist," put it:

> The workers' solidarity weakened after the employer made a minor concession. And there was also suppression from the government, so it inevitably failed. Actually, I knew this strike would fail when they got obsessed with the union election and gathering demands in the [online chat] group because they failed to unify the workers with concerted action and consistent

397 See p. 93.

> demands… Although we returned to work, we still harbour resentment. We all feel aggrieved today. Outwardly, the strike has been resolved but the underlying problems are still there. All in all, we are frustrated. We feel especially dissatisfied because of the government's suppression of workers. All of us feel very angry at being forced to work now…Although the government does not do a good job in some areas, hurling accusations at the government and getting involved in politics is just ill-advised. In China, it is best not to get involved in political issues.[398]

Still, the hard nut of ongoing, grinding economic exploitation leads even this defeated and generally apolitical and somewhat cynical worker to expect ongoing conflict and express some faint hope, albeit within strong limits set by his hegemonic support for his country, the Party and structural reform.

> You see, ordinary workers can get about 2,700 yuan a month, and it will be 2,930 yuan if they get a 230 yuan pay raise, but social security and the housing fund will be deducted from this figure (2,930 × 8 percent (social security) + 2,930 × 5 percent at least (housing fund)). Thus, they will get 2,500 yuan, less than before. Do you think the workers will be content with that? By the way, overtime stays the same. Adidas has made it clear that it will reduce orders, and maybe other brands will follow suit. So we have reasons to believe the workers will be paid less… So I predict there will be a big strike within half a year and there will only be one demand—a raise of at least 30 percent. Workers can't live on 2,300–2,400 yuan!…
>
> Gaobu [where Yue Yuen is located] is my second home and Yue Yuen is like my family. For many workers, this is a simple and honest feeling. We were once proud to be Yue Yuen workers. We just want a decent job and a dignified life. We love the Communist Party and our homeland, and we hope our country can develop better. But when we workers cannot benefit from the sustained economic development, I think it's not right…
>
> The fire was put out but the embers remain and it will ignite again. And in the next strike we will definitely be better organized and combat-ready![399]

And as of this writing in early 2022, the embers have not reignited at Yue Yuen. Like its predecessors in the Manchurian strike wave of 2002 and the strike wave of 2010 that began in the automotive sector, it has not produced political momentum either among its own participants or among fellow Chinese workers.

398 "Defeat will only make us stronger: Workers Look Back at the Yue Yuen Shoe Factory Strike." *China Labour Bulletin*, May 22, 2014, http://www.clb.org.hk/en/content/defeat-will-only-make-us-stronger-workers-look-back-yue-yuen-shoe-factory-strike.

399 "Defeat will only make us stronger."

Yet labor politics have had a detectable effect on the Party/state's response to them. In an important new study, Manfred Elfstrom has offered a novel analysis of its deployment of the carrot and stick. It does not just operate at the level of an extant strike or strike wave, in the form of repression for leaders deemed too aggressive but tolerance and even some partial accession to demands of followers. Consistent with the discussion above of developments in Guangdong,[400] he has uncovered distinct political approaches to the management of labor strife.

> Where resistance remains largely contained... you see authorities adopting an orthodox approach that combines pre-emption of worker mobilisation, caution when it comes to labour law and the programming of the official trade union — why rock the boat policywise and risk introducing disorder when things are already going well? — and subtle nudging to keep both labour and capital in line. In contrast, where resistance ranges from boundary-spanning to outright transgressive, authorities adopt a risk-taking approach that involves giving up on pre-empting everything and instead focusing on experimenting with novel, somewhat pro-worker policies, while coming down harshly on labour organisers and ordinary striking workers alike.[401]

That is, working class politics is shaping the Party/state's management of it.

...

Working class political formation under structural reform, a period that has involved the largest and most rapid spate of proletarianization in history, has charted a complex pathway. Labor politics remained broadly quiescent in the 1980s, when the working class retained some of its latent capacity to limit the transition to the labor market, and the leadership was divided and tentative in its approach to transforming industry. In the 1990s, the rise of wage labor and the labor market, and the decline in workers' relative (and, for some, absolute) economic and social position stimulated workers to resist in a sustained drumbeat of protests and strikes. They deployed a panoply of repertoires, claims and frames. But these lacked the radical, coordinated character of labor politics in the Maoist era. Incipient strike waves in 2002 and 2010 came to naught. So while workers in particular enterprises have often been able to register some small gains from their own political mobilization, what gains the working class more broadly has achieved have more to do with structural factors such as the supply and demand for labor and with trickle down from China's extraordinary economic development than with working class politics. Workers understand this, which only undermines their interest in coordinated class politics.

400 See p. 185.
401 Franceschini, "Workers and Change in China": 145–146.

Conclusion

Structural reform remade China's working class yet again. It transformed them from industrial citizens[402] with employment security, significant benefit entitlements and meaningful roles in enterprise operations back into proletarians subject to the rigors of the wage relationship and the labor market. It disaggregated China's powerful working class along multiple structural cleavages that cut across each other to produce complex differentiation: workers in state *vs.* private and mixed ownership firms; urban-resident workers *vs.* rural migrants; the employed *vs.* the unemployed; younger generations born and raised under structural reform *vs.* Maoist-era workers; more *vs.* less skilled; more *vs.* less educated; rustbelt *vs.* central *vs.* southeast; men *vs.* women; and even, in some cases, Han Chinese *vs.* those of other or mixed nationality. Moreover, in contrast to the Maoist-era work unit institutional system, which separated workers in each enterprise from those in others (but which they did manage to overcome to act in concert in the 1956–57 strike wave and a decade later in the Cultural Revolution), workers are now riven by the hegemony of capitalism itself, whose consumer and labor markets have reoriented most workers' aspirations and strategies to an individual and family-oriented level.

In the context of this structural fragmentation and individuation, workers' economic situations have, not surprisingly, proven rather variegated. Employed urban workers' lives have improved, often significantly, though they have lost the job security that was an entitlement in the Maoist era. Many of the unemployed have actually seen their livelihoods collapse, especially in rustbelt areas where alternative sources of employment, including petty entrepreneurship, are tightly limited. Rural migrants have experienced somewhat increased income and material life compared with the rural existences they have fled, but the absolute levels are still very low, and for many, perhaps most, they have been won only at the very high cost of becoming subject to sweatshop labor régimes and living conditions. And any economic gains realized anywhere in the working class have certainly been much lower than those achieved by middle class officials, professionals and capitalists small and large. The basis for that overarching gap is, of course, the extraordinary levels of surplus value produced by the working class and appropriated by China's new capitalists and its newly capitalistic state enterprises.

Socially, the working class has undergone radical transformations that render it virtually unrecognizable compared with its Maoist-era past. The size of the Chinese proletariat has gyrated wildly, and its composition has altered profoundly as almost 300 million rural migrants eventually came to outnumber their urban-resident predecessors. It also became younger, better educated

402 Andreas, *Disenfranchised.*

and much more feminized. The strict coincidence of workplace and residence in the Maoist-era work unit has been broken apart, and with it the previously high levels of both solidarity and conflict seen off. Shop floor social relations have become far more authoritarian and draconian than those against which the Maoist-era working class inveighed so ardently.

Where in the past workers had conceived of themselves with a strong sense of self-confidence and rightful power, China's new working class generally feels itself weak, subordinate and defeated. Depression and alienation are not uncommon. Where Maoist-era workers fought for, and in some measure actually achieved, their vision of a radically changed world, their successors feel there is no alternative to structural reform, and they are broadly resigned to the hegemony of the market and the state. Drilling deeper, and recognizing the working class's social fragmentation, reveals its political culture as profoundly variegated, ambivalent and contradictory. In the rustbelt many workers feel an overwhelming sense of betrayal and abandonment, tinged with atavistic pride in workers' historical contribution to what structural reform could achieve even as they cannot share in it. In better off areas, workers feel a complex admixture of dynamism and exhaustion, anomie and independence, hope and realist resignation, attraction and repulsion, wonder and anger.

Politically, the powerful, confident working class that emerged from the Maoist era was slow to react to structural reform, which makes sense since it did not begin seriously to threaten them until the early 1990s. When plant closures and layoffs began to bite in the late 1990s, workers in the northeastern heavy industrial heartland did begin to organize waves of protests, but the Party/state's carrot-and-stick tactics and monopoly of political space combined with the working class's fissiparousness brought resistance to an early end. In the new century, labor protest has been on the rise. By and large it has been defensive; the portentous offensive by automobile workers in 2010 has not been repeated as of this writing in 2022. Labor activism has been oriented overwhelmingly to material and humanistic issues, a sharp contrast with the political orientation of most working class politics in the Maoist era. The literally rebellious repertoires of that period have been replaced by legalistic procedures, wildcat strikes, public demonstrations, guerrilla interventions (such as transport blockages and street theater) and occasional violent outbursts against managers and even themselves in the form of suicides. Nationalism has remained an important trope in conflicts against foreign capital (harkening back to pre-1949 days), but gender and anti-migrant discrimination have not despite their seriousness. Discourse around class, potent before 1949 and in the Maoist decades, is gone.

In short, the relative and, in some places, absolute decline in workers' material conditions, social standing and cultural self-understandings have provided ample fodder that has stoked up significant protest. But, hegemonically, structural reform has shaped working class resistance to itself, de-radicalizing workers' politics precisely at a time when the working class might have been expected to deploy the wellsprings of radicalism of its own recent past. The solution to this puzzle lies in the complex dynamics of China's second bout of working class re-formation. That in turn is a product of the historicity, sequencing and other specificities of the transition back to capitalistic economic and social relations, and especially of the adroit hand of the state in managing the process. Those matters are the subject of the concluding chapter.

CONCLUSION

The Making, Apotheosis and Fall of China's Working Class

Since its emergence in the late nineteenth century, China's working class—now the world's largest by far—has been on a roller-coaster ride. Its formation has traversed three periods—revolutionary (through 1949), Maoist (1949–78) and structural reform (1978–present)—each a radical break with what came before. Distinctive, discontinuous patterns of *economic* exploitation, *social* relations and experiences, and *cultural* self-understandings emerged in each. In *political* terms, the working class responded actively throughout, although how it did so shifted fundamentally depending not only on these economic, social and cultural factors but also on the radically different hegemonic political-*cum*-economic projects of each era. That is, *China's working class has stood up for itself throughout, in ways shaped by economic, social and cultural and political forces of the period but that also conformed profoundly with the hegemonic structures of power it was resisting.*

From the dawn of industrialization in the late nineteenth century through the end of the revolutionary period, the severe *economic* maltreatment and exploitation and the wrenching *social* dislocations and reorganizations of early industrialization remained fairly constant. Two co-dominant *cultural* frames of class and nation emerged from China's anti-imperialist and leftist movements, both spontaneously from among the working class itself and also from a range of progressive organizations and parties. They were reinforced by the hegemonic project led by the Nationalist and Communist Parties during their United Front from 1923 to 1927, and they remained robust even after that project's would-be hegemonic bloc of workers, intellectuals and middle classes disintegrated with the rightward, autocratic shift of the Guomindang and the onset of civil war in 1927.

DOI: 10.4324/9781003518228-5

Politically, starting with early industrialization, the working class engaged in significant levels of protest, much of it spontaneous. China's ongoing crisis created a contradictory political opportunity structure for working class politics. Structurally, the country's size, political fragmentation and low level of institutionalization opened political space locally but made it difficult to create regional or trans-regional movements, much less a national one. Thus, working class resistance generally remained fragmented both geographically and sectorally. That is, most strikes and demonstrations remained local and confined to particular enterprises or trades. Politically, China experienced a breathless succession of régime shifts—from the declining imperial system before 1911, to ongoing political crisis through 1923, to the progressive Guomindang-Communist United Front in south China from 1923 to 1927, to the Guomindang's proto-fascism starting in 1927, to the Second United Front from 1937 to 1945 (during which the Japanese and the Guomindang variously remained in control of China's major cities), to the renewal of Civil War and the gradual Communist conquest of major cities from 1945 to 1949. These rapid switches created and removed constraints on working class resistance. During two of these moments—from 1923 to 1927 and again in the mid-1940s—the Communist Party was able to begin to forge fissiparous labor protests into regionally and sectorally coordinated movements that, while still nationalistic in character, were also more class-based in their frames and claims than before. In short, while economic exploitation, social dislocation, a culture of class-based and patriotic resistance, and imperialism propelled working class self-mobilization for much of the pre-1949 period (including even the proto-fascistic years of Guomindang urban dominance), the level, scope and substance of working class politics was a complex resultant of workers' and the Communist Party's *agency*, the complicated political opportunity *structure*, and the *contingencies* of warlord conflict, the Japanese invasion, the Second World War and the course of the revolution. In short, while economic, social and cultural aspects of working class formation, along with ongoing imperialism, certainly shaped the issues, repertoires and claims of working class politics, changes in the frequency and geographic scope of working class politics before 1949 had much more to do with wider political changes. Most generally, the overall disaggregation of working class politics reflected the absence of any robust political hegemony in China, and the complex clashes of several hegemonic projects over this protracted period of crisis.

Moreover, the mutual isolation of the working class and the Communist Party produced by all this had profound effects for both, before and after 1949. The former had to learn to fend for itself, which produced not just some continued, localized activism even under the most unfavorable conditions of Guomindang and Japanese rule, but also powerful senses of proletarian self-confidence, autonomy and hostility to political authority generally, all of which were prominently in evidence in the radical state socialist decades. The latter, founded by radical intellectuals much more than workers, was reshaped as well, maturing into a battle-hardened, disciplined, effective political fighting force without significant roots in or debts to the working class. This legacy would have the profoundest implications for labor politics ever since.

The advent of hegemonic state socialism in its radical Maoist form utterly remade the working class economically and socially, in the context of which it remade itself culturally and politically. *Economically,* workers' incomes, standards of living and employment security rose dramatically. *Social life* was remade in fundamental ways. Enterprises were reorganized into "work units" which integrated work, residence, commercial services, broad welfare provision, education and recreation. Shop floors were increasingly politicized, often (and most controversially) with flatter hierarchies between managers and workers and new institutions of worker participation. At the same time, the working class was now subdivided into a complex set of hierarchies: urban-resident workers in state and collective factories at the top, urban-resident workers sent to rural postings below them, and, still further down, farmers who were given temporary contracts to work in factories in towns and cities; skilled and unskilled workers, and older and younger ones, who were arrayed along an eight-grade wage scale; men and women; "reds" with political positions, experience and connections *vs.* less politically inclined "experts" and others; and, once the momentous Cultural Revolution hit, "rebels," "conservatives" and "economistics." In status terms, the proletariat was now exalted as never before, not just in official propaganda but also in the popular mind—workers had higher prestige than intellectuals, and young people turned down university slots for factory jobs.

Culturally, three new ways of thinking emerged. Many workers celebrated the victory of the revolution by developing loyalty to the Party for the palpable economic and social gains they were experiencing. But significant parts of the working class evinced an astonishing new level of self-confidence, rebelliousness and a "workerist" sensibility. Beginning in the earliest years of the People's Republic, long before the Cultural Revolution, they had the temerity to denounce the new political and military leadership. These workers put forth robust demands for workplace democracy, claimed themselves "masters of the enterprise," and stridently denounced the bureaucratic reorganizations of the First Five-Year Plan, including incentive pay, concentration of power in managers' hands, and draconian discipline on the shop floor. Finally, rural contract workers adopted an equally strident but much more defensive standpoint against their subordination to the urban-resident workers alongside whom they toiled.

Politically, as before 1949, China's working class engaged in a great deal of spontaneous, autonomous, virtuosic political activity. But now they were also able to achieve real results, reversing enterprise-level policies that divided them, undermining bureaucratic and managerial authority, and democratizing the shop floor. Their activity ebbed and flowed in rhythm to openings in the political opportunity structure, rising during the initial "liberation" in the early 1950s, Mao's "Hundred Flowers" policy of 1956 and of course the Cultural Revolution. And thanks to the radical change in the wider political system that came with the triumph of the revolution, the working class could now mobilize itself on regional and even national scales, which had proven much harder before 1949 without the help of the Communist Party. Yet the fact of such *aperturas* should not blind us to the considerable risks that workers were taking at each of these junctures, which many workers actually suffered in the crackdowns against the East China system of management and the consolidation of one-man management in the early 1950s, the Anti-Rightist Campaign of 1957 and the rebels' ultimate defeat in the Cultural Revolution. That is, in their moments of self-mobilization, while radical workers were responding to a new, radical hegemony, they were also acting with considerable gumption against unfathomable odds.

Moreover, where before 1949 (and, as we shall see, after 1978) most working class political mobilization focused on *material* conditions, now it focused much more on *political* questions—of factory power, class relations, and, ultimately, of the very nature of the Party and socialism. To be sure, these were issues raised by Mao and his left supporters; but radical workers also came to them on their own. Arguably, they may even have helped embolden Mao and other radical leaders to pursue them. Indeed, even "economistic" rural contract workers demanding equal material treatment with urban resident workers framed their demands politically, and sought (and briefly received) the backing of top radical élites.

This returns us to the puzzle of why China's working class was most radical during the period when its core stratum was also treated best in economic and social terms. Four forces seem to have been at work. The improvement in material life may finally have opened space for urban resident state and collective enterprise workers to raise deeper, more radical questions. Moreover, in the context of state socialism, the relative material disadvantage of urban-resident workers exiled to the countryside, and of rural migrant workers, may have pointed directly to radical critique. Indeed, Marx and Burawoy suggest that their situation is more likely to produce pushback than even the exploitation of workers under capitalism, which is more subject to ideological obfuscation grounded in the abstract nature of surplus value (compared with state socialism's appropriation of surplus labor and product).[1] Third, the same might be said of workers unhappy at being left out of the clientelist networks of power built up by factory officials. Fourth, radical workers were emboldened by support from Mao and other leftists at the pinnacle of the Party for radical change. In other words, the radical economic and social fragmentation of China's

1 Karl Marx, *Capital*; Burawoy and Lukács, *The Radiant Past*, 18–19.

working class under radical state socialism provided the material basis for the most radical politics it ever evinced. But it still took a great deal of fortitude, daring and political will, as well as support from on high, for China's working class to build its potent political movement on that foundation.

Yet in the end it proved vulnerable. The social capacities of the working class may have expanded tremendously with the victory of the revolution, but those of the Party/state did so even more—not just because of its victory, but also because of the preceding decades of battles that hardened it. The power imbalance became evident from the outset, when the working class's self-initiated radical offensives such as the East China system of factory management were defeated by a Party without significant roots in the working class. Sequencing matters here too: the early defeat of working class radicalism came before the rise of the Maoist critiques that subsequently revived it in the run-up to the Great Leap Forward and then the Cultural Revolution. So does context: both those moments proved too chaotic to enable working class radicalism to secure victories.

Structural reform of Chinese industry, which started hesitantly in 1979 and only got seriously underway in 1992, utterly remade China's working class yet again. *Economically*, capitalistic wage and labor relations replaced state socialist ones, even in enterprises that remained in state and collective ownership. For many of the tens of millions of former (and formerly exalted) workers of now shuttered heavy industries, unemployment actually reduced standards of living. For others, including the plethora of rural migrants, incomes and standards of living rose, though at the high price of marked declines in employment security, shop floor power, and labor conditions and hours, especially in the sweatshops that have proliferated across China. Moreover, the improvements in material conditions experienced by many workers pale in comparison with those of the new middle and upper classes—the distribution of income in urban China went from being one of the most equal in the world to one of the most unequal. That is, the problem is even more horrific when placed in the context of the vast quantities of surplus value the working class has produced and the new middle and upper classes have appropriated directly or indirectly.

Socially too, the working class has been completely transformed. It has ballooned, shrunk, ballooned and shrunk again, almost quintupling in size. Rural migrants, who were a minority of the industrial labor force in the Maoist era, now comprise a hefty majority. A complex tessellation of cleavages has rent the working class: employed *vs.* unemployed, older *vs.* younger, more *vs.* less educated and skilled, male *vs.* female, rustbelt *vs.* sunbelt, rural *vs.* urban, and those employed by state, private and mixed-ownership firms. Factory management has become far more authoritarian and draconian than even the worst practices that Maoist-era workers attacked so ardently. Workers no longer live in all-encompassing "work units" together with all their fellow workers, with two dissimilar exceptions: those living in hellish sweatshop dormitories, which cannot really be termed "communities" in any meaningful sense despite the close but ephemeral bonds they produce; and the aging unemployed trapped in apartments in shuttered rustbelt firms.

The transformation of working class *culture* could hardly have been more extreme. The extraordinarily confident and often strident "workerism" of the Maoist period has been replaced by a range of self-concepts: depressed atavism; resigned, unquestioning acceptance of the hegemony of the market and the state; and, among rural migrants, a complex admixture of attraction, repulsion, depression and resignation concerning urban life and work. Discourse about class, which was important in revolutionary days and absolutely central in the Maoist period, has vanished. In a supreme, bizarre irony that reflects the respective ideological hegemonies of Maoism and structural reform, Chinese workers focused on capitalism and capitalists most when state socialism prevailed and least when it finally returned.

Politically, though, workers have fought back actively and creatively against the worst depredations that the structural reforms visited on them. They have engaged in a wide range of protest repertoires, many of which were time-honored (such as strikes, slowdowns, demonstrations and blockades) and some of which were novel (such as eye-catching street theater). Similar to the revolutionary period, but very different from the Maoist days when workers demanded a new world, the vast majority of stimuli and demands have been defensive—for example, protests against wage arrears, plant closures, abusive management and unpaid overtime. The depoliticization was fostered by sequencing—the defeat of the left in the Cultural Revolution, and structural reform's hesitant start for its first fifteen years—and by the tidal wave of rural entrants. In another contrast with the huge Shanghai strike wave of 1957 and the protracted nationwide outpouring during the Cultural Revolution, under structural reform working class resistance only just began to metastasize twice—in the northeast in 2002 and in nationwide automobile plants in 2010—and both waves soon subsided. In all this, the working class has resisted structural reform in ways fundamentally shaped by the hegemony of structural reform itself.

...

In short, China's working class has been fundamentally remade not once but twice since its birth in the late nineteenth century. This in itself is not particularly surprising for a country that has undergone such extreme revolutionary gyrations from the death rattle of an ancient agrarian monarchy, to decades of international and revolutionary war and failed transitions to capitalism and to both bourgeois democracy and proto-fascism, to radical state socialism, and finally back to a capitalistic economy under a stabilized Leninist state. What is puzzling, though, are the specific patterns of working class formation and re-formation. Before 1949, how can the ebbs and flows of the working class's politics and its sometime ability to coordinate its resistance be explained? Why, having been unable, despite ardent activism, to play a major role in the revolution or gain a strong foothold within the Communist Party in those decades, did the working class nonetheless rise to the apex of the hegemonic bloc that underpinned the People's Republic during its three Maoist decades? Why, despite that exalted position, did it become so very radical, asserting its "workerist" superiority and demanding extraordinary power and compensation precisely when it had never had it so good? And how can the ebbs and flows of its radicalism during those years too be explained? Finally, why, having acted so radically and with such power, did it shift from the socialist or even communist offensive to a much meeker, defensive posture when finally confronted with the profound depredations of a transition to a particularly despotic form of capitalism? At a moment when its proclivity for deep structural critique would have been most appropriate and necessary, why did it revert to material demands? Why, having attacked the very concept of wages and management, did it now militate simply to be paid its wages and to be managed less cruelly?

At the most general level, the explanation is that *working class formation and, perhaps more surprisingly, resistance even in revolutionary China has been shaped by hegemonic forces more than it has challenged them.* During the revolutionary period, China lacked any stable hegemony, but it was awash with competing hegemonic projects and forces. Workers militated on this dizzying terrain: for decent wages and labor conditions, human treatment and national pride. They mobilized effectively within the profoundly new social structures into which history had thrown them, including particularistic ones such as gangs (*bang*), brotherhoods and sisterhoods, and native place networks and groups; philanthropic and self-help outfits; unions; criminal secret societies; militias; and parties. At a time when they were being attacked simultaneously as workers and as Chinese, they developed a political culture of resistance that almost seamlessly mixed class and nation. And in a country that lacked robust national political institutions or even unity and sovereignty, they organized mostly locally, undertaking coordinated attacks across regions only when there were wider institutions—the Guomindang-Communist United Front of the 1920s and the rising Communist Party of the latter 1940s—to which to attach themselves.

With the victory of the revolution in 1949, the Party quickly established a powerful new hegemony that was robust enough to survive even the self-inflicted crises of the Great Leap Forward and the Cultural Revolution. It offered a vastly improved material life to the working class. As David Laitin has argued, hegemony defines not only structures and forms of power but also the contours of controversy and the terms on which struggles for power are fought.[2] The victory of the revolution, then, also created opportunities, political impulses and local and even national leadership—from Mao and other leftists at the very top—for workers to demand control over their factories. But that was a bridge too far for many in the Party who were more focused on economic recovery and rapid industrialization based on the Soviet model. The controversy raged on within the Party and across Chinese shop floors, creating irritants in many factories and fueling the huge Shanghai strike wave of 1957. The Great Leap and especially the economic crisis it precipitated put active politics of radical restructuring of factory power on the back burner. But the Cultural Revolution brought it squarely to the fore, this time complicating matters further by fueling a third strand: the "economistic" demands of rural contract workers for equal pay and treatment. It also deeply divided the proletariat politically, as workers ended up fighting, including against each other, on three sides: rebels, conservatives and "economistics." The Cultural Revolution, and with it the hegemony of Maoist state socialism, ended in tears, especially for the left and its radical working class supporters. In the fullness of time, it would become clear that in fact the entire working class *qua* class had suffered a stunning defeat. This, and much else that happened in working class politics in the Maoist era, had a great deal to do with the fact that during the revolution the working class had never established its power within the Communist Party. So while radical state socialism created opportunities for radical working class politics, the working class was never in a position to dominate.

Through the first half of the 1980s, this was not yet apparent. Efforts by structural reformers to promote more draconian management and labor incentives—exactly the measures that radical workers protested and stopped in the Maoist period—faltered as managers, still terrified of another working class backlash, refused to implement them. And while in general workers were hesitant about joining the 1989 "democracy" movement because it didn't speak to their growing anxieties about market reform, some still proved obstinate and radical enough to take extraordinary risks to attack the Party/state. Beijing authorities may have been hesitant in dealing with student and white-collar protesters throughout April and May, but in Shanghai there were stern crackdowns against protesting workers. Most of the violence and casualties in Beijing on the night of June 4 involved workers, who attacked armed forces approaching Tiananmen Square and were mowed down for their impudence. In the weeks after the crackdown, strikes broke out in Hangzhou and other cities. Working class radicalism born in the radical thrusts of the Maoist era was still alive and kicking at a time when structural reform had not yet become hegemonic. To

2 Laitin, *Hegemony and Culture*, 29.

adapt Žižek's stylized version of Gramsci's famous aphorism: "The old world is dying and the new world struggles to be born: now is the time for monsters."[3]

But of course enraged workers were no match for the Party/state once it decided to crack down ruthlessly. Martial law, which dragged on for years, provided a moment which inadvertently gave economic reformers the political confidence to begin price and labor "reforms" in the early 1990s. As the economy began to boom, structural reform became irresistible, and a new hegemonic order grounded in the market and the Party/state—its midwife—was finally born. China's once radical working class now resigned itself to the new capitalistic political economy. It also fragmented along the deep new cleavages established by breathless proletarianization. Many urban resident workers—some voluntarily, some involuntarily due to layoffs—started their own businesses from the minuscule to the gargantuan. Many hung on in their state and collective firms, enduring tougher management and growing anxiety about their employment and livelihoods. Many went to work in the burgeoning private sector. And they all were eventually dwarfed by an avalanche of rural migrant labor whose willingness to endure the most dreadful forms of wage labor only laid them still lower.

Aside from knocking China's working class from its perch, the new hegemony of the market and the Party/state also set up new terms of conflict between workers on one side and employers and the government on the other. As in previous eras, workers have not been shy about standing up for themselves. But the ways they have done so have changed radically. "Workerist" demands for shopfloor power have been replaced by claims around "bread and butter" issues such as pay, working conditions and employment security. Lacking any of the wider political and institutional support radical workers enjoyed in Maoist days, resistance has remained almost exclusively local and cellular. The very concept of the "working class" disappeared not just from workers' vocabularies but also from their politics. Fragmentation became so extreme that, for example, in some cases retired workers demanding their pensions be paid were abandoned by employed workers in the same enterprises or, even worse, by retired workers in those same enterprises whose differently administered pensions were still being paid.

Over its first 125 years, China's working class has experienced two radical shifts in the mode of production: from despotic, foreign-inflected capitalism before 1949 to radical Maoist state socialism through 1978 and, after an uncertain interregnum in the 1980s, back again to despotic, foreign-inflected capitalistic economy starting in the early 1990s. Each has coevolved the very

3 Slavoj Žižek (@Slavojiek), "As Gramsci said 'the old world is dying and the new world struggles to be born: now is the time for monsters,'" *Twitter* (now *X*) here, since it was Twitter at the time. November 19, 2013, 4:12 p.m., https://twitter.com/slavojiek/status/402801649686958080.

different structures of social life, political culture and conflict. During each period, the working class fought hard, but on the terrain of the hegemonic system of the day. Thus the working class produced a truly radical critique and program only under Maoist state socialism, but not under either of its capitalist phases. At the crest of a revolutionary movement that they hoped would overthrow capitalism, Marx and Engels famously urged the workers of the world to unite: "The proletarians have nothing to lose but their chains. They have a world to win."[4] China's working class actually did begin to win it in the Maoist period, though only after capitalism had already been overthrown. With the triumphant return of capitalistic political economy and a state fully committed to it, China's working class's fleeting, tempestuous triumph proved instead to mark out a world to lose.

4 Karl Marx and Friedrich Engels, "Manifesto of the Communist Party," in Robert C. Tucker, ed., *The Marx-Engels Reader*, 2nd ed. (New York: W. W. Norton, 1978), 500.

Commentaries

4

VIEWING *THE MAKING OF CHINA'S WORKING CLASS* THROUGH A RUSSIAN LENS

Stephen Crowley

Marc Blecher has written a work of incomparable breadth, unpacking the multiple transformations experienced by China's working class. He combines a deep dive into a century of dramatic social and economic changes with the words of Chinese workers themselves, including his own numerous in-depth interviews. Nothing analogous exists for the Russian context.[1] In the comments that follow I will explore the similarities and differences with the transformations of the Russian working class, and then investigate whether Blecher's concept of hegemony provides explanatory power for the Russian case.

Blecher explores the China case across three periods. In Russia that periodic categorization might be different, and here we'll explore the Soviet period, the tumultuous postcommunist 1990s, and the Putin era of stability and stagnation.

In contrast to China, there was considerable working class consciousness leading to the world's first "socialist revolution" in 1917. Unlike the CCP, the Bolshevik Party was indeed a "working class organization," albeit with

1 Donald A. Filtzer, *Soviet Workers and Stalinist Industrialization: The Formation of Modern Soviet Production Relations, 1928–1941* (Armonk, N.Y: M.E. Sharpe, 1986); Donald A. Filtzer, "Soviet Workers and Late Stalinism: Labour and the Restoration of the Stalinist System After World War II," electronic resource, *ACLS Humanities E-Book*, 2002, http://ezproxy.oberlin.edu/login?url=http://hdl.handle.net/2027/heb.05234; Donald A. Filtzer, *Soviet Workers and De-Stalinization: The Consolidation of the Modern System of Soviet Production Relations, 1953–1964*, Soviet and East European Studies 87 (Cambridge [England] ; New York, NY, USA: Cambridge University Press, 1992); Donald A. Filtzer, *Soviet Workers and the Collapse of Perestroika: The Soviet Labour Process and Gorbachev's Reforms, 1985–1991*, Cambridge Russian, Soviet and Post-Soviet Studies 93 (Cambridge ; New York, N.Y: Cambridge University Press, 1994).

DOI: 10.4324/9781003518228-7

revolutionary intellectuals at the helm. In Russia itself there was little countervailing pull toward nationalist identity among workers, and even in peripheral areas of the Russian empire, such as Ukraine and Georgia, the popular sentiment was as much or more socialist as nationalist.

Yet particularly with the Civil War, the Bolsheviks became more of a vanguard party than a bottom-up mass organization. A major challenge, however, was that the "first socialist state" was isolated, and came about in a society that was still overwhelmingly agrarian and peasant-based. Stalinist industrialization soon solved that problem, and the size of the working class soon exploded, drawing in (some would say destroying) the Soviet peasantry in the process. Alongside terror, there was considerable enthusiasm, not least among the new working class, for the building of a new socialist society.[2]

The society that resulted included hundreds of new industrial cities and towns, with working class communities at the center. In a major divergence from China, Soviet industrialization was so overwhelming it left only a minimal "collectivized" peasantry in its wake. This meant the divisions between rural migrant workers and urban-resident workers that characterized China's working class were largely nonexistent in the Soviet Union. Indeed, from the Stalinist period on, there was no unemployment to speak of, no "reserve army" of potential workers; rather, there was continual shortage of labor.

This gave workers a considerable amount of workplace power, as Burawoy discovered in Hungary, another Soviet-type society.[3] Since shortages extended to all kinds of goods in the Soviet economy, enterprises sought to provide for workers' needs, to incentivize them and prevent them from seeking work elsewhere. The provision of these goods and services formed a kind of enterprise paternalism, very much akin to the *danwei* system in China. It also led to a strong workplace bond, a sense of belonging to the work *kollektiv*, in part because enterprises often built the housing and other social infrastructure that workers and their families enjoyed.

Beyond the Stalinist period, the Soviet Union experienced nothing like China's Cultural Revolution. Nor, from Stalin until Gorbachev, were there major strikes to speak of. A telling exception was Novocherkassk, where twenty-five workers protesting price increases were shot and killed by Soviet authorities, with another seven later executed and many more injured and imprisoned.[4] The experience shocked the Communist leadership, as it displayed the latent power of the working class to challenge the central ideological claims of the

2 John Scott, *Behind the Urals* (Boston: Houghton Mifflin, 1942).

3 Burawoy, *The Politics of Production.*

4 Samuel H. Baron, *Bloody Saturday in the Soviet Union: Novocherkassk, 1962* (Stanford, CA: Stanford University Press, 2001).

Soviet leadership: that it ruled in the interests of that class. (The very name "Novocherkassk" continues to resonate with portent in Russia to this day.)[5]

In another contrast with China, Soviet workers in this period hardly exhibited radicalism. On the surface at least, they appeared complacent. While there was grumbling about shortages, they faced little threat of unemployment, and their needs were largely provided for. Given the labor shortage, the running joke was "we pretend to work, and they pretend to pay us."

But as in China, there was a distinct "workerist" mentality. The working class was valorized in official ideology, something workers took obvious pride in. Yet workers complained that intellectuals and others would refer to them as unthinking "cattle." This workerism became explicit—and the complacency shattered—with the strikes of Soviet coal miners in 1989.

With Mikhail Gorbachev's perestroika, independent organizing by workers and others became possible. Coal miners burst on the scene with a nationwide strike. In an indication of the degree to which workers remained central to the Soviet system, both economically and ideologically, Gorbachev later reflected in his memoirs that "the rapid destruction of the social order that existed for seventy years began with the miners' [strike] wave."[6] Interestingly, the miners were not protesting against Gorbachev's reforms—which could potentially threaten many of the privileges they had enjoyed—but instead claimed they were pushing for "perestroika from below."[7]

Two years later the miners struck again, in a self-described "political strike" that—rather surprisingly—backed Yeltsin and other radical reformers and helped bring about the end of the Soviet Union. Yet while the miners claimed they were trying to bring about a "market system," when asked to articulate what they meant by such a system (which they had never experienced), they described an arrangement more akin to an economy based on a labor theory of value and workers' control of their coal mines.[8]

However, when Yeltsin's team unleashed "shock therapy" reforms in the now independent Russia in 1992, the consequences for miners and other workers were quite different and largely devastating. When, as Blecher notes, urban industrial development took off in China, especially from 1992, it "produced the biggest, most rapid spurt of proletarianization in world history."[9] For Russia it was nearly the total opposite.

5 A feature film about the uprising and resulting violence, entitled *Dear Comrades*, co-written and directed by Andrei Konchalovsky, was released in Russia in 2020.
6 Mikhail Sergeevich Gorbachev, *Zhizn' i Reformy* (Moskva: Novosti, 1995).
7 Theodore Friedgut and Lewis Siegelbaum, "Perestroika from Below: The Soviet Miners' Strike and Its Aftermath," *New Left Review*, I/181 (June 1, 1990): 5–32.
8 Crowley, *Hot Coal, Cold Steel*.
9 See p. 106.

With the end of state control over the economy, the labor shortage quickly evaporated, and was replaced by labor surplus. There was a palpable fear of a "social explosion" as outmoded Soviet technologies were now faced with global competition, and factories teetered on bankruptcies alongside predictions of massive unemployment.

However, despite almost unprecedented economic decline, the result wasn't massive unemployment. Instead of a loss of jobs, wages dropped dramatically. Many workers became impoverished, but they were technically still employed. Most of the old Soviet factories somehow hung on, relying on barter and other arrangements rather than profit to remain afloat. Wages dropped so low that they eventually gave way to a crisis of "wage arrears"—that is, wages went unpaid altogether. At the height of the crisis in late 1998, approximately two-thirds of Russian workers reported overdue wages, with those affected reporting close to five months' pay in arrears on average.[10]

Not surprisingly, a considerable strike wave erupted as a result. In 1999 unpaid coal miners blockaded the Trans-Siberian Railway, Russia's main transportation artery, in what became known as the "rail wars." Yet despite this spike in strike action, there was nowhere near the level of social tumult and labor action that China has experienced. For one thing, Russia has experienced very few closures of large industrial enterprises, in contrast to the "rust belt" in China's northeast. However, there has been very little dynamic growth and new job creation in Russia that might absorb the social impact of such "creative destruction."

As Putin came to power in 2000, a boom in oil prices boosted the Russian economy from its nadir. The wage arrears crisis soon ended, with wages rising considerably. Living standards improved overall, and Putin seemed to fulfill his promise of providing stability after the tumultuous 1990s. Yet, having just witnessed a massive strike wave soon after becoming president, Putin pushed a new labor code through parliament, one that greatly strengthened the dominant and rather compliant "legacy" union federation left over from the Communist era and deliberately marginalized the more militant alternative unions. Russia's strike laws became draconian, some of the most restrictive in the world. Hence, for the 2000s at least, stability came to mean higher wages alongside greater restrictions, not least for labor.

As in China, Russian workers experienced a substantial loss in status as well as in their material conditions and witnessed an almost unprecedented spike in inequality. Very much as Blecher describes of China, in Russia "working class struggles have become defensive, focused on 'bread-and-butter' questions

10 John S. Earle and Klara Sabirianova Peter, "Equilibrium Wage Arrears: A Theoretical and Empirical Analysis of Institutional Lock-In," *SSRN ELibrary*, September 2000, http://papers.ssrn.com/sol3/papers.cfm?abstract_id=251999.

such as wage arrears,"[11] with arrears a major concern for workers in both cases. Likewise, as in China the labor protests that have erupted have been "cellular," that is typically confined to individual workplaces. As in China, these often led to small gains but spread no further. In Russia this is partly due to the challenge of trade unions, in that the dominant union federation is only partially transformed from the Communist era, and as in the past seeks to dampen protest rather than support it. Thirty years after the end of the Soviet Union, trade unions enjoy some of the lowest levels of public trust of any social or political institution, in yet another similarity with China.

In Russia, while unemployment remains limited, wages are quite low, and as in the 1990s, in adverse labor markets workers see their wages go down rather than an increase in layoffs. Managers have substantial control over an individual worker's wage packet, with a low base wage topped off with a cash bonus "in the envelope" when times are good. Most often dissatisfied workers will exit into the informal economy rather than engage in collective action, a common trend in China as well.

Still, unlike in China, there has not been a substantial rise in strikes in the new century. There have been notable exceptions, however. As in China, structural factors can explain a good bit of the variation. For instance, during the oil boom of the 2000s, workers in the auto industry were particularly militant in some of the foreign firms that had entered the Russian market, leading to the formation of new, alternative unions which spread across the industry. Thus, their protests became sector-wide rather than cellular, and in a growing economy their demands were "offensive"—demanding more job control and a greater share of profits—rather than defensive. There is a distinct echo here with the more offensive-minded auto workers in China, as seen there in 2010.

In Russia however the structural conditions for autoworkers and others changed dramatically with the 2008–9 global recession. Given the sudden and substantial drop in economic output, there was renewed talk of a potential "social explosion." The Russian leadership was faced with the challenge that, having avoided mass bankruptcies in the 1990s, many Soviet-era industrial enterprises remained in operation and were only partially restructured. These included over 300 "monotowns"—single-industry towns, many of them isolated and struggling to remain competitive. While avoiding major factory closures since the Soviet collapse helped prevent widespread social unrest, the result was an economy that relied on oil and gas revenues to maintain social—and ultimately political—stability. As economic growth slowed over the last decade, Putin's promise of stability began to appear like stagnation. As hardship and grievances mounted, the specter of destabilizing labor protest loomed, even before Russia's disastrous decision to invade Ukraine.

11 See p. 162.

What conclusions might we draw from this comparison? Blecher asks about Chinese workers in the reform era, "Why has the working class deradicalized precisely in an era when it has lost so much power?" Similar questions could be—and have been—asked about Russia.[12] One answer might come from the economic theory of strikes, which posits that strikes tend to take place less during times of economic hardship, and more often when workers have less to fear (from job loss) and more to gain (from demanding a greater share of profits).[13] Such a view would see strikes and labor actions as most often expressions of working class power.[14] That perspective can explain how workplace and marketplace power spurred the offensive protests of auto workers in both China and Russia.

Yet the argument at the center of *The Making of China's Working Class* is Blecher's claim that working class formation in China "has proceeded in a dialectic in which it has resisted the hegemonic forces acting on it in ways fundamentally stamped by those very forces," and further that "resistance even in revolutionary China has been shaped by hegemonic forces more than it has challenged them."[15]

How well does the concept of hegemony explain the Russian case? Quite well, it seems. Lenin and the Bolsheviks certainly seized upon the revolutionary mood among workers in coming to power, but once in power their articulation of workers' interests was by and large well received. Stalinist industrialization was tumultuous, to say the least, but by many accounts workers enthusiastically participated in the "building of socialism." Still speaking in broad strokes, in the post-Stalinist era workers largely perceived the benefit of a society that valued them as a class, and where the absence of unemployment—indeed, a shortage of labor—combined with enterprise paternalism prevented a sense of undue exploitation. Yet, as the uprising in Novocherkassk suggests, workers and others had certain expectations about what that system was meant to provide, and limits to what they would accept. Put differently, while Soviet ideology was clearly hegemonic, the system created expectations that it later found difficult to meet.

12 Sarah Ashwin, *Russian Workers: The Anatomy of Patience* (Manchester: Manchester University Press, 1999); Stephen Crowley, "The Social Explosion That Wasn't: Labor Quiescence in Postcommunist Russia," in *Workers After Workers' States: Labor and Politics in Postcommunist Eastern Europe*, ed. Stephen Crowley and David Ost (Lanham, MD: Rowman & Littlefield, 2001).

13 Roberto Franzosi, *The Puzzle of Strikes: Class and State Strategies in Postwar Italy*, Cambridge Studies in Comparative Politics (Cambridge [England] ; New York, NY, USA: Cambridge University Press, 1995).

14 Erik Olin Wright, "Working-Class Power, Capitalist-Class Interests, and Class Compromise," *The American Journal of Sociology* 105, no. 4 (January 2000): 957–1002.

15 See p. 208.

The miners' strikes in 1989 proved this to be the case. When Gorbachev's reforms inadvertently worsened shortages rather than lessening them, while simultaneously allowing for open dissent, the miners united in demanding greater reform. Their actions were very much "workerist," as in many cases they seized control of their mines, running them for a time through their elected strike committees. As Blecher notes about China, "workerism was the working class's way of thinking about and expressing themselves in terms broadly given by the Party, even when they criticized it—a core indication of ideological hegemony."[16] This became expressly so at the end of the Soviet Union, when miners began demanding an end to the Communist system. They called for its replacement with a "market," but articulated a notion of a market economy that reflected more a labor theory of value and workers' ownership and control.

The parallel continues into the post-Soviet era. Blecher argues that when "state socialism ultimately lost out, China's working class too lost the core of its ways of thinking and understanding itself and its world. So in discursive terms it was left helpless to stand up against the onslaught of structural reform." This describes the Russia case rather precisely. Even when the most militant of workers—the miners—realized what profound hardship capitalism entailed for them in practice, they lacked an ideological framework in which to make sense of it, since they had explicitly rejected "socialism" as exploitative. Thirty years after the Soviet collapse, Russian trade unions find little support, and any left-wing opposition to Putin's régime—from workers or elsewhere—is minimal. This despite the finding of Aleksei Levinson of the Levada Center, Russia's leading independent pollster, that "if we take the left to mean socialist ideas in the strictest sense… then these represent the most widespread views in the bulk of the population.… I believe that the dominant views [in Russia] are without a doubt [those of] the left."[17]

One might argue that the concept of hegemony might explain the subordination of subalterns most everywhere, almost as a tautology. Yet as one looks at China and Russia at the time of this writing, one wonders how long the status quo can last. I will leave it to Blecher and his colleagues to speculate on China's future. But in Russia, despite (or perhaps because of) the oppressiveness of the Putin régime, a socialist (or workerist) mentality still lingers, especially in Russia's quite numerous working class communities. Indeed, as I have

16 See p. 63.
17 As cited in Tom Balmforth, "The Paradox Of Russia's Left," *RadioFreeEurope/RadioLiberty*, February 19, 2012, sec. Russia, http://www.rferl.org/content/the_paradox_of_russias_left /24488988.html.

argued elsewhere, the Putin leadership has refrained from a deep restructuring of Russia's economy in part because it fears unleashing destabilizing social unrest, yet at the cost of stagnation, itself a source of growing dissatisfaction.[18] Thus, in Russia a major challenge loomed, one only worsened by Putin's grievous decision to invade Ukraine.

18 Stephen Crowley, *Putin's Labor Dilemma: Russian Politics Between Stability and Stagnation* (Ithaca, N.Y: Cornell University Press, 2021).

5

COMMENTARY ON *THE MAKING OF CHINA'S WORKING CLASS*

Elaine Sio-ieng Hui

Introduction

Offering a comprehensive and all-embracing analysis of labor politics in China, Marc Blecher's new book, *The Making of China's Working Class: A World to Lose*, interrogates the formation of China's working class in three crucial periods: the revolutionary era (1920 to 1949), the Maoist era (1949 to 1978), and the structural reform era (since 1978). *The Making of China's Working Class* is one of the very few works that adopts a historical perspective to dissect the formation of China's working class over time—and how (and whether) class formation during earlier periods has impacted later periods. It asks three important questions: "[W]hat kind of class is China's working class? What are the historical forces and processes that have formed it? And how does the pattern of class formation help explain the working class's reactions historically, presently, and even prospectively?"[1]

Blecher addresses these questions by drawing insights from three scholarly traditions: a) Ira Katznelson's understanding of class, b) the perspective of political development, c) Gramsci's theory of hegemony. First, using Katznelson's conceptual framework, which underscores the economic, social, cultural and political aspects of class, *The Making of China's Working Class* is structured to explain China's working class formation by scrutinizing the economic structures and materialist conditions (the economic aspect); the organizations of society and social relations (the social aspect); shared dispositions, political predispositions and self-perceived identities of workers (the cultural aspect);

1 See p. 2.

DOI: 10.4324/9781003518228-8

and working class organization and collective action (the political aspect). In a nuanced fashion, Blecher elaborates on how the interconnectedness of these four aspects has contributed to class formation in each of the three periods under study.

Second, Blecher uses the perspective of political development and path dependency to address the aforementioned questions. Instead of considering what happened in the past as a mere background, he views the past as key in shaping outcomes in the present. His approach gives emphasis to both continuity and discontinuity, conjuncture and disjuncture, and sequence:

> On the one hand, the "long century" since the dawn of China's industrial working class has been a time of radical discontinuity. On the other, distinctive features, sequences and conjunctures of working class formation in one era created path dependencies both within it as well as for the succeeding one(s). Yet they also brought the first two periods to their ends in path-independent climacterics.[2]

Blecher illustrates that the working class formation in one period has experienced both path-dependent and path-independent effects from the earlier periods.

Third, at the overarching level, Blecher uses the concept of hegemony to explain why the working class in the three stated periods has responded differently toward economic exploitation. In the revolutionary and state socialist periods, Blecher maintains, the working class was politically engaged and staged radical actions, but in the end, it failed to advance a world in which workers would assert greater power and control. In the structural reform period, workers have lost their previous privileges and faced stronger exploitation, but their resistance has become apolitical and less radical. Blecher highlights one puzzle: why China's working class was the most radical, in terms of actions and political consciousness, during the time that it had gained strongest economic and political power in history, and why after a long period of radicalism, in recent decades, it has turned from being offensive to being defensive, from being political to apolitical, from being full of self-confidence and rebelliousness to resigning to the status quo at a time that it encounters the severest exploitation. For Blecher, the answer to this puzzle is related to hegemony of capitalism (as is elaborated on further in the rest of this section). He argues that the working class formation and workers' resistance in the three periods under study has been "shaped by hegemonic forces more than it has challenged them"[3] and that

2 See p. 8.
3 See p. 208.

"hegemony defines not only structure and forms of power but also the contours of controversy and the terms on which struggles for power are fought."[4]

To sum up Blecher's insights based on the three theoretical traditions explained above, in the revolutionary period economically workers were exploited. Culturally, they drew on both the class discourse and nationalist discourse (against imperialism and Japanese invasion) to fuel their resistance. Politically, labor movements grew at the local level due to political fragmentation and weak institutionalization, but not at the cross-sectoral, regional and national levels. The working class in this period was proactive in fending for itself, had developed strong self-confidence and political autonomy, and had developed hostility toward political authority. In this period, workers' identities and struggles "almost seamlessly mixed class and nation"[5] because of competing hegemonic forces exercised by the Kuomintang and CCP.

During the Maoist period, economically, workers' wages and working and living conditions had improved. Socially, urban workers were connected through work units and their democratic participation in factory management had dramatically increased. Yet the working class was divided along the lines of household registration, skill levels, ages, gender and more. Culturally, workers had achieved a new level of self-confidence and rebelliousness. They were highly critical of working and employment conditions in factories and had framed their demands and actions in ways that stressed workplace democracy and class relations. Politically, workers continued to stage autonomous and spontaneous actions, often taking advantage of the political opportunity structures opened up in the country. Workers' radicalism was articulated through the class languages promoted by the CCP and entangled with the political dynamics at the time. Blecher therefore argues that state socialism had reconstituted the working class economically and socially, yet the hegemony of state socialism had limited the terrain within which the working class "remade itself culturally and politically."[6]

In the structural reform period, economically, capitalist production relations have replaced state socialist ones. Urban state workers have faced layoff, unemployment and deterioration of working and life standards. Rural migrant workers have become new subjects of exploitation by the capitalist economy. Socially, work units that used to connect state workers together were dismantled, and migrant workers mostly live in factory dormitories. The working class continues to be divided along multiple lines, including employment status, age, education, gender, skill levels and origins. Culturally, the working class has lost the self-confidence and rebelliousness they had gained in the previous

4 See p. 209.
5 See p. 208.
6 See p. 204.

era. New hegemony around the market economy and the party-state has been established in ways that many workers, former state and migrant workers alike, have resigned themselves to the new economic and political orders. Class discourse is no longer proactively utilized by the working class or its organizations. Politically, although workers continue to stage collective resistance at the local level, Blecher underscores that their actions are defensive, cellular and depoliticized, different from the working class struggles in the previous eras. He concludes, "...the working class has resisted structural reform in ways fundamentally shaped by the hegemony of structural reform itself"[7] because it has not challenged hegemony pertinent to the capitalist economy and the political power of the CCP.

Having summarized the key insights of *The Making of China's Working Class*, the rest of the commentary will focus on three areas. First, the concept of hegemony is crucial for understanding the powerful arguments Blecher makes, but it is not explained in systemic ways in the book. I will attempt to fill this gap so that readers can grasp the breadth and depth of Blecher's insights effectively. Second, while Blecher discusses the resistance of migrant workers, who make up a majority of the working population in present China, his account misses some crucial changes in their activism; therefore, I will attempt to provide a more updated analysis of migrant workers' struggles. Last, I will discuss the conditions for the present working class to build counter-hegemony to win a world in which workers would assert greater power and control.

Hegemony[8]

With his theorization of "coercion" and "hegemony," Italian revolutionary socialist and political theorist Antonio Gramsci explained how class power is organized by the state in political society and civil society. On the one hand, following the argument of Marx, Engels and Lenin, Gramsci held that the coercive machinery of the state, or what he called political society, helps maintain the capitalist class's domination.[9] On the other, he underscored that at the same

7 See p. 207.

8 The elaborations on the concept of hegemony in this section are based on my previous works, including Elaine Sio-ieng Hui, "The Labour Law System, Capitalist Hegemony and Class Politics in China," *China Quarterly 226* (June, 2016): 431–455; Elaine Sio-ieng Hui, "Putting the Chinese State in Its Place: A March from Passive Revolution to Hegemony," *Journal of Contemporary Asia,* 47, no. 1 (June 2016): 66–92; Elaine Sio-ieng Hui, *The Development of Labor Policies in China: From Passive Revolution to Eroding Hegemony* (Cheltenham, Edward Elgar Publishing, forthcoming); and Elaine Sio-ieng Hui and Chris King-Chi Chan, "The 'Harmonious Society' as a Hegemonic Project: Labour Conflicts and Changing Labour Policies in China," *Labour, Capital and Society* 44, 2 (2011): 153–183.

9 Gramsci, *Selections from the Prison Notebooks*; Antonio Gramsci, *A Gramsci Reader: Selected Writing 1916–1935* (New York: New York University Press, 1988).

time the dominant class seeks to obtain the active consent of the working class to its leadership by establishing "its own moral, political and cultural values as conventional norms of practical behavior."[10] This capitalist class ideological ascendency over the subaltern classes is what Gramsci called hegemony. Due to the intricate workings of coercion and hegemony, working class anti-capitalist consciousness and rebellions against capitalism do not appear as automatically as vulgar Marxism in Gramsci's time predicted.

Many subsequent scholars have delved into Gramsci's insights on hegemony.[11] Building on these works and Gramsci's work, I define hegemony as involving six key elements. First, the exercise of hegemony is to sustain the long-term dominance of the dominant class. Second, hegemony is the active consent obtained by the dominant and ruling class over the subordinate classes by influencing their intellectual, moral and political worldviews. Third, the capitalist class needs to create a national-popular appearance for its parochial interests in order to acquire workers' allegiance to their leadership. Fourth, the reproduction of hegemony involves compromises on secondary issues made by the dominant class—short-term concessions made to the subaltern class are not unusual. Fifth, hegemony is bulwarked by the application of state coercion; even the most hegemonic state cannot rule without the support of military and physical forces. Sixth, the ruling class's hegemony is exercised in the unstable and fragile field of socio-political relations; this means the possibility of a working class counter-hegemony exists. It is with the concept of hegemony that Blecher explains why Chinese workers have not been able to win a better world—hegemonic forces in different periods have significantly shaped workers' struggles and worldviews.

Migrant Workers' Activism: Characteristics and Changes

Because *The Making of China's Working Class* provides such a broad sweep of history, Blecher is unable to provide details on everything—including on how migrant worker activism has changed in recent years, which is important to anyone seeking to understand contemporary China's working class. The changes of migrant worker activism include, first, prior to 2010 migrant workers' collective actions primarily sought to advance their immediate economic interests, such

10 Joseph Femia, *Gramsci's Political Thought: Hegemony, Consciousness, and the Revolutionary Process* (Oxford: Clarendon Press, 1987), 3.

11 For instance, Walter Adamson, *Hegemony and Revolution: A Study of Antonio Gramsci's Political and Cultural Theory* (Berkeley: University of California Press, 1980); Joseph Femia, "Hegemony and Consciousness in the Thought of Antonio Gramsci," *Political Studies, 23,* no. 1 (March 1975): 29–48; Douglas Litowitz, "Gramsci, Hegemony, and the Law," *Brigham Young University Law Review 2* (May 2000): 515–551; Chantal Mouffe, *Hegemony and Ideology in Gramsci* (London: Routledge and Kegan Paul, 1979).

as protesting against outstanding or meagre wages, uncompensated workplace injuries or unpaid overtime, leave or severance pay.[12] However, starting with the strike wave that broke out in the auto industry in 2010, migrant workers have made demands related to trade unions, which could be considered a politicization of their resistance, however minimal. The Honda strike that Blecher highlights in his book drew enormous social attention partly because of the workers' request to initiate democratic reform in their workplace trade union. Since 2010, until Xi Jinping took measures to repress civil society, there were more workers' protests and strikes seeking to obtain workplace institutional power through forming enterprise unions in accordance with legal regulations,[13] including the case of Jasic Technologies in Shenzhen in 2018. The Jasic workers followed the legal process to try to set up a union to safeguard their interest, but their effort was met with strong resistance from the upper-level unions, the company and the government. Several dozens of workers and their student supporters were arrested. Although demanding to form or democratize workplace unions is not the same as demanding to establish independent trade unions, workers questioning the status quo of Chinese trade unions reflects that their dissatisfaction is beyond the economic sphere. Rather, their concerns are partly political as workers have questioned the legitimacy of trade unions which have the blessing of the authoritarian party state.

Second, in the 2010s workers' actions have shifted from focusing on issues of production alone (*e.g.*, wages and overtime compensation) to focusing on both issues of production and reproduction, especially pensions and social insurances. In the structural reform period worker protests have moved from defensive actions associated with production politics before the mid- and late 2000s to offensive actions associated with production politics after the late 2000s, and then shifted to defensive actions associated with reproduction politics after 2010.[14] Migrant workers' struggles pertinent to the reproductive sphere and pension insurance are distinct from previous strikes. For example, mostly old-generation migrant workers participated in and led pension protests; female workers' participation in pension strikes exceeded that of their male counterparts; protests around pensions targeted both the state and employers.

Third, prior to the crackdown of civil society by the Xi government, with the support of movement-oriented labor nongovernmental organizations (NGOs), workers' resistance has witnessed key qualitative changes in some parts of China, such as Guangdong. As summarized in my previous work,[15] workers' resistance without the support of movement-oriented labor NGOs had long

12 Hui, "Movement-Oriented Labor Organizations."
13 Ibid.
14 Hui and Chan, *From Production to Reproduction.*
15 Hui, "Movement-Oriented Labor Organizations."

been characterized by legal mobilization through the mediation, arbitration and litigation systems at the individual level,[16] or by uncoordinated, unorganized and spontaneous group actions at the collective level.[17] Workers' collective defiance was expressed in the form of "strikes, road blockages, sit-ins and threatening suicide...factory occupations, riots and murder (of bosses)" without visible leadership.[18] It usually ended with employers unilaterally adjusting pay or work conditions, without formal negotiations or a formal bilaterally agreed resolution. However, before the crackdown on civil society starting in 2015, movement-oriented NGOs were able to promote among workers one type of modular collective labor action, which was "easily transferrable from one setting or circumstance to another."[19] This type of action consists of three tactics, namely the election of worker representatives, collective negotiation and protest. Movement-oriented labor NGOs guided workers to build mobilizing and connective structures, formulate collective action frames and amass movement resources. The modular collective actions are distinct from the instances of worker defiance without movement-oriented labor NGO intervention. Modular action is marked by coordination and organization achieved through worker representative election, mapping-based mobilization, and a branch-like communication strategy. It is also characterized by visible leadership actualized through the election of worker representatives and by formal conflict resolution attained through collective negotiations backed by protests.

It is true that migrant workers' resistance in present China is not as politicized and radical as workers' struggles in the revolutionary and state-socialist periods. However, crucial changes of their activism as those highlighted above merit attention. Currently, they are the largest and an important part of China's working class. Understanding their struggles will inform the discussions on the possibilities of building counter-hegemony in China.

Conditions for Building Counter-Hegemony

Hegemony is not static or stationary. The ruling bloc needs to keep reproducing its ideological and moral ascendency over the working class so as to forestall the latter's revolt.[20] This means building counter-hegemony is possible. How can the working class in the current economic, political, cultural and

16 Mary Gallagher, *Authoritarian Legality in China: Law, Workers, and the State* (Cambridge: Cambridge University Press, 2017).

17 Elfstrom and Kuruvilla, "The Changing Nature"; Eli Friedman and Ching Kwan Lee, "Remaking the World of Chinese Labour: A 30-Year Retrospective" *British Journal of Industrial Relations, 48, no.* 3 (September 2010): 507–533.

18 Friedman and Lee, "Remaking," 519.

19 Tarrow, *Power in Movement* 2nd ed., 41.

20 Hui, *Hegemonic Transformation.*

social conjuncture establish counter-hegemony to win a world in which they have greater power? To be specific, what conditions need to be created for the working class to construct counter-hegemony? Using Katznelson's conceptual framework and Gramsci's ideas, I will address this question in the following section.

Economically, to reproduce capitalist hegemony the ruling class needs to address and incorporate the subaltern class's interests into theirs. Also, it needs to give economic concessions to the working class in such ways that workers feel 'shared' interests with the former, and as a result render their allegiance to it. If the current Xi Jinping government does not address the material exploitation facing workers, reorient the unevenly developed economy, or give workers greater economic concessions, workers' discontent toward poor working conditions, social inequality, and the widening income gap will lay the material foundation for them to challenge the market economy and the state, just like in the revolutionary and state socialist periods. It is possible that latent worker dissatisfaction will burst into overt resistance against the ruling bloc's leadership should any political opportunities open up in the future.

Culturally, organic intellectuals of the working class play an important role in building counter-hegemony. They promote the homogeneity of the working class, help express its worldviews and build up "an awareness of its own functions not only in the economic but also in the social and political field."[21] Organic intellectuals of China's working class, be they worker activists, labor NGOs, students, labor lawyers, academics or pro-labor individuals, should help workers challenge the kind of common sense associated with capitalist economic relations, such as the ideas around market economy, waged labor, contractualism and private property rights; challenge the kind of juridico-political common sense the state reproduces, such as the ideas of rule of law, legal rights defense, and the leadership of the party-state; construct a kind of good sense and enhance workers' class consciousness and political consciousness; and build up workers' collectivity, spur workers to take concerted actions and engage in system-transforming initiatives.[22]

Socially, *The Making of China's Working Class* meticulously shows how workers' formal and informal networks in the revolutionary and state-socialist periods helped mobilize labor actions. In the Xi era, trade unions do not represent workers' genuine interests and labor groups are severely repressed. However, workers, labor activists and pro-labor individuals should, to the degree they can, maintain formal and informal networks that can be turned into mobilizing structures—"collective vehicles, informal as well as formal,

21 Gramsci, *Selections*, 5.

22 Elaine Sio-ieng Hui, "Labor-Related Civil Society Actors in China: A Gramscian Analysis," *Theory and Society,* 49, no. 1 (January 2020), 49–74.

through which people mobilize and engage in collective action"[23] when political opportunities emerge in the future.

Politically, because of tightening political control and escalating suppression of movement-oriented labor NGOs in the Xi era, collective labor actions have decreased, dropping from 2,670 cases in 2016 to 800 cases in 2020 and 972 cases in 2021.[24] However, while manufacturing workers have been the center of labor conflicts, white-collar workers and service workers have taken greater initiatives to resist exploitation recently. For example, in 2021 a group of food delivery workers in Weinan protested by burning their uniforms in public. In the same year, an online campaign, Worker Lives Matter, was launched to collect information of work hours in industries such as technology and finance. Its aim was to protest the 996 practices, meaning workers work from 9 a.m. to 9 p.m. for six days a week, prevalent in these industries.[25] Despite the politically hostile environment, workers' collective resistance continues because of the economic injustice they face. Acting as organic intellectuals, pro-labor individuals and groups should work toward forming a counter-hegemonic historical bloc that organizes workers, educates the public, advocates for political and economic democracy, and initiates radical collective actions when political opportunities present themselves. In this way, the historic bloc can cultivate a "revolutionary orientation" in the society and emerge as social and political structures that are strong enough to replace the existing ones.[26]

Concluding Remark

The Making of China's Working Class is a thoughtfully crafted work. Drawing on rich data, perceptive theoretical perspectives, and a wide range of sources, it provides a unique account of working class formation over the past hundred years in China and deciphers why Chinese workers failed to achieve an alternative world at the peak of their radicalism. It is thought-provoking for anyone who is concerned about China's working class, interested in building a counter-hegemony to the current authoritarian capitalist régime, and who seeks to pursue a better and fairer society. Its analyses may have conveyed a pessimism of the intellect, but the many valuable lessons that Blecher draws about Chinese workers' movements lay a solid foundation for our optimism about systemic

23 Douglas McAdam, John D. McCarthy and Mayer N. Zald, *Comparative Perspectives on Social Movements: Political Opportunities, Mobilizing Structures, and Cultural Framings* (Cambridge: Cambridge University Press, 1996), 3.

24 Kaye Liang and Elaine Sio-ieng Hui, *Movement-Oriented Labour NGOs in China* (Baden: Nomos Verlagsgesellschaft mbH & Co. KG), 2022.

25 Ibid.

26 Robert W. Cox, "Gramsci, Hegemony and International Relations: An Essay in Method," *Millennium: Journal of International Studies,* 12, no. 2 (Summer 1983): 162–175.

changes in the long run. As Blecher highlights, political opportunities are a key factor in explaining radical labor activism in the revolutionary and state socialist periods. When the next political opportunity emerges, if a pro-labor historical bloc is already in shape and alternative visions of social, economic and political systems are established and promulgated by organic intellectuals of the working class, then the working class will be more likely to stage actions to transcend the hegemonic boundaries set by the ruling class and to build a better world.

6

THE CHALLENGE OF BUILDING DURABLE POLITICAL POWER

Paul Pierson

In the past decade much of the political science literature on path dependence and historical development has turned to the study of *entrenchment*. Under what circumstances can a set of political actors achieve *durable* political victories—ones that cannot be undone (at least not without great difficulty) by those who follow? For students of politics this is an appropriate focus, both because it turns attention to the actions of those engaged in politics rather than historical accidents and because it has the potential to capture what astute and well-resourced political actors are really trying to do in politics. Successful entrenchment is both a way to exercise power and to build it. It creates conditions that confer resources over time, and often force the "losers" from prior conflicts to accommodate in significant ways to the new status quo. Arguments along these lines have been applied to such diverse outcomes as the development of the welfare state,[1] the consolidation of strong labor movements and Social Democratic parties in Scandinavia[2] and the institutionalization of racial inequality.[3]

1 Paul Pierson, *Dismantling the Welfare State? Reagan, Thatcher and the Politics of Retrenchment* (Cambridge: Cambridge University Press), 1994.
2 Gøsta Esping-Anderson, *Three Worlds of Welfare Capitalism* (Princeton, NJ: Princeton University Press), 1990; Evelyne Huber and John D. Stephens, *Development and Crisis of the Welfare State* (Chicago: University of Chicago Press), 2001.
3 Avidit Acharya, Matthew Blackwell and Maya Sen, *Deep Roots: How Slavery Still Shapes Southern Politics* (Princeton, NJ: Princeton University Press), 2018; Paul Starr, *Entrenchment: Wealth, Power and the Constitution of Democratic Societies* (New Haven: Yale University Press), 2019; Jessica Trounstine, *Segregation by Design: Local Politics and Inequality in American Cities* (Princeton, NJ: Princeton University Press), 2018.

DOI: 10.4324/9781003518228-9

This literature provides an interesting vantage point for examining Blecher's sweeping historical treatment of the evolution of China's working class. What is striking, in Blecher's account, is the repeated failure of working class forces to successfully entrench policies, worker organizations or modes of work organization that would durably support worker interests. No doubt, as Blecher demonstrates, this failure can be attributed in part to the sheer volatility of Chinese political and social life—the radicalism of episodes of social disruption—over the long period he studies. Repeated massive dislocations have minimized the prospects for building durable arrangements of any kind. As Blecher emphasizes, previous events and endeavors often leave meaningful traces. Yet we see little that could be recognized as entrenchment—the establishment of consequential arrangements that cannot be dislodged and offer persistent advantages to those who constructed them. Certainly, we do not see entrenchment of arrangements that offered such advantages to China's working class.

I will offer a brief sketch of what we know about processes of entrenchment under other conditions before suggesting how this research might complement Blecher's analysis of the Chinese case. The hope is that despite the vast differences in social circumstances, this perspective offers some insights into understanding the limited ability of China's working class to cement its interests as lasting gains. Entrenchment, at least in the instances that political scientists have explored, seems to rest on the capacity to exercise political authority. It is this capacity that allows political actors to lock in gains and reproduce them over time. The failure to really penetrate the state in meaningful and lasting ways thus represented a fundamental obstacle to the consolidation of protections for working class interests.

Let me briefly flesh out a couple of examples of successful entrenchment. The first, drawing on my own work and a collaboration with John Myles, concerns old-age pensions.[4] In many countries systems of contributory social insurance were established over substantial political opposition. Once these programs were institutionalized, however, they became almost impossible to reverse. A huge constituency for these programs developed—one that was highly sensitive to any effort to take benefits away. Fairly quickly, the notion of reversing course came to be seen as politically inconceivable. Entrenchment was especially evident when the design of these new pension programs followed a "Pay-as-you-go" design, where current payroll contributions pay for the current generation's retirement. Such a design made it almost impossible to design a transition away from the existing system, since it would inevitably be seen as imposing massive losses on either pensioners or taxpayers, or both.

4 Paul Pierson, *Dismantling the Welfare State*; John Myles and Paul Pierson, "The Comparative Political Economy of Pension Reform," in Paul Pierson, ed., *The New Politics of the Welfare State* (Oxford: Oxford University Press), 2001, 305–333.

Almost ninety years later, the quote attributed to President Franklin Roosevelt rings true: "... no damn politician can ever scrap my Social Security program."[5]

The entrenchment of white supremacy in the American South after reconstruction offers a second powerful example.[6] For a brief period after the Civil War there seemed to be a genuine prospect for introducing something like a multi-racial democracy in the states of the former Confederacy. Supported by the presence of federal troops and backed by enforcement from federal courts, a multi-racial Republican coalition began to coalesce and held political power in much of the South. But as Northern enthusiasm for continued enforcement waned and southern "Redeemers" mobilized, employing fraud and terror, this shaky coalition came apart. The process took several decades, but as the forces of white supremacy regained the upper hand they worked on multiple fronts to consolidate power. They rewrote state constitutions, captured law enforcement and introduced a suite of election rules that effectively denied Black people the franchise. All of this was backed by the continued use of fraud and terror to deter challengers and enabled by the retreat of the federal courts and law enforcement. The Jim Crow system—an authoritarian enclave within the U.S. polity[7]—would persist for almost a century. It would only be broken through the application of *external* political force applied through the Civil Rights Act and federal law enforcement.

A final example is the consolidation of Social Democracy in Scandinavia. A rich literature in Comparative Political Economy has developed around the core finding that despite many treatments of advanced capitalism expecting to see nations converging on a single basic framework, the institutional reality has instead been continued *divergence*, with quite different national models able to sustain their viability over the long term.[8] Within this diversity one of the most durable (and arguably the most impressive with respect to a range of social outcomes) is the Social Democratic model developed in Denmark, Finland, Norway and Sweden. This was a very long-term political project. Enacting it required considerable electoral success (through the development of powerful and popular Social Democratic parties, aligned with equally powerful labor movements). The key, however, was translating that electoral success into changes in government policy—the construction of expansive welfare states and strong systems of education and training, supports for full employment, and a framework

5 Larry DeWitt, "Research Note #23: Luther Gulick Memorandum re: Famous FDR Quote," *Research Notes & Special Studies by the Historian's Office*, https://www.ssa.gov/history/Gulick.html.

6 Acharya, Blackwell and Sen, *Deep Roots*; Starr, *Entrenchment*; Trounstine, *Segregation by Design*.

7 Robert Mickey, *Paths Out of Dixie: The Democratization of Authoritarian Enclaves in America's Deep South, 1944-1972* (Princeton, NJ: Princeton University Press), 2015.

8 Esping-Anderson, *Three Worlds*.

for industrial relations that enabled robust and forward-thinking labor unions. Critically, these policies were themselves exercises in power-building, both because they strengthened the constituencies of Social Democrats, and they became popular with a broad swath of voters in all these countries. As Evelyne Huber and John Stephens have documented in detail, Social Democrats were able to create a "policy ratchet effect," in which key political victories not only couldn't be reversed but set the table for additional victories moving forward.[9]

All of these examples of "entrenchment" are taken from the universe of advanced capitalist democracies, because these are the cases I know something about. Do they have implications for thinking about the subject of Blecher's narrative, which explores a far different political terrain a world away? I want to suggest that they do in fact have two relevant implications.

The first concerns power. For political scientists, power is often at the heart of accounts emphasizing the durability and continuity of social outcomes. In many instances, power begets power.[10] Power can be used to change the political rules, so that future political contestation takes place on a level playing field. It can be used to strip resources from one's opponents, and to confer resources on one's allies. Power can be used to change people's expectations, leading them to give up on alternative projects, or defect to those who look to be on the winning side. Power can be used to alter cultural institutions, potentially changing the way people think about what they want or what is possible (what Lukes famously called "the third face of power").[11] In short, power can generate positive feedback loops that embed particular arrangements and relationships over the long term.

Second, and following on this, most of these processes draw on the authority of the state. In all the cases I've described, a political coalition succeeded in gaining considerable control of political authority. The use of that authority was critical to generating the positive feedback loops I've just described. Change the constitutional rules, change the law, change the budgets, change the cultural institutions. All of these things, with the partial exception of the last, require considerable influence over the state.

Indeed, in each of these cases those seeking to use authority to entrench power gain extensive influence over the state *for an extended period of time.* Huber and Stephens, for example, argue explicitly that it is not just the size of Social Democratic Party electoral victories but more important the *durability* of those victories that is critical. The Swedish Social Democrats, famously, were in power continuously from 1932 to 1976. Reconstruction did not collapse

9 Huber and Stephens, *Development and Crisis.*

10 Paul Pierson, "Power and Path Dependence," in James Mahoney and Kathleen Thelen, eds., *Advances in Comparative Historical Analysis* (Cambridge: Cambridge University Press, 2015), 125–46.

11 Steven Lukes, *Power: A Radical View* (New York: Macmillan, 1973).

overnight. There were decades of contestation over the curtailment of Black people's voting rights in the South.[12] As the architects of Jim Crow gained the upper hand they relied on the repeated exercise of state power (everything from multiple restrictions on the franchise to the systematic deployment of organized violence) to consolidate control. The entrenchment of Social Security also depended on sustained political control. After Social Security was enacted in 1935 Republicans sought its repeal. Their 1936 presidential candidate Alf Landon—a fierce critic of the new program—lost in a landslide. Indeed, it was not until 1952 that Republicans recaptured the White House and were in a position to pursue serious reform. By that time, however, it was too late—the program was popular and firmly entrenched, and moderate Republicans decided to make their peace with it.[13]

In all these instances entrenchment required not just the ability to exercise political authority but the ability to do so over time. Holding power increases the opportunity to make repeated interventions that help consolidate the arrangements you are trying to embed. At the very least, it allows you to fend off interventions designed to overturn these arrangements, buying time while they can become deeply institutionalized.

Blecher's fascinating narrative explores political contexts that are radically different than the ones just described. Nonetheless, some of the implications I have highlighted may be instructive. China's working class was never able to gain the capacity to exercise political authority. Absent that authority, it could not build a durable institutional foothold. Given the volatility of the social and political environment, the kind of *sustained* political power that probably would have been necessary remained an even more distant and elusive aspiration. Exploring what allows an ambitious social coalition to exercise power in a manner that allows durable victories underscores just how difficult and uncommon such successful undertakings are.

12 Alexander Keyssar, *The Right to Vote: The Contested History of Democracy in the United States* (New York: Basic Books), 2009.

13 Martha Derthick, *Policymaking for Social Security* (Washington, D.C.: Brookings Institution Press), 1979.

7

RESPONSE

Entrenchment, Hegemony, Russia

Marc Blecher

Entrenchment

Paul Pierson's focus on *entrenchment* resonates with Gramsci's concept of hegemony, which he often described as the construction of *trench* systems of political power and conflict.[1] It involves "political actors achiev[ing] durable political victories—ones that cannot be undone (at least not without great difficulty) by those who follow."[2] Since the foundational work on entrenchment has been done on "real-existing democracies," Pierson expresses the "hope that despite the vast differences in social circumstances, this perspective offers some insights into" autocracies as well[3]—here, to "understanding the limited ability of China's working class to cement its interests as lasting gains." It's a major conceptual and theoretical aspiration that runs against the grain of most thinking about autocracies, since it posits a conceptualization in which classes and groups therein nonetheless are able to act in significant ways that cement institutional and policy gains for themselves. Yet on further reflection the potentiality is certainly plausible. After all, the outcome envisioned here is not power—which by definition an autocracy could not share—but governance practices and even institutional or policy arrangements. Daniel Kelliher and Kate Zhou have argued that collective farmers did so during China's radical state socialist

1 Ira Katznelson invoked this prominently in titling his Gramscian account of urban politics in *New York City Trenches*.

2 See p. 233.

3 Philippe Schmitter and I have made our first cut into régime types by distinguishing real-existing democracies from autocracies. Schmitter and Blecher, *Politics as a Science*, 24 and *passim*.

DOI: 10.4324/9781003518228-10

decades.[4] Manfred Elfstrom has recently demonstrated the capacity of the working class during structural reform to "alter…day-to-day governance in an environment seemingly extremely inhospitable to popular pressures."[5]

The theory of entrenchment opens the question of why, even in a non-real-existing democracy (RED), autocratic Leninist régime, a big social actor such as the working class could not entrench such alterations into *enduring policies or institutions* even as the Party/state continues to monopolize *power*. The answer has to lie in the realm of politics within autocratic régimes, not just the régime types themselves. And hegemony—the political construction of trenches—is an important part of those politics.

And he certainly is right to point to one major obstacle to the working class's capacity to entrench gains in noting that "[r]epeated massive dislocations have minimized the prospects for building durable arrangements of any kind"[6] during both the Republican/revolutionary and radical state socialist decades. Modesty probably accounts for Pierson not also referencing his point about non-ergodic events such as the White Terror.[7]

The structural reform period has been far more stable. Here the obstacle to working class gains, much less entrenched ones, has lain, as Pierson emphasizes, in the realm of power. In the radical state socialist period, the Party/state was able to contain working class efforts to exercise authority within the factory level. And of course those exertions could not extend to the wider Party/state itself. The closest the working class got to the latter was the abortive effort by proletarian politicians and their allies to establish some autonomy for the ACFTU.[8] They then contented themselves with struggles for some authority at the factory level. But the institutions within which they did so before the Cultural Revolution were themselves creatures of the Party/state, not their own, exemplifying the political hegemony of the Party and its factory-level allies among management, technical experts, and even ordinary workers whom it coopted. That is, workers sought authority in their factories through trenches of the Party/state institutions that they were opposing, but that, very skillfully and determinedly, granted them limited political space and material resources. This exemplifies Hui's fourth characteristic of hegemony: "the reproduction of hegemony involves compromises on secondary issues made by the dominant class—short-term concessions made to the subaltern class are not unusual."[9] Interestingly, this is very roughly analogous to the limitations of working class

4 Daniel Kelliher, *Peasant Power and Rural Change in China* (New Haven, Yale University Press, 1993); Kate Zhou, *How the Peasants Changed China* (Boulder: Westview, 1996).

5 Elfstrom, *Workers and Change in China*, 14.

6 See p. 234.

7 See p. 22.

8 See p. 67.

9 See p. 227.

politics in the revolutionary period, which could seek and even achieve some gains locally but not nationally.[10]

But, in line with Hui's sixth point about hegemony,[11] this proved unstable, as it did not satisfy workers' interest aspirations or their desire for actual authority at the factory level and, as the Cultural Revolution would soon make clear, beyond. When the Cultural Revolution created a political opportunity[12] to break the jam, workers and working class politicians stepped forward to make a breakthrough. Here their political efforts fell victim to the volatility it unleashed, as referenced just above.[13] But those dislocations were not external factors to the working class politics of the day; rather, they were stoked by those very politics of counter-hegemony, which helped discredit them when they failed on the broader canvas of Chinese politics. And that failure left the field open for the Cultural Revolution right, which proved anti-proletarian, to triumph, to put paid to the working class's efforts to gain some measure of political authority, and even to blame workers in the bargain. That is, the volatility undermined the working class but, in the fullness of time, strengthened its adversaries in the Party/state and the managerial, technical classes as well as the capitalist ones it called into being.

They founded their hegemony not just on the failure of working class radicalism, but also, hegemonically, on its discreditation even among the working class itself. The proletariat in turn broadly recognized that failure, came to support or at least resign themselves to aspects of the new capitalistic political economy, and insofar as they opposed it, did so by redefining their interests in economic rather than political terms, and seeking them through strikes in which some of those interests could actually be accommodated—all aspects of capitalist hegemony. In Gramscian terms, new trenches were dug and fortified; in Pierson's, the power of the Party/state, and the managers, technicians and capitalists it incorporated into its new hegemonic bloc, became entrenched.

And having done so—having remained in power despite what was surely a legitimacy crisis engendered by the Cultural Revolution and then the 1989 events, and in fact having used both to enact structural reforms that rocketed China's economy into previously unimaginable heights, with significant trickle-down effects for workers (and farmers and the petit bourgeoisie as well)—power now appears, as Pierson points up, to have begotten power.[14] Even if Xi's political project proves ephemeral over the medium term, few expect the Party/state would follow suit.

10 See p. 38 *ff.*
11 See p. 242.
12 See p. 36.
13 See p. 234.
14 See p. 238.

In the end, then, in China the complex pattern of working class formation and deformation has gone hand in hand with that of the country's state formation.

Hegemony

Elaine Sio-Ieng Hui has, literally, written the book on hegemony in China, and readers here are fortunate to have her thoughtful summary of its six elements.[15] Every single one is present in the pattern of working class formation.

- "First, the exercise of hegemony is to sustain the long-term dominance of the dominant class." This is the pattern of entrenchment just discussed.
- "Second, hegemony is the active consent obtained by the dominant and ruling class over the subordinate classes by influencing their intellectual, moral and political worldviews." In the Republican/revolutionary period, there was no dominant and ruling class. In the first seventeen years of the radical state socialist period, despite some early workerist opposition to the new Party/state, the rapid improvements of the economic aspects of working class formation combined with the stabilized and institutionalized social aspects provided through the new enterprise work units, produced active support for or at least participation in the new factory-level institutions established by the Party/state. When these ran into strict limits set by the Party/state in the wake of the Great Leap Forward, the embers of workerism came back to life in the Cultural Revolution with active support for the authority of one segment of the "dominant and ruling class"—the Maoist left. In the structural reform period, the defeat of the working class left by the new Party/state leadership followed by the economic, social and political re-formations of the working class produced working class cultural re-formation ranging from acquiescence to support for the authority of the "dominant and ruling class."
- "Third, the capitalist class needs to create a national-popular appearance for its parochial interests in order to acquire workers' allegiance to their leadership." This certainly pertained in the revolutionary period. There is less evidence for it in the radical state socialist or structural reform periods—a possible avenue of future research.
- "Fourth, the reproduction of hegemony involves compromises on secondary issues made by the dominant class—short-term concessions made to the subaltern class are not unusual." This is the "social contract" the Party/state made with the working class during the first seventeen (pre-Cultural Revolution) years of the radical state socialist period. It traded increased living standards and social status and some limited avenues of political

15 See p. 227.

participation within enterprises for refusal to admit the working class to the corridors of power. In the structural reform period, it relied on a very significant concession to the burgeoning rural migrant stratum by allowing it admission to the working class, which for many outweighed the dreadful terms of their employment. And in cases of labor strife, it often intervened to force employers to agree to a fraction of workers' demands.

- "Fifth, hegemony is bulwarked by the application of state coercion; even the most hegemonic state cannot rule without the support of military and physical forces." Thus, the curtain was brought down on working class radicalism in the Cultural Revolution by military-backed "revolutionary committees" and continues in the role of Party organization and surveillance in factories and of the police in labor disputes.
- "Sixth, the ruling class's hegemony is exercised in the unstable and fragile field of socio-political relations; this means the possibility of a working class counter-hegemony exists." We return to this prospect at the very end.

Migrant Workers' Activism

Hui is right to highlight incipient demands by migrants for workplace unions, broadened focus not just on production but also reproduction, and new forms of legal and social movement activism. I would only add that these straws in the wind are not just blowing among migrants. A small number of urban-resident workers are also getting in on the act. And there is evidence that the very distinction between these two strata is beginning to dissolve.[16] New strata such as service, white collar and gig workers are also emerging and just starting to get mobilized, as Hui herself points out.[17] And Elfstrom shows, they are beginning to have some small effects at least on quotidian governmental practices.[18]

Conditions for Building Counter-Hegemony

Hui argues that "[e]conomically, to reproduce capitalist hegemony the ruling class needs to address and incorporate the subaltern class's interests into theirs. Also, it needs to give economic concessions to the working class in such ways that workers feel 'shared' interests with the former, and as a result render their allegiance to it."[19] Quite right, and Xi (and Hu Jintao before him) clearly recognized as much and took steps in this direction—Hu with his initiatives in

16 Marc Blecher, "The Political Economy of Working Class Re-formation," in *China's Political Economy in the Xi Jinping Epoch: Global and Domestic Dimensions*, ed. Lowell Dittmer (Hackensack, NJ: World Scientific, 2021), chap. 4.

17 See p. 243.

18 Elfstrom, *Workers and Change in China.*

19 See p. 230.

inequality, and Xi with his anti-poverty and anti-corruption programs—which helped build their hegemony.

She also writes that "[c]ulturally, organic intellectuals of the working class play an important role in building counter-hegemony."[20] This is why Xi has cracked down on them. But of course, repression has its limits and can prove counterproductive for a hegemon.

Finally, Hui points out that, as noted just above, "while manufacturing workers have been the center of labor conflicts, white-collar workers and service workers have taken greater initiatives to resist exploitation recently."[21] Indeed, proletarianization beyond the factory could pose potential dangers for Party/state hegemony. But given the structural aspects of such employment, such as its dispersal, precarity and high turnover, it has proven very difficult for labor movements to organize these sectors even in REDs.

Russia

While Pierson has radically expanded the horizons for comparative work on China, there is also much to learn from comparisons with its closest cousin. Steve Crowley leads: "In contrast to China, there was considerable working class consciousness leading to the world's first 'socialist revolution' in 1917. Unlike the CCP, the Bolshevik Party was indeed a 'working class organization,' albeit with revolutionary intellectuals at the helm."[22] This of course was also true of the CCP for its first seven years. But the April 1927 White Terror drove a wedge between the Party and the working class that could never be overcome; for the next 22 years the Party matured into a battle-hardened, victorious revolutionary force in the absence of meaningful contact with China's working class. The consequences for the Party/state's lasting hegemony over the country's proletariat were enormous.

Crowley also reminds us how much population size and rural-urban proportions also matter for working class formation.

> The society that resulted included hundreds of new industrial cities and towns, with working class communities at the center. In a major divergence from China, Soviet industrialization was so overwhelming it left only a minimal "collectivized" peasantry in its wake. This meant the divisions between rural migrant workers and urban-resident workers that characterized China's working class were largely nonexistent in the Soviet Union. Indeed, from

20 See p. 230.
21 See p. 231.
22 See p. 216.

> the Stalinist period on, there was no unemployment to speak of, no "reserve army" of potential workers; rather, there was continual shortage of labor.[23]

By contrast, China had a massive reserve army, and it made itself felt during the Great Leap Forward, when significant numbers of the "best and brightest" farmers left for the burgeoning urban industrial sector (contributing along with many other factors to the collapse of the rural economy during the Leap). In response to that, the Party/state forcibly evicted rural migrants from the working class and enforced the sharp separation of farmers and workers for three more decades. In effect it created an industrial labor shortage, which was often dysfunctional for industrial recovery and a return to growth. To cope with this problem, it invented the rural contract labor system, by which selected factories could arrange with nearby communes to hire their farmers. The enterprises paid the communes, which in turn continued to pay their members in their collectives' work points. This produced a two-tier proletariat in which farmers labored alongside urban resident workers in the very same factories and jobs for lower compensation.[24] That became a major irritant which produced some of the most extreme proletarian radicalism during the Cultural Revolution. The highly complex system of household registration underpinning all this has produced all manner of unequal effects and administrative arrangements up to the present. It has also contributed to the low wage levels and sweatshop conditions that have prevailed throughout the structural reform period, since many and eventually most of the new working class were migratory second-class citizens who have labored and lived under the constant threat of eviction—not unlike the plight of migrant workers worldwide. Interestingly, amid all the labor protest of the last several decades, the two-tier household registration system that underpins these high levels of labor exploitation and has structurally split the proletariat has not itself become particularly politicized—at least not yet.

Crowley further points out the political implications of the Russian labor shortage.

> This gave workers a considerable amount of workplace power, as Burawoy discovered in Hungary, another Soviet-type society. Since shortages extended to all kinds of goods in the Soviet economy, enterprises sought to provide for workers' needs, to incentivize them and prevent them from seeking work elsewhere. The provision of these goods and services formed a kind of enterprise paternalism, very much akin to the danwei system in China. It also led to a strong workplace bond, a sense of belonging to the work

23 See p. 216.
24 Blecher, "Peasant Labour for Urban Industry," 731–746.

> *kollektiv*, in part because enterprises often built the housing and other social infrastructure that workers and their families enjoyed.[25]

Here China is very similar in a way that helps explain the radicalism of the working class in the Maoist decades—a factor to which *The Making of China's Working Class* does not sufficiently attend. But in turn the comparison also raises the question of why the labor shortage did not produce those same political impulses in the USSR and Eastern Europe. Here the answer has to do with the incorporation of their working classes early on (especially in the USSR), and the absence of radical criticism of state socialism by the highest levels which appeared uniquely and so astonishingly in China during the Cultural Revolution, and which workers adopted (hegemonically) to advance their cause.

In another similarity, in Russia "as in China, there was a distinct 'workerist' mentality. The working class was valorized in official ideology, something workers took obvious pride in."[26] But in China workerism stemmed from the proletariat's having developed apart from the Party/state and, both in the early years of the People's Republic and again in the Cultural Revolution, feelings among many workers of resentment of and superiority to it.

"With Mikhail Gorbachev's perestroika, independent organizing by workers and others became possible" and led to a wave of strikes that eventually toppled the USSR.[27] No wonder the Chinese Party/state has never permitted independent labor organizing. If there is anything that keeps Xi Jinping up at night, it is the prospect of a "colored revolution" in which the working class could play a major role.[28]

Workers in both countries have experienced wage arrears, but for very different reasons. In Russia, they were a result of and adaptation to deep structural crisis.

> ...despite almost unprecedented economic decline, the result wasn't massive unemployment. Instead of a loss of jobs, wages dropped dramatically. Many workers became impoverished, but they were technically still employed. Most of the old Soviet factories somehow hung on, relying on barter and other arrangements rather than profit to remain afloat. Wages dropped so low that they eventually gave way to a crisis of "wage arrears"—that is, wages went unpaid altogether. At the height of the crisis in late 1998, approximately

25 See p. 216.
26 See p. 217.
27 See p. 217 *ff.*
28 That is why, soon after he came to power, Xi ordered social science institutes across China to research the question of why the Soviet Union collapsed. It also explains why working class politics has been one of the most sensitive and tightly regulated subjects for research by foreign scholars.

> two-thirds of Russian workers reported overdue wages, with those affected reporting close to five months' pay in arrears on average.[29]

By contrast, the Chinese Party/state engineered sweeping structural change through massive enterprise closures and consolidations.[30] Wage arrears, also serious, resulted not so much from bankrupt state enterprises being kept open as from employers' avarice or the problems experienced by new private enterprises in the new capitalistic environment.[31] But whatever the reasons, arrears have proven a major stimulant of strikes in both countries.

Crowley re-poses a core question of this book:

> "Why has the working class deradicalized precisely in an era when it has lost so much power?" Similar questions could be—and have—been asked about Russia. One answer might come from the economic theory of strikes, which posits that strikes tend to take place less during times of economic hardship, and more often when workers have less to fear (from job loss) and more to gain (from demanding a greater share of profits). Such a view would see strikes and labor actions as most often expressions of working class power. That perspective can explain how workplace and marketplace power spurred the offensive protests of auto workers in both China and Russia.[32]

His propensity to ground protest politics in structural change is most welcome, surely right, and something that should have gotten more attention in this book. Yet here it still does not explain the proliferation of defensive strikes across the structural reform period, a time of labor shortages when workers could easily change jobs (and often did).

On another core issue of this book, Crowley opines:

> How well does the concept of hegemony explain the Russian case? Quite well it seems. Lenin and the Bolsheviks certainly seized upon the revolutionary mood among workers in coming to power, but once in power their articulation of workers' interests was by and large well received. Stalinist industrialization was tumultuous, to say the least, but by many accounts workers enthusiastically participated in the "building of socialism." Still speaking in broad strokes, in the post-Stalinist era workers largely perceived the benefit of a society that valued them as a class, and where the absence of unemployment—indeed, a shortage of labor—combined with enterprise

29 See p. 218.
30 See p. 103.
31 See p. 95 and *passim*.
32 See p. 220.

> paternalism prevented a sense of undue exploitation. Yet, as the uprising in Novocherkassk suggests, workers and others had certain expectations about what that system was meant to provide, and limits to what they would accept. Put differently, while Soviet ideology was clearly hegemonic, the system created expectations that it later found difficult to meet.
>
> The miners' strikes in 1989 proved this to be the case.[33]

And when they did strike, they focused on the structural transformations that had led to their dashed hopes. In China, by contrast, state socialist cultural hegemony had already collapsed in the maelstrom of the Cultural Revolution. So strikes and protest in the structural reform period generally focused, hegemonically, more on the economic issues characteristic of the new capitalist political economy, such as wages, pensions and corruption.

Yet once state socialism collapsed, Russian workers rejected it as exploitative.[34] By contrast, in China they did not do so despite the economic privation they clearly recalled. They often reminisced about the security, respect, relative equality (with each other and with shop floor managers), power (however limited), honesty, and sense of community and *esprit de corps* of radical state socialist days. Insofar as they had criticisms, they found it insufficiently empowering ("workerist").

Crowley's closing coda begins with a key question: "One might argue that the concept of hegemony might explain the subordination of subalterns most everywhere, almost as a tautology."[35] Not necessarily. As Hui has put it so well, hegemony can also entail coercion as a backstop where consent has evaporated. Where coercion plays a major role in achieving the subordination of subalterns, hegemony is weak and failing. Moreover, Gramsci's dyad of coercion and consent is too limited. Subordination can also be based on co-optation, manipulation, compromise, or mere unconscious habit. Moreover, it can be active (support) or passive (acquiescence).[36] So the politics of the development and decline of hegemony, and of subordination, is exceedingly complex, open-ended, dependent on a wide range of factors, and unpredictable.

Crowley and Hui are wise to gesture in this direction at the end of their sagacious commentaries. This book is subtitled *A World to Lose* not just as a catchy negation of the famous, stirring close of *The Communist Manifesto.* It is meant to convey the same sense that Marx and Engels had not of deterministic certainty—a world that will be won—but rather of potentiality: a world that is being lost, or that has been lost for now but that could be, if not re-won in its

33 See p. 221.
34 See p. 221.
35 See p. 221.
36 Schmitter and Blecher, *Politics as a Science*, 48 *ff.*

original form (which would be impossible in any dialectical conception of history), then reconstituted and transcended (*aufgehoben*) in some measure as part of a new phase of history. Gramsci famously said, "pessimism of the intellect, optimism of the will." But, with Hui, and surely Gramsci too (though he could not specify it writing in prison), we can also add some potential "optimism of the intellect."

INDEX

For Product Safety Concerns and Information please contact our EU
representative GPSR@taylorandfrancis.com
Taylor & Francis Verlag GmbH, Kaufingerstraße 24, 80331 München, Germany

www.ingramcontent.com/pod-product-compliance
Ingram Content Group UK Ltd.
Pitfield, Milton Keynes, MK11 3LW, UK
UKHW022350190926
475702UK00015B/2216
* 9 7 8 1 0 3 2 7 6 9 1 1 0 *